Expert Python Programming

Learn best practices to designing, coding, and
distributing your Python software

Tarek Ziadé

BIRMINGHAM - MUMBAI

Expert Python Programming

Copyright © 2009 Packt Publishing

All rights reserved. No part of this book may be reproduced, stored in a retrieval system, or transmitted in any form or by any means, without the prior written permission of the publisher, except in the case of brief quotations embedded in critical articles or reviews.

Every effort has been made in the preparation of this book to ensure the accuracy of the information presented. However, the information contained in this book is sold without warranty, either express or implied. Neither the author, Packt Publishing, nor its dealers or distributors will be held liable for any damages caused or alleged to be caused directly or indirectly by this book.

Packt Publishing has endeavored to provide trademark information about all the companies and products mentioned in this book by the appropriate use of capitals. However, Packt Publishing cannot guarantee the accuracy of this information.

First published: September 2008

First reprint: April 2009

Production Reference: 2220409

Published by Packt Publishing Ltd.
32 Lincoln Road
Olton
Birmingham, B27 6PA, UK.

ISBN 978-1-847194-94-7

www.packtpub.com

Cover Image by Javier BarrXa C. (jbarriac@yahoo.com)

Credits

Author

Tarek Ziadé

Reviewers

Shannon -jj Behrens

Paul Kennedy

Wendy Langer

Acquisition Editor

Douglas Paterson

Development Editors

Ved Prakash Jha

Technical Editors

Siddharth Mangarole

Abhinav Prasoon

Copy Editor

Sneha Kulkarni

Editorial Team Leader

Mithil Kulkarni

Project Manager

Abhijeet Deobhakta

Project Coordinator

Patricia Weir

Indexer

Rekha Nair

Proofreader

Chris Smith

Production Coordinators

Aparna Bhagat

Rajni Thorat

Adline Swetha Jesuthas

Shantanu Zagade

Cover Work

Aparna Bhagat

Foreword

Python has come a long way.

There was a time when companies would call me crazy when I insisted on using Python. These days, there simply aren't enough Python coders to go around. Major companies such as Google, YouTube, VMware, and DreamWorks are in a constant scramble to snatch up all the good Python talent they can find.

Python used to lag behind Perl because Perl had CPAN. These days, `setuptools` and PyPI have led to an explosion of readily available, high-quality, third-party Python libraries. Python also used to lag behind Java Servlets and Ruby on Rails because there was no standard API for interacting with web servers. These days, the Web Server Gateway Interface (WSGI) has led to a renaissance in the Python web world. Thanks to Google App Engine, I think we'll see even more.

Python seems to attract programmers who are highly opinionated and have a real taste for elegance. Very few people become Python programmers because it's what they learned in college, or because it's what all the big companies are using. Rather, people are drawn to Python when they discover its intrinsic beauty. Because of this, there are a surprising number of Python books. I don't have the statistics to prove it, but it seems to me that Python has a higher ratio of books to programmers than any other language. However, historically, there haven't been enough advanced Python books. That's about to change.

This book presents an interesting list of topics. It covers a range of Python features and how to use them in unexpected ways. It also covers a selection of interesting third-party libraries and tools. Along the way, agile programming with Python tools and libraries is covered. This includes test-driven development with `Nose`, document-driven development with `doctest`, source control with Mercurial, continuous integration with `Buildbot`, and project management with Trac. Finally, it covers more traditional topics such as profiling, optimization, and design patterns such as Alex Martelli's infamous Borg approach to Singletons.

If you're looking to progress from knowing Python to mastering Python, this is the book for you. In fact, this is exactly the type of book I wish I had had five years ago. What took me years to discover by steadfastly attending talks at PyCon and my local Python users' group is now available in a succinct book form.

There has never been a more exciting time to be a Python programmer!

Shannon -jj Behrens
Moderator of the San Francisco Bay Area Python Interest Group
`http://jjinux.blogspot.com`

About the Author

Tarek Ziadé is CTO at Ingeniweb in Paris, working on Python, Zope, and Plone technology and on Quality Assurance. He has been involved for five years in the Zope community and has contributed to the Zope code itself.

Tarek has also created Afpy, the French Python User Group and has written two books in French about Python. He has gave numerous talks and tutorials in French and international events like Solutions Linux, Pycon, OSCON, and EuroPython.

Before starting with Chapter 1, I would like to thank a few people that helped me while I was writing this book:

The whole Python community of course, the AFPY user group, Stefan Schwarzer for his slides on optimization, his quote and his great feedback and reviews, Georg Brandl for reviewing Chapter 10 about Sphinx, Peter Bulychev for assistance on CloneDigger, Ian Bicking for assistance on minimock, the Logilab team for assistance on PyLint, Gael Pasgrimaud, Jean-François Roche, and Kai Lautaportti for their work on collective.buildbot, Cyrille Lebeaupin, Olivier Grisel, Sebastien Douche and Stéfane Fermigier for various reviews.

Thanks to the OmniGroup and their great OmniGraffle tool; all diagrams were made with it (see `http://www.omnigroup.com/applications/OmniGraffle`).

A very special thanks goes to Shannon "jj" Behrens who did a deep reviewing of this book.

About the Reviewers

Shannon -jj Behrens is the moderator of the San Francisco Bay Area Python Interest Group. While not technical editing Python books and hopping from startup to startup, he enjoys playing with his four kids and blogging at `http://jjinux.blogspot.com`.

> I'd like to thank Tarek for patiently listening to all my critiques, and I'd like to thank my lovely wife, Gina-Marie Behrens, for protecting me from the kids long enough to finish editing the book.

Paul Kennedy is a Senior Lecturer in the Faculty of Engineering and Information Technology at the University of Technology, Sydney. He is also Director of the Knowledge Infrastructure Laboratory in the UTS Centre for Quantum Computation and Intelligent Systems. Dr Kennedy has been developing software professionally since 1989 with a career bridging industry and academia. He has worked with languages including C/C++ and Python and in such diverse areas as computer graphics, artificial intelligence, bioinformatics, and data mining. For the last ten years he has been teaching undergraduate and postgraduate students in software engineering and data mining. He completed his PhD in Computing Science in 1998 and regularly consults to industry in data mining projects. He has been General Chair of the Australasian Data Mining Conference for 2006-2008, has actively contributed to international Program Committees, reviewed for international journals, and has more than 30 publications.

Wendy Langer first learned to program in Microbee Basic, in between bouts of playing 'Hunt the Wumpus' and 'Colossal Caves'. This all happened a long time ago, in a galaxy far, far, away. Many years later, she learned Fortran whilst studying for a physics degree at University. Finally, after a long period of wandering in the outer darkness, she discovered the perfect programming language—Python! Even though she currently spends more actual coding time using C++, her heart will always belong to Python.

She has worked as a programmer in web development using technologies such as Python, Zope, Django, MySQL, and PostgreSQL, and was a reviewer on the previous Packt title *Learning Website Development with Django* by Ayman Hourieh.

I would like to thank my mum, and also Jesse-the-dog, for protecting me during the reviewing of this book from the many dangerous creatures (such as possums, cats, and postmen) to be found in the local area.

Table of Contents

Preface

Python rocks!

From the earliest version in the late 1980s to the current version, it has evolved with the same philosophy: providing a multi-paradigm programming language with readability and productivity in mind.

People used to see Python as yet another scripting language and wouldn't feel right about using it to build large systems. But through the years and thanks to some pioneer companies, it became obvious that Python could be used to build almost any kind of a system.

In fact, many developers that come from another language are charmed by Python and make it their first choice.

This is something you are probably aware of if you have bought this book, so there's no need to convince you about the merits of the language any further.

This book was written to express many years of experience in building all kinds of applications with Python, from small system scripts done in a couple of hours to very large applications written by dozens of developers over several years.

It describes the best practices used by developers to work with Python.

The first title that came up was *Python Best Practices* but it eventually became *Expert Python Programming* because it covers some topics that are not focused on the language itself but rather on the tools and techniques used to work with it.

In other words this book describes how an advanced Python developer works every day.

What This Book Covers

Chapter 1 explains how to install Python and makes sure all readers have the closest, standardized environment. I almost removed this chapter since the book is not intended for beginners. But it was kept because there are definitely some experienced Python programmers out there who are not aware of some of the things presented. If you are, don't feel frustrated about it, as the rest of the book will probably meet your needs.

Chapter 2 is about syntax best practices, below the class level. It presents iterators, generators, descriptors, and so on, in an advanced way.

Chapter 3 is also about syntax best practices, but focuses above the class level.

Chapter 4 is about choosing good names. It is an extension to PEP 8 with naming best practices, but also gives tips on designing good APIs.

Chapter 5 explains how to write a package and how to use code templates and then focuses on how to release and distribute your code.

Chapter 6 extends *Chapter 5* by describing how a full application can be written. It demonstrates it through a small case study called *Atomisator*.

Chapter 7 is about `zc.buildout`, a system for managing a development environment and releasing applications, which is widely used in the Zope and Plone community and is now used outside the Zope world.

Chapter 8 gives some insight on how a project code base can be managed and explains how to set up continuous integration.

Chapter 9 presents how to manage software life cycle through an iterative and incremental approach.

Chapter 10 is about documentation and gives tips on technical writing and how Python projects should be documented.

Chapter 11 explains Test-Driven Development and the tools that can be used to do it.

Chapter 12 is about optimization. It gives profiling techniques and an optimization strategy guideline.

Chapter 13 extends *Chapter 12* by providing some solutions to speed up your programs.

Chapter 14 ends the book with a set of useful design patterns.

Last, keep an eye on `http://atomisator.ziade.org`, which is the website that was build throughout the book. It has all code sources presented and will contain errata and other add-ons.

What You Need for This Book

This book is written for developers who work under Linux, Mac OS X or Windows. All pre-requisites are described in the first chapter to make sure your system is Python-enabled and meets a few requirements.

This is important for Windows developers because they need to make sure they have a command-line environment that is close to what Mac OS X and Linux users have from scratch. In general, all the examples should work on any platform.

Last, keep in mind that this book is not intended to replace online resources, but rather aims at complementing them. So obviously you will need internet access to complete your reading experience at some points, through provided links.

Who This Book Is For

This book was written for Python developers who wish to go further in mastering Python. Some sections of the book, such as the section on continuous integration, are targeted at project leads.

It complements the usual *How To Program In Python* reference books and online resources and goes deeper in the syntax usage.

It also explains how to be agile while coding. While this can be applied to any language, the book concentrates on providing examples with Python. So, if you are not practicing tests nor using version control systems, you will probably learn a lot through this book that will help you even in other languages.

From Test-Driven Development to distributed version control systems and continuous integration, you will learn the latest programming techniques used by experienced Python developers on big projects.

While these topics are quickly evolving, this book will not get obsolete that easily because it rather focuses on whys instead of hows.

So, even if a given tool presented is not used anymore, you will understand why it was useful and you will be able to pick the right one with a critical point of view.

Conventions

In this book, you will find a number of styles of text that distinguish between different kinds of information. Here are some examples of these styles, and an explanation of their meaning.

Code words in text are shown as follows: This environment can be built using the `buildout` command. A block of code will be set as follows:

```
>>> from script_engine import run
>>> print run('a + b', context={'a': 1, 'b':3})
4
```

Any command-line input and output is written as follows:

```
$ python setup.py --help-commands
```

New terms and **important words** are introduced in a bold-type font. Words that you see on the screen, in menus or dialog boxes for example, appear in our text like this: "clicking the **Next** button moves you to the next screen".

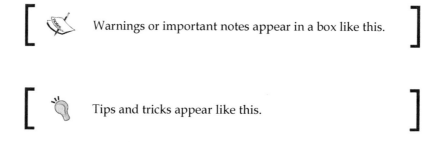

Warnings or important notes appear in a box like this.

Tips and tricks appear like this.

Reader Feedback

Feedback from our readers is always welcome. Let us know what you think about this book, what you liked or may have disliked. Reader feedback is important for us to develop titles that you really get the most out of.

To send us general feedback, simply drop an email to feedback@packtpub.com, making sure to mention the book title in the subject of your message.

If there is a book that you need and would like to see us publish, please send us a note in the **SUGGEST A TITLE** form on www.packtpub.com or email suggest@packtpub.com.

If there is a topic that you have expertise in and you are interested in either writing or contributing to a book, see our author guide on www.packtpub.com/authors.

Customer Support

Now that you are the proud owner of a Packt book, we have a number of things to help you to get the most from your purchase.

Downloading the Example Code for the Book

Visit `http://www.packtpub.com/files/code/4947_Code.zip` to directly download the example code.

The downloadable files contain instructions on how to use them.

The author owns a site: `http://atomisator.ziade.org` where the code mentioned in this book are available.

Errata

Although we have taken every care to ensure the accuracy of our contents, mistakes do happen. If you find a mistake in one of our books—maybe a mistake in text or code—we would be grateful if you would report this to us. By doing this you can save other readers from frustration, and help to improve subsequent versions of this book. If you find any errata, report them by visiting `http://www.packtpub.com/support`, selecting your book, clicking on the **let us know** link, and entering the details of your errata. Once your errata are verified, your submission will be accepted and the errata added to the list of existing errata. The existing errata can be viewed by selecting your title from `http://www.packtpub.com/support`.

Piracy

Piracy of copyright material on the Internet is an ongoing problem across all media. At Packt, we take the protection of our copyright and licenses very seriously. If you come across any illegal copies of our works in any form on the Internet, please provide the location address or website name immediately so we can pursue a remedy.

Please contact us at `copyright@packtpub.com` with a link to the suspected pirated material.

We appreciate your help in protecting our authors, and our ability to bring you valuable content.

Questions

You can contact us at `questions@packtpub.com` if you are having a problem with some aspect of the book, and we will do our best to address it.

Last, this book is dedicated to Milo and Amina.

1
Getting started

Python is good for developers.

No matter what operating system you or your customers are running, it will work. Unless you are coding platform-specific things, or using a platform-specific library, you can work on Linux and deploy on other systems, for example. However, thats not uncommon anymore. (Ruby, Java, and many other languages work in the same way.) Combined with the other qualities that we will discover throughout this book, Python becomes a smart choice for a company's primary development language.

This chapter gathers everything required to get started with Python, no matter what your environment is. It presents:

- How to install Python
- How to use and enhance the prompt
- How to be ready to extend Python, by installing `setuptools`
- How to set up a development environment, using the *old school* or the *new school* ways

A book always starts with some appetizers. So if you are already familiar with Python, and have it installed and reachable from your favorite code editor, you can skip the first section of this chapter, and just read other sections quickly. You might find in them interesting points to enhance your environment. Be sure to read the section on `setuptools` though, as its installation is mandatory for the rest of the book.

If you are using Windows, make sure you have installed the software described in this chapter, as it will be required to run all the examples this book provides.

Installing Python

The Python programming language runs on almost any system such as Linux, Macintosh, and Windows. The distributions are made available by the core team on the main download page of the Python website at: http://www.python.org/download. Other platforms are maintained by the people from the community, and summarized on a dedicated page. (See http://www.python.org/download/other.) Here, you'll probably find the distributions for operating systems that will remind you of your college years, if you are thirty-years old or more.

 If you have a computer, you will be able to use Python no matter what operating system this computer runs on.

If not, ditch it.

Before installing Python, let's have a quick tour of the existing implementations.

Python Implementations

The main Python implementation is written in the C language and is called **CPython**. It is the one that majority of people refer to, when they talk about Python. When the language evolves, the C implementation is changed accordingly. Besides C, Python is available in a few other implementations that are trying to keep up with the mainstream. Most of them are a few milestones behind CPython, but provide a great opportunity to use and promote the language in a specific environment.

Jython

Jython is a Java implementation of the language. It compiles the code into Java byte code, and allows the developers to seamlessly use Java classes within their Python modules. (In Python, a file containing code is called a module.) Jython allows people to use Python as the top-level scripting language on complex application systems, for example J2EE. It also brings Java applications into Python applications. Making Apache Jackrabbit (which is a document repository API based on JCR; see http://jackrabbit.apache.org) available in a Python program is a good example of what Jython allows. The current milestone is 2.2.1, but the Jython team is heading over to 2.5. Some Python web frameworks such as Pylons are currently boosting Jython development to make it available in Java world.

See http://www.jython.org/Project/index.html.

IronPython

IronPython brings Python into .NET. The project is supported by Microsoft, where IronPython's lead developers work. The latest stable version is 1.1 (released in April 2007) and implements Python 2.4.3. It is available in ASP.NET, and lets people use the Python code in their .NET application in the same way as Jython does in Java. It is quite an important implementation for the promotion of a language. Besides Java, the .NET community is one of the biggest developer communities out there. The TIOBE community index also shows that .NET languages are among the rising stars. (For more information, visit `http://www.tiobe.com/tpci.htm`.)

Also see `http://www.codeplex.com/Wiki/View.aspx?ProjectName=IronPython`.

PyPy

PyPy is probably the most exciting implementation, as its goal is to rewrite Python into Python. In PyPy, the Python interpreter is itself written in Python. We have a C code layer carrying out the nuts-and-bolts work for the CPython implementation of Python. But in the PyPy implementation, this C code layer is rewritten in pure Python. This means that you can change the interpreter's behavior during execution time, and implement code patterns that couldn't be easily done in CPython. (See `http://codespeak.net/pypy/dist/pypy/doc/objspace-proxies.html`.) PyPy used to be 2000 times slower than CPython, but this has improved a lot in the past years. The introduction of techniques such as the **JIT (Just-In-Time)** compiler is promising. The current speed factor is between 1.7 and 4, and the current implementation target is Python 2.4. PyPy can be seen as the head of R&D in the compilation matters, and the starting point of many innovations that the mainstream implementation can benefit from later. On the whole though, PyPy is interesting for theoretical reasons, and interests those who enjoy going deep into the internals of the language. It is not generally used in production.

See `http://codespeak.net/pypy`.

Other Implementations

There are other implementations and ports of Python. For example, Nokia has made Python 2.2.2 available in the S60 phone series (`http://opensource.nokia.com/projects/pythonfors60/`), and Michael Lauer maintains a port on ARM Linux that makes it available in devices such as *Sharp Zaurus* (`http://www.vanille-media.de/site/index.php/projects/python-for-arm-linux`).

There are many other examples, but this book will focus installing the CPython implementation on Linux, Windows, and Mac OS X.

Linux Installation

If you are running Linux, you probably have Python installed. So, try to call it from the shell:

```
tarek@dabox:~$ python
Python 2.3.5 (#1, Jul  4 2007, 17:28:59)
[GCC 4.1.2 20061115 (prerelease) (Debian 4.1.1-21)] on linux2
Type "help", "copyright", "credits" or "license" for more information.
>>>
```

If the command is found, you will be placed into the interactive shell that comes with Python, represented by the >>> sign. The information about the compiler used to build Python (here GCC) and the target system (Linux) is displayed. If you are using Windows, you will get Microsoft Visual Studio as the compiler. The Python version is also displayed in the result. Make sure you are running the latest stable release (probably 2.6 by the time this book is printed).

If it is not the case, you can install several versions of Python on your system without any unexpected interaction. Each Python version will be reachable with its full name, or with the Python command, depending on your path environment:

```
tarek@dabox:~$ which python
/usr/bin/python
tarek@dabox:~$ python<tab>
python              python2.3           python2.5
python2.4
```

If the command is not found, which is very uncommon under Linux, you need to install it using the package-management tools for your Linux system, such as **apt** for Debian, or **rpm** for Red Hat, or by compiling the sources.

While it is preferable to stick with a package installation, we will now discuss each of the two installation methods (package-managed installation and source installation) in a little more detail. However, the latest Python version might not always be available in your package-management tools as yet.

Package Installation

Using the Linux package system of the Linux distribution is the common way to install Python, and to make sure that you can easily upgrade it. Depending on your system, you will have to run one of these commands:

- `apt-get install python` for Debian-based distributions, such as Ubuntu
- `urpmi python` for rpm-based ones, such as Fedora or Red Hat series
- `emerge python` for Gentoo

If the latest version does not show up, a manual installation will be needed.

Finally, some extra packages should be installed in order to have a full installation. They are optional and you can work without them. But they are useful if you want to code C extensions, or to profile your programs. The packages that should be installed in order to have a full installation are:

- **python-dev**: It contains Python headers needed when the C modules are compiled.
- **python-profiler**: It contains non-GPL modules (Hotshot profiler) for full GPL distributions such as Debian or Ubuntu.
- **gcc**: It is used to compile extensions that contain C code.

Compiling the Sources

A manual installation is done with the **cmmi** process (**configure, make, make install** sequence) that performs a compilation of Python and deploys it on the system. The latest Python archive can be found on `http://python.org/download`.

> **Using wget for downloads:**
> The **wget** program, from the Gnu project, is a command line utility that can perform downloads. It is available under all platforms. Under Windows, you can get a binary distribution at: `http://gnuwin32.sourceforge.net/packages/wget.htm`.
> On Linux or Mac OS X, it is installable through the package systems such as **apt** or **MacPorts**.
> See `http://www.gnu.org/software/wget`.

To build Python, we will use `make` and `gcc`.

- `make` is a program that is used to read configuration files, usually named `Makefile`, and check that all requirements to compile the program are met. It is also used to drive the compilation. It is invoked with the `configure` and `make` commands.
- `gcc` is the GNU C Compiler, an open-source compiler widely used to build programs.

Make sure they are both installed on your system. Under some versions of Linux such as Ubuntu, you can install build tools with the `build-essentials` package.

To build and install Python, run this sequence:

```
cd /tmp
wget http://python.org/ftp/python/2.5.1/Python-2.5.1.tgz
tar -xzvf Python-2.5.1.tgz
```

```
cd Python-2.5.1
./configure
make
sudo make install
```

This installation will also install the headers provided for binary installations that are usually included in the **python-dev** package. The Hotshot profiler is also bundled into the source releases. The result should be the same when you are done, that is, Python should be reachable in the shell.

[At this point, your system is Python-enabled. So, let's celebrate!]

Windows Installation

Python can be compiled on Windows in the same way as for Linux. But this can be quite painful because you will need to set up a complicated compilation environment. Standard installers are provided in the python.org download section, and the wizard to achieve the installation is pretty straightforward.

Installing Python

If you leave all the options at default, Python will be installed under c:\Python25, and not under the usual Program Files folder. This prevents any space in the path.

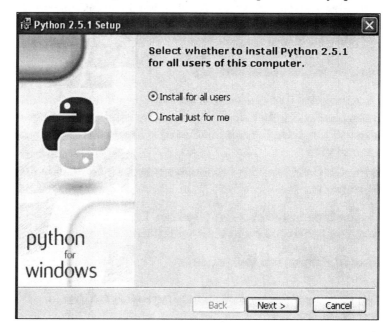

The last step is changing your PATH environment variable, so that we can call Python from the DOS shell.

On most Windows installations, this is done by:

- Right-clicking on the **My Computer** icon that is located on the desktop or the start menu, to get to the **System Properties** dialog box
- Getting in the **Advanced** tab
- Clicking on the **Environment Variables** button
- Editing the PATH system variable to add two new paths, separated by ";" (a semi-colon)

The paths to be added are:

- c:\Python25, to be able to call python.exe
- c:\Python25\Scripts, to be able to call third-party scripts that are installed in your Python by extensions

You should be able to run Python in the Command Prompt. To get there, open the **Run** shortcut in the **Start** menu, open **cmd**, and then call python:

```
C:\> python
Python 2.5.2 (#71, Oct 18 2006, 08:34:43) [MSC v.1310 32 bit (Intel)] on
win32
Type "help", "copyright", "credits" or "license" for more information.
>>>
```

This is enough to run Python. But this environment is not quite complete, when compared to that of a Linux user. To perform everything that is presented in this book, **MinGW** needs to be installed.

Installing MinGW

MinGW is a compiler for Windows platforms. It provides the gcc compiler in all flavors, and a set of libraries and headers. MinGW can be used as a full replacement for Microsoft's Visual C++. You could also choose to keep both compilers on your system and use them for different purposes, depending upon your requirements.

To install MinGW, get the distribution from http://sourceforge.net/project/showfiles.php?group_id=2435&package_id=240780. There you will find a link to **Sourceforge**. (See http://sourceforge.net, the largest developer website for Open Source projects.) The automated installer is the best choice, as everything will be bundled. Get the installer and run it.

Just as for Python, the PATH environment variable in the system properties needs to be extended with c:\MinGW\bin, in order to be able to invoke its commands. You should be able to run MinGW commands from the shell after the path is set:

```
C:\>gcc -v

Reading specs from c:/MinGW/bin/../lib/gcc-lib/mingw32/3.2.3/specs

Configured with: ../gcc/configure --with-gcc --with-gnu-ld --with-gnu-as
--host=

mingw32 --target=mingw32 --prefix=/mingw --enable-threads --disable-nls
--enable

-languages=c++,f77,objc --disable-win32-registry --disable-shared --
enable-sjlj-

exceptions

Thread model: win32

gcc version 3.2.3 (mingw special 20030504-1)
```

These commands will never be run manually, but are used automatically by Python when a compiler needs to be used.

Installing MSYS

Another tool that should be installed under Windows is **MSYS (Minimal SYStem)**. It provides a Bourne Shell command-line interpreter environment under Windows that provides all the usual commands Linux or Mac OS X has, such as cp, rm and so on.

This may sound overkill, since Windows has the same set of tools whether they are graphical or available in an MS-DOS prompt. But this helps the developers who work on several systems to have a universal set of commands to work with.

Get the download link for MSYS from http://sourceforge.net/project/showfiles.php?group_id=2435&package_id=240780 and install it on your system.

If you perform a standard installation, MSYS will be installed in c:\msys. You must add C:\msys\1.0\bin in your PATH variable in the same way as you added MinGW.

The rest of this book uses Bourne Shell commands in its examples. So if you are under Windows, you should install MSYS.

Now that you have MinGW and MSYS, there's no need to be jealous of those with a Linux installation anymore, since they implement in your system the most important parts of a Linux development environment.

Mac OS X Installation

Mac OS X is based on Darwin, which in turn is based on FreeBSD. This makes the platform quite similar and compatible to Linux. Apple, on the top of it, added a graphical engine (Quartz) and a specific file tree.

From the shell point of view, the major difference is how the system tree is organized. You will not find, for example a /home root folder, but you can find a /Users folder. The applications are also usually installed in /Library. /usr/bin is used though, as it is used on Linux.

Just as for Linux and Windows, there are two ways you can install Python on Mac OS X. You can install it using a package installer, or you can compile it from the source. The package installation is the simplest way, but you might want to build Python yourself. However, the latest version might not be available yet, as a binary distribution.

Package Installation

The latest Mac OS X version (Leopard at this time) comes with an installed Python. To install an extra Python, get a universal binary at http://www.pythonmac.org/packages for Python 2.5.x. You will get a .dmg file that you can mount. It contains a .pkg file that you can launch.

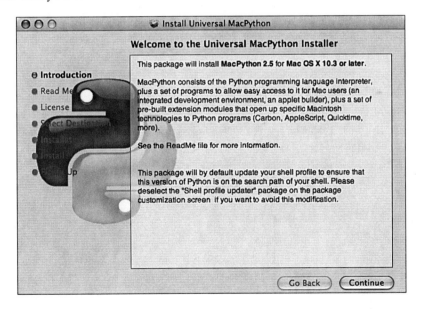

This will install Python in the /Library folder and create the proper links in the system so you can run it from the shell.

Compiling the Source

To compile Python, you need to install:

- The gcc compiler: It is provided in the Xcode Tools, and is available on the install disk or online at: http://developer.apple.com/tools/xcode.

- **MacPorts**: This is a package system comparable to Debian's package-management system **apt** that will help you install dependencies, for instance the same way Linux users can with apt. See http://www.macports.org.

From here, you can follow the same process explained for compiling under Linux.

The Python Prompt

The Python prompt, which comes when the python command is called, allows you to interact with the interpreter. It is very common, for example, to use it as a small calculator:

```
macziade:/home/tziade tziade$ python
Python 2.5 (r25:51918, Sep 19 2006, 08:49:13)
[GCC 4.0.1 (Apple Computer, Inc. build 5341)] on darwin
Type "help", "copyright", "credits" or "license" for more information.
>>>1 + 3
4
>>>5 * 8
40
```

When the enter key is hit, the line is interpreted and the result is immediately displayed. This particularity, inherited from the **ABC** language, affects the way Python the programmers work. In code documentation, all usage examples are shown in small prompt sessions.

Getting out of the prompt:
To get out of the prompt, use Ctrl+D under Linux or Mac OS X, and Ctrl+Z under Windows.

Since the prompt interactive mode will play an important role in the coding process, we need to make it very easy to use.

Customizing the Interactive Prompt

The interactive prompt can be configured with a startup file. When it starts, it looks for the PYTHONSTARTUP environment variable and executes the code in the file pointed to by this variable. Some Linux distributions provide a default startup script, which is generally located in your home directory. It is called .pythonstartup. Tab completion and command history are often provided to enhance the prompt, and are based on the the readline module. (You need the readline library.) If you don't have such a file, you can easily create one.

Here's an example of the simplest startup file that adds completion with the <*Tab*> key, and history:

```
# python startup file
import readline
import rlcompleter
import atexit
import os
# tab completion
readline.parse_and_bind('tab: complete')
# history file
histfile = os.path.join(os.environ['HOME'], '.pythonhistory')
try:
    readline.read_history_file(histfile)
except IOError:
    pass
atexit.register(readline.write_history_file, histfile)
del os, histfile, readline, rlcompleter
```

Create this file in your home directory and call it .pythonstartup. Then add a PYTHONSTARTUP variable in your environment using the path of your file.

 The python script is available in the pbp.script package under the 'pythonstartup.py' name. You can get this file at http://pypi.python.org/pypi/pbp.scripts and rename it to '.pythonstartup'

 Setting up the PYTHONSTARTUP environment variable:

If you are running Linux or Mac OS X, the simplest way is to create the startup script in your home folder. Then link it with a PYTHONSTARTUP environment variable set into the system shell startup script. For example, Bash and Korn shell use the .profile file, where you can insert a line such as:

`export PYTHONSTARTUP=~/.pythonstartup`

If you are running Windows, it is easy to set a new environment variable as an administrator in the system preferences, and save the script in a common place instead of using a specific user location.

When the interactive prompt is called for, the `.pythonstartup` script should be executed, and the new functionalities made available. For instance, tab completion is really useful to recall module contents:

```
>>> import md5
>>> md5.<tab>
md5.__class__          md5.__file__            md5.__name__
md5.__repr__           md5.digest_size
md5.__delattr__        md5.__getattribute__    md5.__new__
md5.__setattr__        md5.md5
md5.__dict__           md5.__hash__            md5.__reduce__
md5.__str__            md5.new
md5.__doc__            md5.__init__            md5.__reduce_ex__    md5.
blocksize
```

You can adapt the script for more automation, as Python provides an entry point with a module. Further, a module provides the interpreter base classes. (See the `code` module at: `http://docs.python.org/lib/module-code.html`.) But if you want an advanced interactive prompt, you can use an existing tool: iPython.

iPython: An Advanced Prompt

iPython (`http://ipython.scipy.org`) is a project aiming to provide an extended prompt. Among the features provided, the most interesting ones are:

- Dynamic object introspection
- System shell access from the prompt
- Profiling direct support
- Debugging facilities

See the full list at: `http://ipython.scipy.org/doc/manual/index.html`.

To install iPython, go to the download page `http://ipython.scipy.org/moin/Download` and follow the instructions in accordance with your platform.

The iPython shell in action looks like this:

```
tarek@luvdit:~$ ipython
Python 2.4.4 (#2, Apr  5 2007, 20:11:18)
Type "copyright", "credits" or "license" for more information.
IPython 0.7.2 -- An enhanced Interactive Python.
?        -> Introduction to IPython's features.
%magic   -> Information about IPython's 'magic' % functions.
help     -> Python's own help system.
object? -> Details about 'object'. ?object also works, ?? prints more.
In [1]:
```

iPython and application debugging:
iPython is a friendly prompt when it comes to debugging, especially for server-side code that runs daemonized.

Installing setuptools

Perl has a great collection of third-party libraries, and a simple way to install them. The Perl CPAN system lets any developer publish a new library with a simple set of commands. A similar technology has been used in the Python world for the past few years, and is becoming the standard way to install extensions. It is based on:

- A centralized repository on Python's official website called the **Python Package Index (PyPI)**, which was formerly the **Cheeseshop** (with reference to a Monty Python sketch from the BBC)
- A packaging system called `setuptools` that is based on `distutils`, to deliver the code in archives and interact with PyPI

Before installing these extensions, a few explanations are necessary to get the whole picture.

Understanding How It Works

Python comes with a module called `distutils` that provides a set of tools to distribute your Python applications. It provides the following:

- A skeleton to provide standard metadata fields such as the author name, the license type, and many others
- A set of helpers who know how to build a distribution over the code of a package (in Python, a package is a system folder containing one or more modules) and let you create either a set of pre-compiled python files, or a real installer for Windows.

But `distutils` is limited to the package, and doesn't provide a way to define its dependencies over other packages. `setuptools` enhances this by adding a basic dependency system and a lot of other features. It also provides an automatic package finder that knows how to fetch dependencies, and install them automatically. In other words, `setuptools` is to Python what `apt` is to Debian.

 Preparing a setuptools wrapper in Python is becoming the standard way to deploy it. Chapter 5 will cover it extensively.

This tool has become very popular, and is now almost mandatory when writing Python applications that are meant to be distributed to others. It will hopefully be integrated in the standard library that comes with Python within the next few years. Until then, if you want a fully-enabled Python system for yourself with all the power of setuptools, you will need to separately install setuptools. This is because it is not yet a part of the standard Python install.

setuptools Installation Using EasyInstall

To install setuptools, you need to install **EasyInstall**, which is a package downloader and installer. This program is complementary to setuptools because it knows how to handle packages built with it. Installing it will also install setuptools.

Download and run the ez_setup.py script provided on Peak's website. You can find it on http://peak.telecommunity.com/DevCenter/EasyInstall, and its location is usually http://peak.telecommunity.com/dist/ez_setup.py:

```
macziade:~ tziade$ wget http://peak.telecommunity.com/dist/ez_setup.py
08:31:40 (29.26 KB/s) - « ez_setup.py » saved [8960/8960]

macziade:~ tziade$ python ez_setup.py setuptools
Searching for setuptools
Reading http://pypi.python.org/simple/setuptools/
Best match: setuptools 0.6c7
...
Processing dependencies for setuptools
Finished processing dependencies for setuptools
```

If you have a previous installation, you will get a warning, and you will need to use the upgrade option (-U setuptools):

```
macziade:~ tziade$ python ez_setup.py
Setuptools version 0.6c7 or greater has been installed.
(Run "ez_setup.py -U setuptools" to reinstall or upgrade.)

macziade:~ tziade$ python ez_setup.py -U setuptools
Searching for setuptools
Reading http://pypi.python.org/simple/setuptools/
Best match: setuptools 0.6c7
...
Processing dependencies for setuptools
Finished processing dependencies for setuptools
```

When everything is installed, a new command is available on your system called `easy_install`. Any installation or upgrade of an extension will be done through this command. For example, if the `py.test` extension (which is a set of tools to practice agile development; see `http://codespeak.net/py/dist`) needs to be installed, you can run the following code:

```
tarek@luvdit:/tmp$ sudo easy_install py
Searching for py
Reading http://cheeseshop.python.org/pypi/py/
Reading http://codespeak.net/py
Reading http://cheeseshop.python.org/pypi/py/0.9.0
Best match: py 0.9.0
Downloading http://codespeak.net/download/py/py-0.9.0.tar.gz
...
Installing pytest.cmd script to /usr/local/bin
Installed /usr/local/lib/python2.3/site-packages/py-0.9.0-py2.3.egg
Processing dependencies for py
Finished processing dependencies for py
```

If you are under Windows, the script is called `easy_install.exe`, and is located in the `Scripts` folder of your Python installation. So as long as this folder, similar to the one configured in the Windows installation section, is in your PATH, you will be able to call it with `easy_install` as well (without the `sudo` prefix that is used to have root privileges under Linux and Mac OS X).

This tool makes it really easy to extend Python, as every dependency is automatically installed. If an extension needs to be compiled when you are under Windows, an extra step is needed for MinGW to be automatically called.

Hooking MinGW into distutils

When a compilation is needed, a compiler can be indicated to Python with a configuration file. This has to be done explicitly under Windows. Create a new file called `distutils.cfg`, in the `python-installation-path\lib\distutils` folder (`Lib` folder comes with a capital L under Windows) with the following content:

```
[build]
compiler = mingw32
```

This will link MinGW and Python, so that every time Python builds a package that has some C code inside, it will use MinGW transparently.

 Now everything is ready to write some code, at last!

Working Environment

Taking time to set up the working environment is important for productivity. The time used to sharpen the tools is never wasted. It is a bad idea to force the usage of a specific set of tools on all developers when you lead a project. It is better to let each person take care of his or her desk as long as a common set of standards is adopted.

Working on a Python project means writing code, but it also means interacting with data files and third-party servers such as code repositories.

[A developer spends most of his or her time doing something else on his computer, other than writing code.]

There are two paths to set such an environment: either by building it with a composition of small tools (the *old school way*), or by using an all-in-one tool (the *new school way*). Of course, there are various blends between these, and every developer should build his or her environment the way he or she likes it.

Using an Editor and Complementary Tools

This kind of environment is the longest one to prepare, but probably the most productive one. This is because you will be able to tweak it to make it fit with the way you are working. If you always use the same computer, it is easier to install and configure a set of chosen tools. But preparing a portable environment is even better. You can bundle it, for example, in a USB key and use it on any computer. It is also a good practice to use the same tools no matter what the platform is. This will help you in working efficiently anywhere.

[
Portable Python and similar projects:

Portable Python is a project that provides such a feature for Windows, by offering a ready-to-use embedded version of Python and a code editor. We will not create such an exhaustive environment if the target already has Python installed. But this project has an interesting approach and should be looked over. See http://www.portablepython.com.

 Damn Small Linux (DSL) is also an interesting solution to embed a set of tools in a USB drive. It knows how to run a Linux embed into a system emulator called *Qemu*, which runs on any platform. So having a tweaked DSL with Python installed can provide the same features. See http://www.damnsmalllinux.org/usb-qemu.html.

Dragon technology provides a live Ubuntu system that can be used to build a portable Python environment. See http://www.dragontechnology.com/ubuntu_usb.php.
]

Starting from there, a working environment will be composed of:

- A **code editor** that can be found on all platforms, preferably open-source and free
- A few **extra binaries** that provide some features we do not want to rewrite in Python

Code Editor

Many editors are available that are compatible with Python. In a working environment composed of multiple tools, the best pick is an editor that is focused on editing the code and nothing else. That said, the boundary between a simple code editor and an **Integrated Development Environment (IDE)** will always be a bit fuzzy. Even simple editors provide ways to extend or interact with the system. But a well-configured code editor will not bother you with superfluous features.

For many years, the best choices in this area have been **Vim** (http://www.vim.org) or **Emacs** (http://www.gnu.org/software/emacs). They seem unfriendly at first because they have their own standards based on specific keyboard shortcuts, and it takes quite a while to get familiar with them. But when the commands are under control, they are the most productive tools a developer can have. They provide Python-specific modes, and know how to edit other files with a dedicated mode on each format.

Vim is a Python-friendly editor, and lately, the community has shown a lot of interest in it. It can be easily extended with Python. As an example, look up this Pycon 2007 talk: http://www.tummy.com/Community/Presentations/vimpython-20070225/vim.html.

 A big advantage of Vim is that it has been installed on all Linux systems for years, so if you have to work on someone else's system or on a server, it will be available.

The next section presents Vim installation and configuration. If you are more likely to use Emacs, a good starting point is this page: http://www.python.org/emacs.

Installing and Configuring Vim

The latest version is 7.1 and comes with nice features such as a bundled code completer.

If you are under Linux, a version of Vim should already be installed, but probably a version older than 7.1. Check this with the vim --version command. If your version is below 7.0, you should upgrade it either by using the package system of your distribution, or by compiling Vim.

On other systems, Vim needs to be installed. Windows users can get the self-installing executable that provides **gvim** (a version that comes with a graphical user interface) and also a console version. Mac OS X users need to compile the 7.1 version because binaries for the latest version are not currently available.

Get the right version from the download page here: `http://www.vim.org/download.php`, and compile if necessary.

If you need to compile Vim while working with multi-byte characters (such as accented letters in French), you need to call `configure` with the `--enable-multibyte` command. The compilation sequence will look like this:

```
    ./configure --enable-multibyte
make
sudo make install
```

This will install Vim in `/usr/local`, and the binary will be available at: `/usr/local/bin/vim`.

The last thing to do is to create a `.vimrc` file in your home directory if you are under Linux or Mac OS X, and a `_vimrc` file under Windows. In this last case, you should save it in the installation folder, and add an environment variable called `VIM` containing this path, so Vim will know where to get it.

The `vimrc` file content is as follows:

```
    set encoding=utf8
    set paste
    set expandtab
    set textwidth=0
    set tabstop=4
    set softtabstop=4
    set shiftwidth=4
    set autoindent
    set backspace=indent,eol,start
    set incsearch
    set ignorecase
    set ruler
    set wildmenu
    set commentstring=\ #\ %s
    set foldlevel=0
    set clipboard+=unnamed
    syntax on
```

For instance, the `tabstop` option will transform a *<Tab>* stroke into four spaces.

 Remember that the `:help` command under Vim can be called on each option, to understand what it does.

For example, `:help ruler` will display a help screen on the `ruler` option.

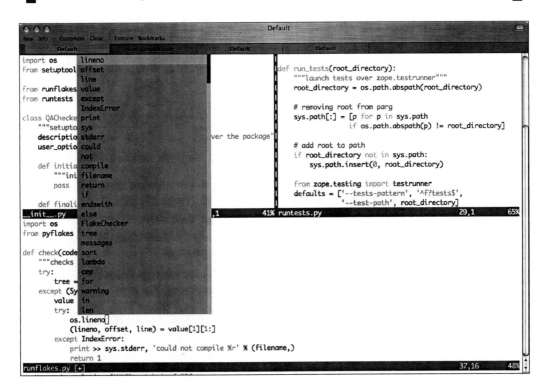

Vim should be ready to run from here.

Using Another Editor

If you cannot get used to Vim or Emacs and want a visual mode editor that interacts a little more with the mouse, you can pick another editor. But it should provide a Python mode and respect the following criteria:

- Replacing the *<Tab>* keystroke by four spaces: This is the most important feature and is now handled correctly by most editors. If the editor you try does not have it, just drop it. Otherwise, you will end up with mixing the tab and spaces in your code, which is a mess for the compiler.

- Removing the trailing spaces on save

- Offering smart cursor placement on new lines, to speed up the writing
- Providing a standard color-code highlighting
- Offering simple code completion

There are a lot of other criteria that can be looked over to compare the code editors. Some are a bit unnecessary such as the code folding, whereas others are quite useful such as API searching. But having the Python interactive prompt, besides the editor, covers enough features to be efficient with the five criteria just mentioned.

 If you really feel uncomfortable with editors such as Vim or Emacs, you probably belong to the new school crew.

Extra Binaries

To complete the editor, a few binaries can be installed to cover common needs:

- **diff**, from GNU `diffutils`, helps comparing the content of two folders or files. This program is available by default on all Linux distributions and Mac OS X. It has to be installed on Windows, and an installer can be found here: `http://gnuwin32.sourceforge.net/packages/diffutils.htm`. When it is installed, the diff command is available in the prompt.

- **grep** provides a command-line utility to search for strings from files. It is more powerful than the system tools, and works in the same way on all platforms. It is available by default on Linux and Mac OS X. It has to be installed on Windows, and can be found here: `http://gnuwin32.sourceforge.net/packages/grep.htm`.

Notice that both grep Under Windows, these are available with MSYS.

Using an Integrated Development Environment

Besides a code editor, all complementary tools are integrated in an IDE. This makes it really fast to deploy and use.

The best free open-source IDE for Python available at this time is Eclipse (`http://www.eclipse.org`) combined with the **PyDev** (`http://pydev.sourceforge.net`) plug-in. This add-on is not free.

A very good commercial alternative is Wingware IDE. See `http://wingware.com`.

Eclipse is portable and will let you work in the same way on any computer. PyDev is a plug-in that enriches Eclipse with certain Python features such as:

- Code completion
- Syntax highlighting
- **Quality Assurance (QA)** tools such as **PyLint** and **Bicycle Repair Man**
- Code coverage
- An integrated debugger

Installing Eclipse with PyDev

Eclipse is written in Java, so the first step is to install the **Java Runtime Environment (JRE)**. If you are running Mac OS X, JRE is already installed. The latest version of JRE can be found on Sun's website at: `http://java.sun.com/javase/downloads/index.jsp`. Download the correct installer and follow the instructions to deploy it on your system.

Eclipse does not provide an installer, since it is just a folder with Java scripts. So its installation is just a matter of getting an archive and uncompressing it on the system. The plug-ins can then be added through the Eclipse interface with a neat package system. But it can be really painful to install the correct set of plug-ins as the latest Eclipse version might not be compatible with them.

Since the extra plug-ins can be bundled in an archive, the simplest way is to get a custom distribution of Eclipse. There are no specialized distributions for Python, but you can create them online on your own.

Yoxos provides this feature through an AJAX installer located at: `http://ondemand.yoxos.com/geteclipse/W4TDelegate`. This web page lets you pick the plug-ins you need and prepares a downloadable archive. Search PyDev for an Eclipse plug-in, and double-click on it in the plug-in list tree on the left. This will add it with all its dependencies. You can then click on the **Download** button on the top right corner to get your archive.

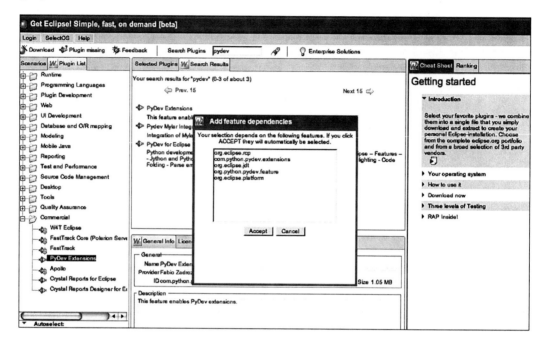

Uncompress the archive on your system, for example in `c:\Program Files\Eclipse` under Windows, and in your home directory under Linux or Mac OS X. You will find a shortcut in this folder to launch the application. Eclipse will then be ready to use.

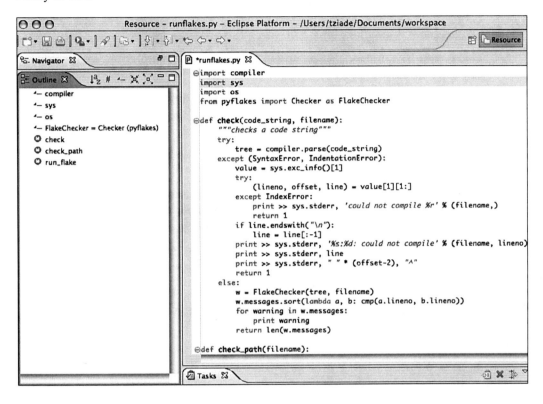

Summary

This chapter covered four points:

- **Python installation**: Python comes in many flavors, but this book focuses on CPython. It can be installed on Linux, Mac OS X, and Windows, but can also be compiled. Using available binaries is simple, though.

- **setuptools installation**: To complete Python-based installation, setuptools has to be deployed as well.

- **Prompt customization**: Python comes with an interactive prompt that can be customized using a startup file. It plays an important role when writing code because small sequences of code can be tested in it.

- **Working environment**: Lastly, to complete the prompt, the developers can use:

  ○ A classical code editor such as Vim or Emacs, or any other can be used as long as it provides a friendly mode for Python code. This editor has to be completed with a set of tools.

  ○ An Integrated Development Environment that integrates everything can be used. Eclipse with PyDev is the best pick at this time.

The next chapter covers the syntax best-practices below the class level.

2

Syntax Best Practices— Below the Class Level

The ability to write an efficient syntax comes naturally with time. If you take a look back at your first program, you will probably agree with this. The right syntax will appear to your eyes as a good-looking piece of code, and the wrong syntax as something disturbing.

Besides the algorithms that are implemented and the architectural thought for your program, taking great care over how it is written weighs heavily on how it will evolve. Many programs are ditched and rewritten from scratch because of their obtuse syntax, unclear APIs, or unconventional standards.

But Python has evolved a lot in the last few years. So if you were kidnapped for a while by your neighbor (a jealous guy from the local Ruby developers' user group) and kept away from the news, you will probably be astonished by its new features. From the earliest version to the current one (2.6 at this time), a lot of enhancements have been made to make the language clearer, cleaner, and easier to write. Python basics have not changed drastically, but the tools to play with them are now a lot more ergonomic.

This chapter presents the most important elements of modern syntax, and the tips on their usage:

- List comprehensions
- Iterators and generators
- Descriptors and properties
- Decorators
- `with` and `contextlib`

 Code performance tips such as for speed improvement or memory usage are covered in Chapter 12.

If you need a reminder on the Python syntax throughout the chapter, the three elements from the official documentation that you can refer to are:

- The help function at the prompt
- The online tutorial at: `http://docs.python.org/tut/tut.html`
- The style guide at: `http://www.python.org/dev/peps/pep-0008`

List Comprehensions

As you probably know, writing a piece of code such as this is painful:

```
>>> numbers = range(10)
>>> size = len(numbers)
>>> evens = []
>>> i = 0
>>> while i < size:
...     if i % 2 == 0 and i != 4:
...         evens.append(i)
...     i += 1
...
>>> evens
[0, 2, 4, 6, 8]
```

This may work for C, but it actually makes things slower for Python because:

- It makes the interpreter work on each loop to determine what part of the sequence has to be changed.
- It makes you keep a counter to track what element has to be treated.

A list comprehension is the correct answer to this pattern. It uses wired features that automate parts of the previous syntax:

```
>>> [i for i in range(10) if i % 2 == 0 and i != 4]
[0, 2, 6, 8]
```

Besides the fact that this writing is more efficient, it is way shorter and involves fewer elements. In a bigger program, this means less bugs and code that is easy to read and understand.

Another typical example of a Pythonic syntax is the usage of `enumerate`. This built-in function provides a convenient way to get an index when a sequence is used in a loop. For example, this piece of code:

```
>>> i = 0
>>> seq = ["one", "two", "three"]
>>> for element in seq:
...       seq[i] = '%d: %s' % (i, seq[i])
...       i += 1
...
>>> seq
['0: one', '1: two', '2: three']
```

can be replaced by the following shorter code:

```
>>> seq = ["one", "two", "three"]
>>> for i, element in enumerate(seq):
...       seq[i] = '%d: %s' % (i, seq[i])
...
>>> seq
['0: one', '1: two', '2: three']
```

and then refactored in a list comprehension like this:

```
>>> def _treatment(pos, element):
...       return '%d: %s' % (pos, element)
...
>>> seq = ["one", "two", "three"]
>>> [_treatment(i, el) for i, el in enumerate(seq)]
['0: one', '1: two', '2: three']
```

This last version is also making it easy to vectorize the code, by sharing small functions that work over a single item of a sequence.

What does a Pythonic syntax mean?

A Pythonic syntax is a syntax that uses the most efficient idioms for the small code patterns. This word can also apply to high-level matters such as libraries. In that case, the library will be considered Pythonic if it plays well with the Pythonic idioms. This term is used sometimes in the community to classify pieces of code, and a tentative definition can be found here: http://faassen.n-tree.net/blog/view/weblog/2005/08/06/0.

Every time a loop is run to massage the contents of a sequence, try to replace it with a list comprehension.

Iterators and Generators

An `iterator` is nothing more than a container object that implements the iterator protocol. It is based on two methods:

- `next`, which returns the next item of the container
- `__iter__`, which returns the iterator itself

Iterators can be created with a sequence using the `iter` built-in function, for example:

```
>>> i = iter('abc')
>>> i.next()
'a'
>>> i.next()
'b'
>>> i.next()
'c'
>>> i.next()
Traceback (most recent call last):
  File "<stdin>", line 1, in <module>
StopIteration
```

When the sequence is exhausted, a `StopIteration` exception is raised. It makes iterators compatible with loops since they catch this exception to stop cycling. To create a custom iterator, a class with a `next` method can be written, as long as it provides the special method `__iter__` that returns an instance of the iterator:

```
>>> class MyIterator(object):
...     def __init__(self, step):
...         self.step = step
...     def next(self):
...         """Returns the next element."""
...         if self.step == 0:
...             raise StopIteration
...         self.step -= 1
...         return self.step
...     def __iter__(self):
...         """Returns the iterator itself."""
...         return self
...
>>> for el in MyIterator(4):
...     print el
...
3
2
1
0
```

Iterators themselves are a low-level feature and concept, and a program can live without them. But they provide the base for a much more interesting feature: generators.

Generators

Since Python 2.2, generators provide an elegant way to write simple and efficient code for functions that return a list of elements. Based on the `yield` directive, they allow you to pause a function and return an intermediate result. The function saves its execution context and can be resumed later if necessary.

For example (this is the example provided in the **PEP** about iterators), the Fibonacci series can be written with an iterator:

```
>>> def fibonacci():
...     a, b = 0, 1
...     while True:
...         yield b
...         a, b = b, a + b
...
>>> fib = fibonacci()
>>> fib.next()
1
>>> fib.next()
1
>>> fib.next()
2
>>> [fib.next() for i in range(10)]
[3, 5, 8, 13, 21, 34, 55, 89, 144, 233]
```

This function returns a `generator` object, a special iterator, which knows how to save the execution context. It can be called indefinitely, yielding the next element of the suite each time. The syntax is concise, and the infinite nature of the algorithm does not disturb the readability of the code anymore. It does not have to provide a way to make the function stoppable. In fact, it looks similar to how the series would be designed in pseudo-code.

A PEP is a **Python Enhancement Proposal**. It is a paper written to make a change on Python, and a start-point for the community to discuss it. See PEP 1 for further information: http://www.python.org/dev/peps/pep-0001

In the community, generators are not used so often because the developers are not used to thinking this way. The developers have been used to working with straight functions for years. `generators` **should be considered every time you deal with a function that returns a sequence or works in a loop**. Returning the elements one at a time can improve the overall performance, when they are passed to another function for further work.

In that case, the resources used to work out one element are most of the time less important than the resources used for the whole process. Therefore, they can be kept low, making the program more efficient. For instance, the Fibonacci sequence is infinite, and yet the generator that generates it does not require an infinite amount of memory to provide the values one at a time. A common use case is to stream data buffers with generators. They can be paused, resumed, and stopped by third-party code that plays over the data, and all the data need not be loaded before starting the process.

The `tokenize` module from the standard library, for instance, generates tokens out of a stream of text and returns an `iterator` for each treated line, that can be passed along to some processing:

```
>>> import tokenize
>>> reader = open('amina.py').next
>>> tokens = tokenize.generate_tokens(reader)
>>> tokens.next()
(1, 'from', (1, 0), (1, 4), 'from amina.quality import
                                        similarities\n')
>>> tokens.next()
(1, 'amina', (1, 5), (1, 10), 'from amina.quality import
                                        similarities\n')
>>> tokens.next()
```

Here we see that `open` iterates over the lines of the file and `generate_tokens` iterates over them in a pipeline, doing additional work.

`generators` can also help in breaking the complexity, and raising the efficiency of some data transformation algorithms that are based on several suites. Thinking of each suite as an `iterator`, and then combining them into a high-level function is a great way to avoid a big, ugly, and unreadable function. Moreover, this can provide a live feedback to the whole processing chain.

In the example below, each function defines a transformation over a sequence. They are then chained and applied. Each call processes one element and returns its result:

```
>>> def power(values):
...     for value in values:
...         print 'powering %s' % value
...         yield value
```

```
...
>>> def adder(values):
...     for value in values:
...         print 'adding to %s' % value
...         if value % 2 == 0:
...             yield value + 3
...         else:
...             yield value + 2
...
>>> elements = [1, 4, 7, 9, 12, 19]
>>> res = adder(power(elements))
>>> res.next()
powering 1
adding to 1
3
>>> res.next()
powering 4
adding to 4
7
>>> res.next()
powering 7
adding to 7
9
```

[
Keep the code simple, not the data:

It is better to have a lot of simple iterable functions that work over sequences of values than a complex function that computes the result for one value at a time.
]

The last feature introduced in Python regarding generators is the ability to interact with the code called with the next method. yield becomes an expression, and a value can be passed along with a new method called send:

```
>>> def psychologist():
...     print 'Please tell me your problems'
...     while True:
...         answer = (yield)
...         if answer is not None:
...             if answer.endswith('?'):
...                 print ("Don't ask yourself
...                        "too much questions")
...             elif 'good' in answer:
...                 print "A that's good, go on"
...             elif 'bad' in answer:
...                 print "Don't be so negative"
...
>>> free = psychologist()
```

```
>>> free.next()
Please tell me your problems
>>> free.send('I feel bad')
Don't be so negative
>>> free.send("Why I shouldn't ?")
Don't ask yourself too much questions
>>> free.send("ok then i should find what is good for me")
A that's good, go on
```

send acts like next, but makes yield return the value passed. The function can, therefore, change its behavior depending on the client code. Two other functions were added to complete this behavior: throw and close. They raise an error into the generator:

- throw allows the client code to send any kind of exception to be raised.
- close acts in the same way, but raises a specific exception: GeneratorExit. In that case, the generator function must raise GeneratorExit again, or StopIteration.

Therefore, a typical template for a generator would look like the following:

```
>>> def my_generator():
...     try:
...         yield 'something'
...     except ValueError:
...         yield 'dealing with the exception'
...     finally:
...         print "ok let's clean"
...
>>> gen = my_generator()
>>> gen.next()
'something'
>>> gen.throw(ValueError('mean mean mean'))
'dealing with the exception'
>>> gen.close()
ok let's clean
>>> gen.next()
Traceback (most recent call last):
  File "<stdin>", line 1, in <module>
StopIteration
```

The `finally` section, which was not allowed on previous versions, will catch any `close` call or `throw` call that is not caught, and is the recommended way to do some cleanup. The `GeneratorExit` exception must not be caught in the generator because it is used by the compiler to make sure it exits cleanly, when `close` is called. If some code is associated with this exception, the interpreter will raise a system error and quit.

These three new methods make it possible to use generators to write coroutines.

Coroutines

A `coroutine` is a function that can be suspended and resumed, and can have multiple entry points. Some languages provide this feature natively such as **Io** (`http://iolanguage.com`) or **Lua** (`http://www.lua.org`). They allow the implementation of cooperative multitasking and pipelines. For example, each `coroutine` consumes or produces data, then pauses until other data are passed along.

Threading is an alternative to coroutines in Python. It can be used to run an interaction between pieces of code. But they need to take care of resource locking since they behave in a pre-emptive manner, whereas coroutines don't. Such code can become fairly complex to create and debug. Though `generators` are almost coroutines, the addition of `send`, `throw`, and `close` was originally meant to provide a coroutine-like feature to the language.

PEP 342 (`http://www.python.org/dev/peps/pep-0342`) that initiated the new behavior of generators also provides a full example on how to create a coroutine scheduler. The pattern is called **Trampoline,** and can be seen as a mediator between coroutines that produce and consume data. It works with a queue where coroutines are wired together.

The `multitask` module available at PyPI (install it with `easy_install multitask`) implements this pattern and can be used straightforwardly:

```
>>> import multitask
>>> def coroutine_1():
...     for i in range(3):
...         print 'c1'
...         yield i
...
>>> def coroutine_2():
...     for i in range(3):
...         print 'c2'
...         yield i
...
>>> multitask.add(coroutine_1())
>>> multitask.add(coroutine_2())
```

```
>>> multitask.run()
c1
c2
c1
c2
c1
c2
```

A classical example of cooperative work between coroutines is a server application that receives queries from multiple clients, and delegates each one to a new thread that responds to it. Implementing this pattern with coroutines is a matter of writing a coroutine (server) that is in charge of receiving queries, and another one (handler) for treating them. The first coroutine places a new handler call for each request in the trampoline.

The `multitask` package adds good APIs to play with sockets, and an echo server, for example, is done straightforward with it:

```python
from __future__ import with_statement
from contextlib import closing
import socket
import multitask
def client_handler(sock):
    with closing(sock):
        while True:
            data = (yield multitask.recv(sock, 1024))
            if not data:
                break
            yield multitask.send(sock, data)
def echo_server(hostname, port):
    addrinfo = socket.getaddrinfo(hostname, port,
                                   socket.AF_UNSPEC,
                                   socket.SOCK_STREAM)
    (family, socktype, proto,
     canonname, sockaddr) = addrinfo[0]
    with closing(socket.socket(family,
                                socktype,
                                proto)) as sock:
        sock.setsockopt(socket.SOL_SOCKET,
                        socket.SO_REUSEADDR, 1)
        sock.bind(sockaddr)
        sock.listen(5)
        while True:
            multitask.add(client_handler((
                    yield multitask.accept(sock))[0]))
```

```
if __name__ == '__main__':
    import sys
    hostname = None
    port = 1111
    if len(sys.argv) > 1:
        hostname = sys.argv[1]
    if len(sys.argv) > 2:
        port = int(sys.argv[2])
    multitask.add(echo_server(hostname, port))
    try:
        multitask.run()
    except KeyboardInterrupt:
        pass
```

 `contextlib` is discussed a bit later in this chapter.

 Another coroutine implementation:
greenlet (`http://codespeak.net/py/dist/greenlet.html`) is another library that provides a good implementation of coroutines for Python, among other features.

Generator Expressions

Python provides a shortcut to write simple generators over a sequence. A syntax similar to list comprehensions can be used to replace `yield`. Parentheses are used instead of brackets:

```
>>> iter = (x**2 for x in range(10) if x % 2 == 0)
>>> for el in iter:
...     print el
...
0
4
16
36
64
```

These kinds of expressions are called generator expressions or **genexp**. They are used in the way the list comprehensions are used to reduce the size of a sequence of code. They also yield elements one at a time like regular generators do. So the whole sequence is not computed ahead of time as list comprehensions. They should be used every time a simple loop is made on a `yield` expression, or to replace a list comprehension that can behave as an iterator.

The itertools Module

When iterators were added in Python, a new module was provided to implement common patterns. Since it is written in the C language, it provides the most efficient iterators. `itertools` covers many patterns, but the most interesting ones are `islice`, `tee`, and `groupby`.

islice: The Window Iterator

`islice` returns an iterator that works over a subgroup of a sequence. The following example reads the lines in a standard input, and yields the elements of each line starting from the fifth one, as long as the line has more than four elements:

```
>>> import itertools
>>> def starting_at_five():
...      value = raw_input().strip()
...      while value != '':
...          for el in itertools.islice(value.split(),
...                                     4, None):
...              yield el
...          value = raw_input().strip()
...
>>> iter = starting_at_five()
>>> iter.next()
one two three four five six
'five'
>>> iter.next()
'six'
>>> iter.next()
one two
one two three four five six
'five'
>>> iter.next()
'six'
>>> iter.next()
one
one two three four five six seven eight
'five'
>>> iter.next()
'six'
>>> iter.next()
'seven'
>>> iter.next()
'eight'
```

One can use `islice` every time to extract data located in a particular position in a stream. This can be a file in a special format using records for instance, or a stream that presents data encapsulated with metadata, like a **SOAP** envelope, for example. In that case, `islice` can be seen as a window that slides over each line of data.

tee: The Back and Forth Iterator

An iterator consumes the sequence it works with. There is no turning back. `tee` provides a pattern to run several iterators over a sequence. This helps us to run over the data again, if provided with the information of the first run. For instance, reading the header of a file can provide information on its nature before running a process over it:

```
>>> import itertools
>>> seq = range(10)
>>> def with_head(iterable, headsize=1):
...     a, b = itertools.tee(iterable)
...     return list(itertools.islice(a, headsize)), b
...
>>> with_head(seq)
([0], <itertools.tee object at 0x8a6e8>)
>>> with_head(seq, 4)
([0, 1, 2, 3], <itertools.tee object at 0x8a698>)
```

In this function, if two iterators are generated with `tee`, then the first one is used with `islice` to get the first `headsize` elements of the iteration, and return them as a flat list. The second element returned is a fresh iterator that can be used to perform work over the whole sequence.

groupby: The uniq Iterator

This function works a little like the Unix command `uniq`. It is able to group the duplicate elements from an iterator, as long as they are adjacent. A function can be given to the function for it to compare the elements. Otherwise, the identity comparison is used.

An example use case for `groupby` is compressing data with **run-length encoding (RLE)**. Each group of adjacent repeated characters of a string is replaced by the character itself and the number of occurrences. When the character is alone, 1 is used.

For example:

get uuuuuuuuuuuuuuuuuup

will be replaced by:

1g1e1t1 18u1p

Just a few lines are necessary with `groupby` to obtain RLE:

```
>>> from itertools import groupby
>>> def compress(data):
...     return ((len(list(group)), name)
...                for name, group in groupby(data))
...
>>> def decompress(data):
...     return (car * size for size, car in data)
...
>>> list(compress('get uuuuuuuuuuuuuuuuuup'))
[(1, 'g'), (1, 'e'), (1, 't'), (1, ' '),
 (18, 'u'), (1, 'p')]
>>> compressed = compress('get uuuuuuuuuuuuuuuuuup')
>>> ''.join(decompress(compressed))
'get uuuuuuuuuuuuuuuuuup'
```

Compression algorithms:

If you are interested in compression, consider the **LZ77** algorithm. It is an enhanced version of RLE that looks for adjacent matching patterns instead of matching characters: `http://en.wikipedia.org/wiki/LZ77`.

`groupby` can be used each time a summary has to be done over data. In this matter, the built-in function `sorted` is very useful to make the similar elements adjacent from data passed to it.

Other Functions

`http://docs.python.org/lib/itertools-functions.html` will give you an exhaustive list of `itertools` functions that were not shown in this section. Each of them is presented with its corresponding code in pure Python to understand how it works:

- `chain(*iterables)`: This makes an iterator that iterates over the first iterable, then proceeds to the next one, and so on.
- `count([n])`: This returns an iterator that gives consecutive integers, such as a range. Starts with `0` or with `n`, when given.
- `cycle(iterable)`: This iterates over each element of the iterable, and then restarts. This repeats indefinitely.
- `dropwhile(predicate, iterable)`: This drops each element from the iterable, as long as the predicate returns `True`. When the predicate returns `False`, it starts to yield the rest of the elements.
- `ifilter(predicate, iterable)`: This is similar to the built-in function `filter`.

- `ifilterfalse(predicate, iterable)`: This is similar to `ifilter`, but will iterate on elements when the predicate is `False`.

- `imap(function, *iterables)`: This is similar to the built-in function `map`, but works over several iterables. It stops when the shortest iterable is exhausted.

- `izip(*iterables)`: This works like `zip` but returns an iterator.

- `repeat(object [, times])`: This returns an iterator that returns `object` on each call. Run `times` times or indefinitely when `times` is not given.

- `starmap(function, iterable)`: This works like `imap` but passes the iterable element as a star argument to `function`. This is helpful when returned elements are tuples that can be passed as arguments to `function`.

- `takewhile(predicate, iterable)`: This returns the elements from the iterable, and stops when `predicate` turns `False`.

Decorators

Decorators were added in Python 2.4 to make function and method wrapping (a function that receives a function and returns an enhanced one) easier to read and understand. The original use case was to be able to define the methods as class methods or static methods, on the head of their definition. The syntax before the decorators was:

```
>>> class WhatFor(object):
...     def it(cls):
...         print 'work with %s' % cls
...     it = classmethod(it)
...     def uncommon():
...         print 'I could be a global function'
...     uncommon = staticmethod(uncommon)
...
```

This syntax was getting hard to read when the methods were getting big, or several transformations over the methods were done.

The decorator syntax is lighter and easier to understand:

```
>>> class WhatFor(object):
...     @classmethod
...     def it(cls):
...         print 'work with %s' % cls
...     @staticmethod
...     def uncommon():
...         print 'I could be a global function'
...
```

```
>>> this_is = WhatFor()
>>> this_is.it()
work with <class '__main__.WhatFor'>
>>> this_is.uncommon()
I could be a global function
```

When the decorators appeared, many developers in the community started to use them because they became an obvious way to implement some patterns. One of the original mail threads on this was initiated by Jim Hugunin, the IronPython lead developer.

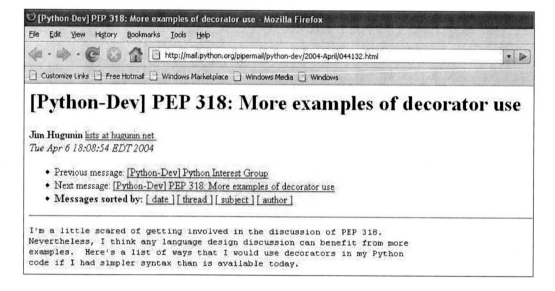

The rest of this section presents how to write decorators, and provides a few examples.

How to Write a Decorator

There are many ways to write custom decorators, but the simplest and most readable way is to write a function that returns a sub-function that wraps the original function call.

A generic pattern is:

```
>>> def mydecorator(function):
...     def _mydecorator(*args, **kw):
...         # do some stuff before the real
...         # function gets called
...         res = function(*args, **kw)
```

```
...          # do some stuff after
...             return res
...          # returns the sub-function
...          return _mydecorator
...
```

It is a good practice to give an explicit name to the sub-function like _mydecorator, instead of a generic name like wrapper, because it will be easier to read tracebacks when an error is raised in the chain: you will know you are dealing with the given decorator.

When arguments are needed for the decorator to work on, a second level of wrapping has to be used.

```
def mydecorator(arg1, arg2):
    def _mydecorator(function):
        def __mydecorator(*args, **kw):
            # do some stuff before the real
            # function gets called
            res = function(*args, **kw)
            # do some stuff after
            return res
        # returns the sub-function
        return __mydecorator
    return _mydecorator
```

Since decorators are loaded by the interpreter when the module is first read, their usage should be limited to wrappers that can be generically applied. If a decorator is tied to the method's class or to the function's signature it enhances, it should be refactored into a regular callable to avoid complexity. In any case, when the decorators are dealing with APIs, a good practice is to group them in a module that is easy to maintain.

 A decorator should focus on arguments that the wrapped function or method receives and returns, and if needed, should limit its introspection work as much as possible.

The common patterns for decorators are:

- Argument checking
- Caching
- Proxy
- Context provider

Argument checking

Checking the arguments that a function receives or returns can be useful when it is executed in a specific context. For example, if a function is to be called through XML-RPC, Python will not be able to directly provide its full signature as in the statically-typed languages. This feature is needed to provide introspection capabilities, when the XML-RPC client asks for the function signatures.

The XML-RPC protocol:

The XML-RPC protocol is a lightweight **Remote Procedure Call** protocol that uses XML over HTTP to encode its calls. It is often used instead of SOAP for simple client-server exchanges.

Unlike SOAP, which provides a page that lists all callable functions (WSDL), XML-RPC does not have a directory of available functions. An extension of the protocol that allows discovering the server API was proposed, and Python's xmlrpclib module implements it. (See http://docs.python.org/lib/serverproxy-objects.html.)

A decorator can provide this type of signature, and make sure that what goes in and out respects it:

```
>>> from itertools import izip
>>> rpc_info = {}
>>> def xmlrpc(in_=(), out=(type(None),)):
...     def _xmlrpc(function):
...         # registering the signature
...         func_name = function.func_name
...         rpc_info[func_name] = (in_, out)
...
...         def _check_types(elements, types):
...             """Subfunction that checks the types."""
...             if len(elements) != len(types):
...                 raise TypeError('argument count is wrong')
...             typed = enumerate(izip(elements, types))
...             for index, couple in typed:
...                 arg, of_the_right_type = couple
...                 if isinstance(arg, of_the_right_type):
...                     continue
...                 raise TypeError('arg #%d should be %s' % \
...                         (index, of_the_right_type)
...
...         # wrapped function
...         def __xmlrpc(*args):   # no keywords allowed
...             # checking what goes in
...             checkable_args = args[1:]   # removing self
...             _check_types(checkable_args, in_)
...
```

```
...              # running the function
...              res = function(*args)
...
...              # checking what goes out
...              if not type(res) in (tuple, list):
...                  checkable_res = (res,)
...              else:
...                  checkable_res = res
...              _check_types(checkable_res, out)
...
...              # the function and the type
...              # checking succeeded
...              return res
...          return __xmlrpc
...      return _xmlrpc
...
```

The decorator registers the function into a global dictionary, and keeps a list of the types for its arguments and for the returned values. Note that the example was highly simplified to demonstrate argument-checking decorators.

A usage example would be:

```
>>> class RPCView(object):
...
...     @xmlrpc((int, int))      # two int -> None
...     def meth1(self, int1, int2):
...         print 'received %d and %d' % (int1, int2)
...
...     @xmlrpc((str,), (int,))      # string -> int
...     def meth2(self, phrase):
...         print 'received %s' % phrase
...         return 12
...
```

When it is read, this class definition populates the rpc_info dictionary and can be used in a specific environment, where the argument types are checked:

```
>>> rpc_info
{'meth2': ((<type 'str'>,), (<type 'int'>,)),
 'meth1': ((<type 'int'>, <type 'int'>),
           (<type 'NoneType'>,))}
>>> my = RPCView()
>>> my.meth1(1, 2)
received 1 and 2
>>> my.meth2(2)
Traceback (most recent call last):
  File "<stdin>", line 1, in <module>
  File "<stdin>", line 16, in _wrapper
  File "<stdin>", line 11, in _check_types
TypeError: arg #0 should be <type 'str'>
```

There are many other use cases for argument-checking decorators, such as type enforcement (see http://wiki.python.org/moin/PythonDecoratorLibrary#head-308f2b3507ca91800def19d813348f78db34303e) where you can define several levels of type checking, given a global configuration value:

- Nothing is checked.
- The checker just pops warnings.
- The checker raises `TypeError` exceptions.

Caching

The caching decorator is quite similar to argument checking, but focuses on those functions whose internal state does not affect the output. Each set of arguments can be linked to a unique result. This style of programming is the characteristic of *functional programming* (see http://en.wikipedia.org/wiki/Functional_programming), and can be used when the set of input values is finite.

Therefore, a caching decorator can keep the output together with the arguments that were needed to compute it, and return it directly on subsequent calls. This behavior is called *memoizing* (see http://en.wikipedia.org/wiki/Memoizing), and is quite simple to implement as a decorator:

```
>>> import time
>>> import hashlib
>>> import pickle
>>> from itertools import chain
>>> cache = {}
>>> def is_obsolete(entry, duration):
...     return time.time() - entry['time'] > duration
...
>>> def compute_key(function, args, kw):
...     key = pickle.dumps((function.func_name, args, kw))
...     return hashlib.sha1(key).hexdigest()
...
>>> def memoize(duration=10):
...     def _memoize(function):
...         def __memoize(*args, **kw):
...             key = compute_key(function, args, kw)
...
...             # do we have it already ?
...             if (key in cache and
...                 not is_obsolete(cache[key], duration)):
...                 print 'we got a winner'
...                 return cache[key]['value']
...
...             # computing
...             result = function(*args, **kw)
```

```
...
...                     # storing the result
...                     cache[key] = {'value': result,
...                                     'time': time.time()}
...                 return result
...             return __memoize
...         return _memoize
...
```

A *SHA* hash key is built using the ordered argument values, and the result is stored in a global dictionary. The hash is made using a pickle, which is a bit of a shortcut to freeze the state of all objects passed as arguments, ensuring that all arguments are good candidates. If a thread or a socket is used as an argument, for instance, a `PicklingError` will occur. (See `http://docs.python.org/lib/node318.html`.)

The `duration` parameter is used to invalidate the cached value when too much time has passed since the last function call.

Here's an example of usage:

```
>>> @memoize()
... def very_very_very_complex_stuff(a, b):
...     # if your computer gets too hot on this calculation
...     # consider stopping it
...     return a + b
...
>>> very_very_very_complex_stuff(2, 2)
4
>>> very_very_very_complex_stuff(2, 2)
we got a winner
4
>>> @memoize(1)        # invalidates the cache after 1 second
... def very_very_very_complex_stuff(a, b):
...     return a + b
...
>>> very_very_very_complex_stuff(2, 2)
4
>>> very_very_very_complex_stuff(2, 2)
we got a winner
4
>>> cache
{'c2727f43c6e39b3694649ee0883234cf': {'value': 4, 'time':
 1199734132.7102251}}
>>> time.sleep(2)
>>> very_very_very_complex_stuff(2, 2)
4
```

Notice that the first call used empty parenthesis because of the two-level wrapping.

Caching expensive functions can dramatically increase the overall performance of a program, but it has to be used with care. The cached value could also be tied to the function itself to manage its scope and life cycle, instead of a centralized dictionary. But in any case, a more efficient decorator would use a specialized cache library based on advanced caching algorithms, and for the web applications on distributed caching features. **Memcached** is one of those and can be used in Python.

[Chapter 13 provides detailed information and techniques on caching]

Proxy

Proxy decorators are used to tag and register functions with a global mechanism. For instance, a security layer that protects the access of the code, depending on the current user, can be implemented using a centralized checker with an associated permission required by the callable:

```
>>> class User(object):
...     def __init__(self, roles):
...         self.roles = roles
...
>>> class Unauthorized(Exception):
...     pass
...
>>> def protect(role):
...     def _protect(function):
...         def __protect(*args, **kw):
...             user = globals().get('user')
...             if user is None or role not in user.roles:
...                 raise Unauthorized("I won't tell you")
...             return function(*args, **kw)
...         return __protect
...     return _protect
...
```

This model is often used in Python web frameworks to define the security over publishable classes. For instance, Django provides decorators to secure function access. (See *Chapter 12* called *Sessions, Users, and Registration* in the Django book at http://www.djangobook.com.)

Here's an example, where the current user is kept in a global variable. The decorator checks his or her roles when the method is accessed:

```
>>> tarek = User(('admin', 'user'))
>>> bill = User(('user',))
>>> class MySecrets(object):
...     @protect('admin')
...     def waffle_recipe(self):
...         print 'use tons of butter!'
...
>>> these_are = MySecrets()
>>> user = tarek
>>> these_are.waffle_recipe()
use tons of butter!
>>> user = bill
>>> these_are.waffle_recipe()
Traceback (most recent call last):
  File "<stdin>", line 1, in <module>
  File "<stdin>", line 7, in wrap
__main__.Unauthorized: I won't tell you
```

Context Provider

A context decorator makes sure that the function can run in the correct context, or run some code before and after the function. In other words, it sets and unsets a specific execution environment. For example, when a data item has to be shared among several threads, a lock has to be used to ensure that it is protected from multiple access. This lock can be coded in a decorator as follows:

```
>>> from threading import RLock
>>> lock = RLock()
>>> def synchronized(function):
...     def _synchronized(*args, **kw):
...         lock.acquire()
...         try:
...             return function(*args, **kw)
...         finally:
...             lock.release()
...     return _synchronized
...
>>> @synchronized
... def thread_safe():    # make sure it locks the resource
...     pass
...
```

Context decorators are being replaced by the usage of the `with` statement that appeared in Python 2.5. This statement was created to streamline the `try..finally` pattern, and in some cases, covers the context decorator use cases.

A good place to start to get more decorator use cases is: `http://wiki.python.org/moin/PythonDecoratorLibrary`.

with and contextlib

The `try..finally` statement is useful to ensure some cleanup code is run even if an error is raised. There are many use cases for this, such as:

- Closing a file
- Releasing a lock
- Making a temporary code patch
- Running protected code in a special environment

The `with` statement factors out these use cases, by providing a simple way to call some code before and after a block of code. For example, working with a file is usually done like this:

```
>>> hosts = file('/etc/hosts')
>>> try:
...      for line in hosts:
...           if line.startswith('#'):
...                continue
...           print line
... finally:
...      hosts.close()
...
127.0.0.1        localhost
255.255.255.255 broadcasthost
::1              localhost
```

 This example is specific to Linux since it reads the host file located in `etc`, but any text file could have been used here in the same way.

By using the `with` statement, it can be rewritten like this:

```
>>> from __future__ import with_statement
>>> with file('/etc/hosts') as hosts:
...      for line in hosts:
...           if line.startswith('#'):
```

```
...             continue
...         print line
...
127.0.0.1         localhost
255.255.255.255 broadcasthost
::1               localhost
```

Notice that the `with` statement is still located in the __future__ module for the 2.5 series and will be directly available in 2.6. It is described in: http://www.python. org/dev/peps/pep-0343.

The other items that are compatible with this statement are classes from the `thread` and `threading` module:

- thread.LockType
- threading.Lock
- threading.RLock
- threading.Condition
- threading.Semaphore
- threading.BoundedSemaphore

All these classes implement two methods: __enter__ and __exit__, which together form the **with** protocol. In other words, any class can implement it:

```
>>> class Context(object):
...     def __enter__(self):
...         print 'entering the zone'
...     def __exit__(self, exception_type, exception_value,
...                     exception_traceback):
...         print 'leaving the zone'
...         if exception_type is None:
...             print 'with no error'
...         else:
...             print 'with an error (%s)' % exception_value
...
>>> with Context():
...     print 'i am the zone'
...
entering the zone
i am the zone
leaving the zone
with no error
>>> with Context():
...     print 'i am the buggy zone'
...     raise TypeError('i am the bug')
```

```
...
entering the zone
i am the buggy zone
leaving the zone
with an error (i am the bug)
Traceback (most recent call last):
   File "<stdin>", line 3, in <module>
TypeError: i am the bug
```

__exit__ receives three arguments that are filled when an error occurs within the code block. If no error occurs, all three arguments are set to None. When an error occurs, __exit__ should not re-raise it, as this is the responsibility of the caller. It can prevent the exception being raised though, by returning True. This is provided to implement some specific use cases, such as the contextmanager decorator that we will see in the next section. But for most use cases, the right behavior for this method is to do some cleaning like what would be done by finally; no matter what happens in the block it does not returning anything.

The contextlib Module

A module was added to the standard library to provide helpers to use the with statement. The most useful item is contextmanager, a decorator that will enhance a generator that provides both __enter__ and __exit__ parts, separated by a yield statement. The previous example written with this decorator will look like this:

```
>>> from contextlib import contextmanager
>>> from __future__ import with_statement
>>> @contextmanager
... def context():
...     print 'entering the zone'
...     try:
...         yield
...     except Exception, e:
...         print 'with an error (%s)' % e
...         # we need to re-raise here
...         raise e
...     else:
...         print 'with no error'
...
```

If any exception occurs, the function needs to re-raise it in order to pass it along. Note that context could have some arguments if needed, as long as they are provided in the call. This small helper simplifies the normal class-based context API exactly as generators do with the classed-based iterator API.

The two other helpers provided by this module are:

- `closing(element)`: This is a `contextmanager` decorated function that yields an element, and then calls the element's close method on exit. This is useful for classes that deal with streams, for instance.

- `nested(context1, context2, ...)`: This is a function that will combine contexts and make nested `with` calls with them.

Context Example

An interesting usage of `with` is logging the code that can be decorated when entering the context, and then set back as it was when it is over. This prevents changing the code itself and allows, for example, a unit test to get some feedback on the code usage.

In the following example, a context is created to equip all public APIs of a given class:

```
>>> from __future__ import with_statement
>>> from contextlib import contextmanager
>>> @contextmanager
... def logged(klass, logger):
...     # logger
...     def _log(f):
...         def __log(*args, **kw):
...             logger(f, args, kw)
...             return f(*args, **kw)
...         return __log
...
...     # let's equip the class
...     for attribute in dir(klass):
...         if attribute.startswith('_'):
...             continue
...         element = getattr(klass, attribute)
...         setattr(klass, '__logged_%s' % attribute, element)
...         setattr(klass, attribute, _log(element))
...
...     # let's work
...     yield klass
...
...     # let's remove the logging
...     for attribute in dir(klass):
...         if not attribute.startswith('__logged_')
```

```
...          continue
...          element = getattr(klass, attribute)
...          setattr(klass, attribute[len('__logged_'):],
...                  element)
...          delattr(klass, attribute)
...
```

The logger function can then be used to record what APIs are being called in a given context. In the following example, the calls are added in a list to track the API usage, and then to perform some assertions. For instance, if the same API is called for more than once, it could mean that the public signature of the class could be refactored to avoid duplicate calls:

```
>>> class One(object):
...     def _private(self):
...         pass
...     def one(self, other):
...         self.two()
...         other.thing(self)
...         self._private()
...     def two(self):
...         pass
...
>>> class Two(object):
...     def thing(self, other):
...         other.two()
...
>>> calls = []
>>> def called(meth, args, kw):
...     calls.append(meth.im_func.func_name)
...
>>> with logged(One, called):
...     one = One()
...     two = Two()
...     one.one(two)
...
>>> calls
['one', 'two', 'two']
```

Summary

In this chapter, we have learned that:

- List comprehensions are the most convenient way to take existing iterables, do something with them, and then produce new lists.
- Iterators and generators provide an efficient set of tools to generate and work with sequences.
- Decorators provide a readable way to wrap existing functions and methods with an additional behavior. This leads to new code-patterns that are very simple to implement and use.
- The `with` statement streamlines the `try..finally` pattern.

The next chapter also covers syntax best-practices, but those dedicated to classes.

3

Syntax Best Practices— Above the Class Level

We will now focus on syntax best practices for classes. It is not intended to cover design patterns here, as they will be discussed in Chapter 14. This chapter gives an overview of the advanced Python syntax to manipulate and enhance the class code. Though the Python object model is still evolving in some subtle, but fundamental ways in the 2x series, it still presents some of the language internals to fully understand how classes work. This is quite important to avoid some common pitfalls and misuses of the object model.

The following topics will be discussed:

- Subclassing built-in types
- Accessing methods from super classes
- Slots
- Meta-programming

Subclassing Built-in Types

Python 2.2 introduced the unification of types and classes (see the draft here: http://www.python.org/download/releases/2.2.3/descrintro) that made the subclassing of the built-in types possible. A new built-in type called `object` was added to provide a common ancestor for all built-in types. This had a subtle, but minor effect on the mechanics of OOP in Python, and allowed programmers to subclass the built-in types such as `list`, `tuple`, or `dict`. So every time a class that behaves almost like one of the built-in types needs to be implemented, the best practice is to subtype it.

Next, we will show the code for a class called `distinctdict`, which uses this technique. It is a subclass of the usual Python `dict` type. This new class behaves in most ways like an ordinary Python `dict`. But instead of allowing multiple keys with the same value, when someone tries to add a new entry with an identical value, it raises a `ValueError` with a help message:

```
>>> class DistinctError(Exception):
...     pass
>>> class distinctdict(dict):
...     def __setitem__(self, key, value):
...         try:
...             value_index = self.values().index(value)
...             # keys() and values() will return
...             # corresponding lists
...             # as long as the dict is not changed
...             # between the two calls
...             # otherwise the dict type does not guarantee
...             # the ordering.
...             existing_key = self.keys()[value_index]
...             if existing_key != key:
...                 raise DistinctError(("This value already
...                                     "exists for '%s'") % \
...                             str(self[existing_key]))
...         except ValueError:
...             pass
...
...         super(distinctdict, self).__setitem__(key, value)
...
>>> my = distinctdict()
>>> my['key'] = 'value'
>>> my['other_key'] = 'value'
Traceback (most recent call last):
  File "<stdin>", line 1, in <module>
  File "<stdin>", line 14, in __setitem__
DistinctError: This value already exists for 'value'
>>> my['other_key'] = 'value2'
>>> my
{'other_key': 'value2', 'key': 'value'}
```

If you take a look at your existing code, you may find a lot of classes that partially implement the built-in types, and are faster and cleaner as subtypes. The `list` type, for instance, manages the sequences that should be used every time a class works internally with a sequence:

```
>>> class folder(list):
...     def __init__(self, name):
...         self.name = name
...     def dir(self):
...         print 'I am the %s folder.' % self.name
```

```
...            for element in self:
...                print element
...
>>> the = folder('secret')
>>> the
[]
>>> the.append('pics')
>>> the.append('videos')
>>> the.dir()
I am the secret folder:
pics
videos
```

Since Python 2.4, the `collections` module has provided types that can be used to implement efficient container classes:

- The `deque` type implements a double-ended queue.
- The `defaultdict` type provides a dictionary-like object with default values for unknown keys. This type is similar to the way hashes work in Perl or Ruby.

Built-in types cover most of the use cases.

When you are about to create a new class that acts like a sequence or a mapping, think about its features and look over the existing built-in types. You will end up using one of them most of the time.

Accessing Methods from Superclasses

`super` is a built-in type that can be used to access an attribute belonging to an object's superclass.

The Python official documentation lists `super` as a built-in function. But it's a built-in type, even if it is used like a function.

```
>>> super
<type 'super'>
```

Its usage is a bit confusing, when you are used to accessing a class attribute or method by calling the parent class directly and passing `self` as the first argument. Refer to the following code:

```
>>> class Mama(object):  # this is the old way
...     def says(self):
...         print 'do your homework'
...
>>> class Sister(Mama):
```

```
...         def says(self):
...             Mama.says(self)
...             print 'and clean your bedroom'
...
>>> anita = Sister()
>>> anita.says()
do your homework
and clean your bedroom
```

Look particularly at the line `Mama.says(self)`, where we use the technique just described to call the `says()` method of the superclass (that is, the `Mama` class), and pass `self` as the argument. This means that the `says()` method belonging to `Mama` will be called. But the instance on which it will be called will return `self`, which is an instance of `Sister` in this case.

Instead, the `super` usage would be:

```
>>> class Sister(Mama):  # this is the new way
...     def says(self):
...         super(Sister, self).says()
...         print 'and clean your bedroom'
...
```

This use case is very simple to follow and understand, but when you face a multiple inheritance schema, `super` becomes hard to be used. Before explaining these problems, including when `super` should be avoided, understanding how the **Method Resolution Order (MRO)** works in Python is important.

Understanding Python's Method Resolution Order (MRO)

Python 2.3 added a new MRO based on **C3**, the MRO built for Dylan (http://www.opendylan.org). The reference document, written by Michele Simionato, is located here: http://www.python.org/download/releases/2.3/mro. It describes how C3 builds the **linearization** of a class, also called **precedence**, which is an ordered list of the ancestors. This list is used to seek an attribute.

[The C3 algorithm is described later in this section.]

The MRO change was made to resolve an issue introduced with the creation of a common base type (`object`). Before the change to the C3 linearization method, if a class had two ancestors (see *Illustration 1*), the MRO was quite simple to compute:

```
>>> class Base1:
...     pass
```

```
...
>>> class Base2:
...       def method(self):
...           print 'Base2'
...
>>> class MyClass(Base1, Base2):
...       pass
...
>>> here = MyClass()
>>> here.method()
Base2
```

When `here.method` is called, the interpreter looks for the method in `MyClass`, then `Base1`, and then eventually finds it in `Base2`.

Now a `BaseBase` class on the top of the two base classes (both `Base1` and `Base2` inherit from it, see *Illustration 2*) was introduced. As a result, the old MRO that behaved according to the "left-to-right depth-first" rule was getting back to the top through the `Base1` class before looking in `Base2`.

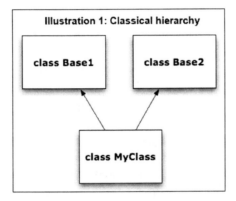

Illustration 1: Classical hierarchy

class Base1   class Base2

class MyClass

The following code was making this weird behavior happen:

```
>>> class BaseBase:
...       def method(self):
...           print 'BaseBase'
...
>>> class Base1(BaseBase):
...       pass
...
>>> class Base2(BaseBase):
...       def method(self):
...           print 'Base2'
...
>>> class MyClass(Base1, Base2):
...       pass
```

```
    . . .
>>> here = MyClass()
>>> here.method()
BaseBase
```

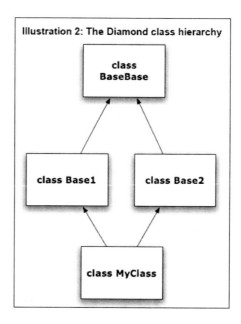

Illustration 2: The Diamond class hierarchy

This inheritance scenario is extremely uncommon, so this is more a problem of theory than practice. The standard library does not structure the inheritance hierarchies in this way, and many developers think it is a bad practice. But with the introduction of `object` at the top of the types hierarchy, the multiple inheritance problem pops up on the C side of the language, resulting in conflicts when doing subtyping. Since making it work properly with the existing MRO involved too much work, a new MRO was a simpler and quicker solution.

So the same example under a recent Python (at least 2.3) is as shown:

```
>>> class BaseBase(object):
...     def method(self):
...         print 'BaseBase'
...
>>> class Base1(BaseBase):
...     pass
...
>>> class Base2(BaseBase):
...     def method(self):
...         print 'Base2'
...
```

```
>>> class MyClass(Base1, Base2):
...      pass
...
>>> here = MyClass()
>>> here.method()
Base2
```

The new MRO is based on a recursive call over the base classes. To summarize the Michele Simionato paper referenced in the beginning of this section, the C3 symbolic notation applied to our example is:

```
L[MyClass(Base1, Base2)] =
      MyClass + merge(L[Base1], L[Base2], Base1, Base2)
```

Where L[MyClass] is the linearization of the MyClass class and merge is a specific algorithm that merges several linearization results.

So a synthetic description would be, as Simionato says:

> *The linearization of C is the sum of C plus the merge of the*
> *linearizations of the parents and the list of the parents*

The merge algorithm is responsible for removing the duplicates and preserving the correct ordering. It is described in the paper like this (adapted to our example):

> *Take the head of the first list, i.e L[Base1][0]; if this head*
> *is not in the tail of any of the other lists, then add it to the*
> *linearization of MyClass and remove it from the lists in the merge,*
> *otherwise look at the head of the next list and take it, if it is a*
> *good head.*

> *Then repeat the operation until all the class are removed or it is*
> *impossible to find good heads. In this case, it is impossible to*
> *construct the merge, Python 2.3 will refuse to create the class*
> *MyClass and will raise an exception.*

The head is the first element of a list and tail contains the rest of the elements. For example, in (Base1, Base2, ..., BaseN), Base1 is the head, and (Base2, ..., BaseN) the tail.

In other words, C3 does a recursive depth lookup on each parent to get a sequence of lists. Then it computes a left-to-right rule to merge all lists with a hierarchy disambiguation, when a class is involved in several lists.

So the result is:

```
>>> def L(klass):
...      return [k.__name__ for k in klass.__mro__]
...
>>> L(MyClass)
['MyClass', 'Base1', 'Base2', 'BaseBase', 'object']
```

> The __mro__ attribute of a class (which is read-only) stores the result of the linearization computation, which is done when the class definition is loaded.
>
> You can also call MyClass.mro() to compute and get the result.
>
> Notice that this will only work for the new-style classes, so it is a bad practice to mix old-style and new-style classes in the code base. The MRO behavior will differ.

super Pitfalls

Back to super. Its usage, when using multiple inheritance hierarchy, can be quite dangerous mainly because of initialization of classes. In Python, the base classes are not implicitly called in __init__, and so it is up to the developer to call them. Here are a few examples.

Mixing super and classic Calls

In the following example taken from James Knight's website (http://fuhm.net/ super-harmful), a C class that calls its base classes using the __init__ method will make B class be called twice!

```
>>> class A(object):
...     def __init__(self):
...         print "A"
...         super(A, self).__init__()
...
>>> class B(object):
...     def __init__(self):
...         print "B"
...         super(B, self).__init__()
...
>>> class C(A,B):
...     def __init__(self):
...         print "C"
...         A.__init__(self)
...         B.__init__(self)
...
>>> print "MRO:", [x.__name__ for x in C.__mro__]
MRO: ['C', 'A', 'B', 'object']
>>> C()
C A B B
<__main__.C object at 0xc4910>
```

This happens due to the A.__init__(self) call, which is made with the C instance, thus making super(A, self).__init__() call B's constructor. In other words, super should be used into the whole class hierarchy. The problem is that sometimes a part of this hierarchy is located in third-party code. Many related pitfalls on the hierarchy calls introduced by multiple inheritances can be found on James's page.

To avoid these problems, you should always take a look at the __mro__ attribute before you subclass it. If it is not available, you are dealing with an old-style class and it is probably safer to avoid super:

```
>>> from SimpleHTTPServer import SimpleHTTPRequestHandler
>>> SimpleHTTPRequestHandler.__mro__
Traceback (most recent call last):
  File "<stdin>", line 1, in <module>
AttributeError: class SimpleHTTPRequestHandler has no attribute '__mro__'
```

If __mro__ is available, have a quick look at the code of the constructor of each class involved in the MRO. If super is used everywhere, it is super! You can use it. If not, try to be consistent.

In the following example, we can see that collections.deque can be safely subclassed and super can be used, because it directly subclasses object:

```
>>> from collections import deque
>>> deque.__mro__
(<type 'collections.deque'>, <type 'object'>)
```

In this example, it seems that random.Random is a wrapper around another class that lives in a _random module:

```
>>> from random import Random
>>> random.Random.__mro__
(<class 'random.Random'>, <type '_random.Random'>, <type 'object'>)
```

This is a C module, so we should be safe as well.

The last example is of a Zope class, where the constructors should be carefully checked:

```
>>> from zope.app.container.browser.adding import Adding
>>> Adding.__mro__
(<class 'zope.app.container.browser.adding.Adding'>,
 <class 'zope.publisher.browser.BrowserView'>,
 <class 'zope.location.location.Location'>,
 <type 'object'>)
```

Heterogeneous Arguments

Another issue with `super` usage is argument passing in initialization. How can a class call its base class __init__ code if it doesn't have the same signature? This leads to the following problem:

```
>>> class BaseBase(object):
...     def __init__(self):
...         print 'basebase'
...         super(BaseBase, self).__init__()
...
>>> class Base1(BaseBase):
...     def __init__(self):
...         print 'base1'
...         super(Base1, self).__init__()
...
>>> class Base2(BaseBase):
...     def __init__(self, arg):
...         print 'base2'
...         super(Base2, self).__init__()
...
>>> class MyClass(Base1 , Base2):
...     def __init__(self, arg):
...         print 'my base'
...         super(MyClass, self).__init__(arg)
...
>>> m = MyClass(10)
my base
Traceback (most recent call last):
  File "<stdin>", line 1, in <module>
  File "<stdin>", line 4, in __init__
TypeError: __init__() takes exactly 1 argument (2 given)
```

One solution would be to use `*args` and `**kw` magic, so that all constructors pass along all the parameters even if they do not use them:

```
>>> class BaseBase(object):
...     def __init__(self, *args, **kw):
...         print 'basebase'
...         super(BaseBase, self).__init__(*args, **kw)
...
>>> class Base1(BaseBase):
...     def __init__(self, *args, **kw):
...         print 'base1'
...         super(Base1, self).__init__(*args, **kw)
```

```
...
>>> class Base2(BaseBase):
...      def __init__(self, arg, *args, **kw):
...          print 'base2'
...          super(Base2, self).__init__(*args, **kw)
...
>>> class MyClass(Base1 , Base2):
...      def __init__(self, arg):
...          print 'my base'
...          super(MyClass, self).__init__(arg)
...
>>> m = MyClass(10)
my base
base1
base2
basebase
```

This is an awful fix though, because it makes all constructors accept any kind of parameters. It leads to weak code, since anything can be passed and gone through. Another solution is to use the classic __init__ calls in MyClass, but this would lead to the first pitfall.

Best Practices

To avoid all the mentioned problems, and until Python has evolved in this field, we need to take into consideration the following points:

- **Multiple inheritance should be avoided:** It can be replaced with some design patterns presented in Chapter 14.

- super **usage has to be consistent:** In a class hierarchy, super should be used everywhere or nowhere. Mixing super and classic calls is a confusing practice. People tend to avoid super, for their code to be more explicit.

- **Don't mix** old-style **and** new-style **classes:** Having a code base with both results in a varying MRO behavior.

- **Class hierarchy has to be looked over when a parent class is called:** To avoid any problems, every time a parent class is called, a quick glance at the involved MRO (with __mro__) has to be done.

Descriptors and Properties

When many C++ and Java programmers first learn Python, they are surprised by Python's lack of a `private` keyword. The nearest concept is 'name mangling'. Every time an attribute is prefixed by "__", it is renamed by the interpreter on the fly:

```
>>> class MyClass(object):
...        __secret_value = 1
...
>>> instance_of = MyClass()
>>> instance_of.__secret_value
Traceback (most recent call last):
  File "<stdin>", line 1, in <module>
AttributeError: 'MyClass' object has no attribute '__secret_value'
>>> dir(MyClass)
['_MyClass__secret_value', '__class__', '__delattr__', '__dict__',
'__doc__', '__getattribute__', '__hash__', '__init__', '__module__',
'__new__', '__reduce__', '__reduce_ex__', '__repr__', '__setattr__',
'__str__', '__weakref__']
>>> instance_of._MyClass__secret_value
1
```

This is provided to avoid name collision under inheritance, as the attribute is renamed with the class name as a prefix. It is not a real lock, since the attribute can be accessed through its composed name. This feature could be used to protect the access of some attributes, but in practice, "__" should never be used. When an attribute is not public, the convention is to use a "_" prefix. This does not call any mangling algorithm, but just documents the attribute as being a private element of the class and is the prevailing style.

Other mechanisms are available in Python to build the public part of the class together with the private code. The descriptors and properties that are key features of OOP design should be used to design a clean API.

Descriptors

A descriptor lets you customize what should be done when you refer to an attribute of an object.

Descriptors are the basis of complex attribute access in Python. They are used internally to implement properties, class, static methods, and the `super` type. They are classes that define how attributes of another class can be accessed. In other words, a class can delegate to another one the management of an attribute.

Descriptor classes are based on three special methods they have to implement:

- __set__: This is called whenever the attribute is set. In the following examples, I will refer to this as a **setter.**
- __get__: This is called whenever the attribute is read (referred as a **getter**).
- __delete__: This is called when del is invoked on the attribute.

These methods are called prior to the __dict__ attribute. For example, given `instance`, an instance of `MyClass`, the algorithm used when `instance.attribute` is read is:

```
# 1. looking for definition
if hasattr(MyClass, 'attribute'):
    attribute = MyClass.attribute
    AttributeClass = attribute.__class__
    # 2. found a getter, using it
    if hasattr(AttributeClass, '__get__':
        return AttributeClass.__get__(attribute, instance, MyClass)
# 3 - regular access with __dict__
return instance.__dict__['attribute']
```

In other words, the usual __dict__ mapping that contains all elements of an object instance is hijacked when a class attribute is defined and has a getter method.

A descriptor that implements __get__ and __set__ is called a **data descriptor.**

A descriptor that just implements __get__ is called a **non-data descriptor.**

Let's create a data descriptor, and use it through an instance:

```
>>> class UpperString(object):
...     def __init__(self):
...         self._value = ''
...     def __get__(self, instance, klass):
...         return self._value
...     def __set__(self, instance, value):
...         self._value = value.upper()
...
>>> class MyClass(object):
...     attribute = UpperString()
...
>>> instance_of = MyClass()
>>> instance_of.attribute
''
>>> instance_of.attribute = 'my value'
>>> instance_of.attribute
'MY VALUE'
>>> instance_of.__dict__
```
{}

Now if we add a new attribute in the instance, it will be stored in its __dict__ mapping:

```
>>> instance_of.new_att  = 1
>>> instance_of.__dict__
{'new_att': 1}
```

But if a new data descriptor is added in the class, it will take precedence over the instance __dict__:

```
>>> MyClass.new_att = Upperstring()
>>> instance_of.__dict__
{'new_att': 1}
>>> instance_of.new_att
''
>>> instance_of.new_att = 'other value'
>>> instance_of.new_att
'OTHER VALUE'
>>> instance_of.__dict__
{'new_att': 1}
```

This will not work with non-data descriptors. In that case, the instance will take a precedence over the descriptor:

```
>>> class Whatever(object):
...     def __get__(self, instance, klass):
...         return 'whatever'
```

```
...
>>> MyClass.whatever = Whatever()
>>> instance_of.__dict__
{'new_att': 1}
>>> instance_of.whatever
'whatever'
>>> instance_of.whatever = 1
>>> instance_of.__dict__
{'new_att': 1, 'whatever': 1}
```

This extra rule is made to avoid a recursive attribute lookup.

The algorithm used to set an attribute to a value (which is similar to the one used to delete it) is:

```
# 1- looking for definition
if hasattr(MyClass, 'attribute'):
    attribute = MyClass.attribute
    AttributeClass = attribute.__class__
    # 2 - does attribute definition has a setter ?
    if hasattr(AttributeClass, '__set__'):
        # let's use it
        AttributeClass.__set__(attribute, instance,
                                value)
        return
# 3 - regular way
instance.__dict__['attribute'] = value
```

 Raymond Hettinger wrote an interesting document called *How-To Guide for Descriptors* at http://users.rcn.com/python/download/Descriptor.htm. It is complementary to this section.

Besides their primary role of hiding the internals of a class, some interesting code patterns can be implemented with descriptors, such as:

- **Introspection descriptor:** This works over the hosting class's signature itself to compute some information.
- **Meta descriptor:** This computes values with the class methods itself.

Introspection Descriptor

A common need when working on classes is doing an introspection over their attributes. This is done, for example, in Zope (http://zope.org) when a security mapping is calculated on publishable classes. Epydoc (http://epydoc.sourceforge.net) does similar work to compute documentation.

A property class that computes such documentation can work over the public methods to render a readable documentation. Here's an example of such a non-data descriptor based on the `dir` built-in function, which works on any type of object:

```
>>> class API(object):
...     def _print_values(self, obj):
...         def _print_value(key):
...             if key.startswith('_'):
...                 return ''
...             value = getattr(obj, key)
...             if not hasattr(value, 'im_func'):
...                 doc = type(value).__name__
...             else:
...                 if value.__doc__ is None:
...                     doc = 'no docstring'
...                 else:
...                     doc = value.__doc__
...             return '    %s : %s' % (key, doc)
...         res = [_print_value(el) for el in dir(obj)]
...         return '\n'.join([el for el in res
...                           if el != ''])
...     def __get__(self, instance, klass):
...         if instance is not None:
...             return self._print_values(instance)
...         else:
...             return self._print_values(klass)
...
>>> class MyClass(object):
...     __doc__ = API()
...     def __init__(self):
...         self.a = 2
...     def meth(self):
...         """my method"""
...         return 1
...
>>> MyClass.__doc__
'    meth : my method'
>>> instance = MyClass()
>>> print instance.__doc__
    a : int
    meth : my method
```

The descriptor filters out elements that start with an underscore and displays `docstrings` for methods.

Meta-descriptor

A meta-descriptor uses one or more methods in the hosting class to perform a task. This can be useful, for example, to lower the quantity of code needed to use a class that provides steps. For example, a chaining descriptor can call a list of methods over a class to return an array of results. It can be stopped on failure and equipped with a callback mechanism to get more control over the process:

```
>>> class Chainer(object):
...     def __init__(self, methods, callback=None):
...         self._methods = methods
...         self._callback = callback
...     def __get__(self, instance, klass):
...         if instance is None:
...             # only for instances
...             return self
...         results = []
...         for method in self._methods:
...             results.append(method(instance))
...             if self._callback is not None:
...                 if not self._callback(instance,
...                                       method,
...                                       results):
...                     break
...         return results
```

This implementation allows all kinds of computation over the class methods, combined with external elements such as a logger:

```
>>> class TextProcessor(object):
...     def __init__(self, text):
...         self.text = text
...     def normalize(self):
...         if isinstance(self.text, list):
...             self.text = [t.lower()
...                          for t in self.text]
...         else:
...             self.text = self.text.lower()
...     def split(self):
...         if not isinstance(self.text, list):
...             self.text = self.text.split()
...     def treshold(self):
...         if not isinstance(self.text, list):
...             if len(self.text) < 2:
...                 self.text = ''
...         self.text = [w for w in self.text
```

```
...                          if len(w) > 2]
...
>>> def logger(instance, method, results):
...      print 'calling %s' % method.__name__
...      return True
...
>>> def add_sequence(name, sequence):
...      setattr(TextProcessor, name,
...           Chainer([getattr(TextProcessor, n)
...                 for n in sequence], logger))
```

add_sequence will let you define dynamically a new descriptor that chains calls over methods. The result of this combination can be saved in the class definition:

```
>>> add_sequence('simple_clean', ('split', 'treshold'))
>>> my = TextProcessor(' My Taylor is   Rich ')
>>> my.simple_clean
calling split
calling treshold
[None, None]
>>> my.text
['Taylor', 'Rich']
>>> # let's perform another sequence
>>> add_sequence('full_work', ('normalize',
...                            'split', 'treshold'))
>>> my.full_work
calling normalize
calling split
calling treshold
[None, None, None]
>>> my.text
['taylor', 'rich']
```

Given the dynamic nature of Python, these kinds of descriptors can be added at run-time to perform meta programming.

Definition

Meta-programming is the art of changing a program behavior at run time by either adding new computed functionalities, or changing the existing ones. It differs from generic programming, which might be familiar to those coming from a C++ background. In C++, it creates new pieces of code instead of providing a simple piece of code that can handle a maximum number of cases.

It is also different from "*generative programming*", which generates a static source code out of templates. See: http://en.wikipedia.org/wiki/Generative_programming.

Properties

Properties provide a built-in descriptor type that knows how to link an attribute to a set of methods. A property takes the `fget` argument and three optional ones: `fset`, `fdel`, and `doc`. The last one can be provided to define a `docstring` that is linked to the attribute as if it were a method:

```
>>> class MyClass(object):
...     def __init__(self):
...         self._my_secret_thing = 1
...
...     def _i_get(self):
...         return self._my_secret_thing
...
...     def _i_set(self, value):
...         self._my_secret_thing = value
...
...     def _i_delete(self):
...         print 'neh!'
...
...     my_thing = property(_i_get, _i_set, _i_delete,
...                         'the thing')
...
>>> instance_of = MyClass()
>>> instance_of.my_thing
1
>>> instance_of.my_thing = 3
>>> instance_of.my_thing
3
>>> del instance_of.my_thing
neh !
>>> help(instance_of)
```

```
Help on MyClass in module __main__ object:
class MyClass(__built-in__.object)
 |  Methods defined here:
 |
 |  __init__(self)
 |
 |  ----------------------------------------------------
 |  Data descriptors defined here:
 |  ...
 |  my_thing
 |      the thing
```

Properties make it easier to write descriptors, but must be handled carefully when using inheritance over classes. The created attribute is made on the fly using the methods of the current class and will not use methods that are overridden in the derived classes. This is a bit disruptive, since that is the logical behavior in most languages implementing properties.

For instance, the following example will fail to work as expected:

```
>>> class FirstClass(object):
...     def _get_price(self):
...         return '$ 500'
...     price = property(_get_price)
...
>>> class SecondClass(FirstClass):
...     def _get_price(self):
...         return '$ 20'
...
...
>>> plane_ticket = SecondClass()
>>> plane_ticket.price
'$ 500'
```

A workaround for this behavior is to manually redirect the property instance to the correct method using another method:

```
>>> class FirstClass(object):
...     def _get_price(self):
...         return '$ 500'
...     def _get_the_price(self):
...         return self._get_price()
...     price = property(_get_the_price)
...
```

```
>>> class SecondClass(FirstClass):
...        def _get_price(self):
...            return '$ 20'
...
>>> plane_ticket = SecondClass()
>>> plane_ticket.price
'$ 20'
```

That said, most of the time properties are added in a class to hide its complexity and the methods linked to it are private. So overriding them is a bad practice. It is better to override the property itself in that case:

```
>>> class FirstClass(object):
...        def _get_price(self):
...            return '$ 500'
...        price = property(_get_price)
...
>>> class SecondClass(FirstClass):
...        def _cheap_price(self):
...            return '$ 20'
...        price = property(_cheap_price)
...
>>> plane_ticket = SecondClass()
>>> plane_ticket.price
'$ 20'
```

Slots

An interesting feature that is almost never used by developers is **slots**. They allow you to set a static attribute list for a given class with the __slots__ attribute, and skip the creation of the __dict__ list in each instance of the class. They were intended to save memory space for classes with a very few attributes, since __dict__ is not created at every instance.

Besides this, they can help to design classes whose signature needs to be frozen. For instance, if you need to restrict the dynamic features of the language over a class, defining slots can help:

```
>>> class Frozen(object):
...        __slots__ = ['ice', 'cream']
...
>>> '__dict__' in dir(Frozen)
False
>>> 'ice' in dir(Frozen)
True
>>> glagla = Frozen()
```

```
>>> glagla.ice = 1
>>> glagla.cream = 1
>>> glagla.icy = 1
Traceback (most recent call last):
  File "<stdin>", line 1, in <module>
AttributeError: 'Frozen' object has no attribute 'icy'
```

This won't work on the derived class since any new attribute will be added in __dict__.

Meta-programming

The new-style classes brought the ability to change classes' and objects' definitions on the fly, through two special methods: __new__ and __metaclass__.

The __new__ Method

The special method __new__ is a meta-constructor. It is called every time an object has to be instantiated by the class factory:

```
>>> class MyClass(object):
...     def __new__(cls):
...         print '__new__ called'
...         return object.__new__(cls)  # default factory
...     def __init__(self):
...         print '__init__ called'
...         self.a = 1
...
>>> instance = MyClass()
__new__ called
__init__ called
```

The __new__ method must return an instance of the class. Therefore, it can make changes to the class before or after the object has been created. This is helpful to ensure that the object constructor did not set an undesirable state, or add an initialization that cannot be removed by a constructor.

For example, since __init__ calls are not implicitly called in subclasses, __new__ can be used to make sure that an initialization is done throughout the class hierarchy:

```
>>> class MyOtherClassWithoutAConstructor(MyClass):
...     pass
>>> instance = MyOtherClassWithoutAConstructor()
__new__ called
__init__ called
>>> class MyOtherClass(MyClass):
```

```
...        def __init__(self):
...            print 'MyOther class __init__ called'
...            super(MyOtherClass, self).__init__()
...            self.b = 2
...
>>> instance = MyOtherClass()
__new__ called
MyOther class __init__ called
__init__ called
```

Network socket or database initializations, for instance, should be controlled in __new__ rather than in __init__. It tells us when the initialization **must** be done for the class to work and when it might be derived.

For example, the `Thread` class in the `threading` module uses this mechanism to avoid having an instance uninitialized:

```
>>> from threading import Thread
>>> class MyThread(Thread):
...        def __init__(self):
...            pass
...
>>> MyThread()
Traceback (most recent call last):
  File "<stdin>", line 1, in <module>
  File "/Library/Frameworks/Python.framework/Versions/2.5/lib/
python2.5/threading.py", line 416, in __repr__
    assert self.__initialized, "Thread.__init__() was not called"
AssertionError: Thread.__init__() was not called
```

This is actually done through assertions all over the methods (`assert self.__initialized`), and could be simplified by a single call in __new__, since the instance would not be functional otherwise.

> **Avoiding chained initialization headaches**
>
> __new__ is the answer to the need for implicit initialization of object states. It will let you define an initialization at a lower level than __init__, which is always called.

__metaclass__ Method

Metaclasses give the ability to interact when a class object is created in memory through its factory. They act like __new__ but at the class level. The built-in type type is the built-in base factory. It is used to generate instances of any kind of class given its name, its base classes, and a mapping containing its attributes:

```
>>> def method(self):
...        return 1
...
>>> klass = type('MyClass', (object,), {'method': method})
>>> instance = klass()
>>> instance.method()
1
```

This is similar to an explicit definition of the class:

```
>>> class MyClass(object):
...        def method(self):
...            return 1
...
>>> instance = MyClass()
>>> instance.method()
1
```

Given that feature, a developer can interact with the class creation after or before type has been called. A special attribute has been created to link a class to a custom factory.

__metaclass__ (which will be replaced by an explicit constructor argument in Python 3000) can be added in a class definition to interact with the creation process.

The __metaclass__ attribute must be set to something that will:

1. Accept the same arguments as those that type accepts (namely, a class name, a tuple of base classes, and a mapping of attributes)

2. Return a class object

It doesn't matter whether the thing which does the above is an unbound function such as we use below (the equip function), or a method on another class object, so long as it fulfils criteria 1 and 2. In this example, the API descriptor presented in the descriptor section of this chapter is automatically added to the class if it has an empty docstring:

```
>>> def equip(classname, base_types, dict):
...        if '__doc__' not in dict:
...            dict['__doc__'] = API()
...        return type(classname, base_types, dict)
...
```

```
>>> class MyClass(object):
...       __metaclass__ = equip
...       def alright(self):
...           """the ok method"""
...           return 'okay'
...
>>> ma = MyClass()
>>> ma.__class__
<class '__main__.MyClass'>
>>> ma.__class__.__dict__['__doc__']    # __doc__ is replaced !
<__main__.API object at 0x621d0>
>>> ma.y = 6
>>> print ma.__doc__
    alright : the ok method
    y : int
```

This change would not have been doable otherwise, since __doc__ is a read-only attribute of the built-in base metaclass `type`.

Metaclasses though, complicate the code and make it less robust when they are intended to work over any kind of classes. For instance, you may encounter bad interactions when slots are used in the class, or when some base class already implements a metaclass, which conflicts with what yours does. They just do not compose well.

For changing the read-write attributes or adding new ones, metaclasses can be avoided for simpler solutions, based on dynamic changes over the class instance. These changes are even simpler to manage since they don't have to be grouped in one class (a class can only have a single metaclass). For example, if two specific behaviors have to be applied to one class, an "enhancement function" can be used to append them à la carte:

```
>>> def enhancer_1(klass):
...       c = [l for l in klass.__name__ if l.isupper()]
...       klass.contracted_name = ''.join(c)
...
>>> def enhancer_2(klass):
...       def logger(function):
...           def wrap(*args, **kw):
...               print 'I log everything !'
...               return function(*args, **kw)
...           return wrap
...       for el in dir(klass):
...           if el.startswith('_'):
...               continue
...           value = getattr(klass, el)
...           if not hasattr(value, 'im_func'):
...               continue
```

```
...             setattr(klass, el, logger(value))
...
>>> def enhance(klass, *enhancers):
...     for enhancer in enhancers:
...         enhancer(klass)
...
>>> class MySimpleClass(object):
...     def ok(self):
...         """I return ok"""
...         return 'I lied'
...
>>> enhance(MySimpleClass, enhancer_1, enhancer_2)
>>> thats = MySimpleClass()
>>> thats.ok()
I log everything !
'I lied'
>>> thats.score
>>> thats.contracted_name
'MSC'
```

This is a very powerful behavior, since you can dynamically create many different variations over one class definition that has already been instantiated.

In any case, remember that metaclasses or dynamic enhancers are nothing more than "patches", and they can quickly turn your clean, well-defined class hierarchy into a big mess. They should be done only in these cases:

- At framework level, when a behavior has to be forced in many classes.

- When a special behavior is added for a purpose that does not interact with the features provided by the classes, such as logging.

 For more examples, there's a great introduction to metaclass programming by David Mertz at: http://www.onlamp.com/pub/a/python/2003/04/17/metaclasses.html?page=1.

Summary

The important points covered by this chapter are:

- Subtyping built-in types is a great feature, but before doing it, make sure that the existing types aren't suitable without subclassing.
- Since `super` usage is tricky:
    ◦ Avoid multiple inheritance in your code.
    ◦ Be consistent with its usage and don't mix new-style and old-style.
    ◦ Check the class hierarchy before calling its methods in your subclass.
- **Descriptors** let you customize what should be done when you reference an attribute on an object.
- **Properties** are great to build a public API.
- Meta-programming is very powerful, but remember that it obfuscates the readability of the class design.

The next chapter focuses on choosing good names for code elements, and on API design best practices.

4
Choosing Good Names

Most of the standard library was built keeping usability in mind. For instance, working with built-in types is done naturally and was designed to be easy to use. Python can be compared to the pseudo-code you might think about when working on a program. Most of the code can be read out loud. For instance, this snippet is understandable by anyone:

```
>>> if 'd' not in my_list:
...     my_list.append('d')
```

This is one of the reasons why writing Python is so easy when compared to other languages. When you are writing a program, the flow of your thoughts is quickly translated into lines of code.

This chapter focuses on the best practices writing code that is easy to understand and use, through:

- The usage of naming conventions, described in **PEP 8**, and a set of **naming best practices**
- **namespace refactoring**
- **Working on an API**, from its initial shape to its refactoring

PEP 8 and Naming Best Practices

PEP 8 (`http://www.python.org/dev/peps/pep-0008`) provides a style guide for writing Python code. Besides some basic rules such as space indentation, maximum line length, and other details concerning the code layout, PEP 8 also provides a section on naming conventions that most of the code bases follow.

This section provides a quick summary of this PEP, and adds to it a naming best-practice guide for each kind of element.

Naming Styles

The different naming styles used in Python are:

- **CamelCase**, where words are capitalized and grouped
- **mixedCase**, which is like CamelCase, but starts with a lower case character
- **UPPERCASE**, and **UPPER_CASE_WITH_UNDERSCORES**
- **lowercase** and **lower_case_with_underscores**
- **_leading** and **trailing_** underscores, and sometimes **__doubled__**

Lower case and upper case elements are often a single word, and sometimes a few words concatenated. Names with underscores are usually abbreviated phrases. Using a single word is better. The leading and trailing underscores are used to mark privacy and special elements.

These styles are applied to:

- Variables
- Functions and methods
- Properties
- Classes
- Modules
- Packages

Variables

There are two kinds of variables in Python:

- Constants
- Public and private variables

Constants

For constant global variables, use upper case with userscores. This informs the developer that the given variable represents a constant value.

 There are no real constants in Python like those in C++ where `const` can be used. You can change the value of any variable. That's why Python uses a naming convention to mark a variable as a constant.

For example, the `doctest` module provides a list of option flags and directives (see `http://docs.python.org/lib/doctest-options.html`) that are small sentences, clearly defining what each option is intended for:

```
>>> from doctest import IGNORE_EXCEPTION_DETAIL
>>> from doctest import REPORT_ONLY_FIRST_FAILURE
```

These variable names seem rather long, but it is important to clearly describe them. Their usage is mostly located in initialization code rather than in the body of the code itself, so this verbosity is not annoying.

 Abbreviated names obfuscate the code most of the time. Don't be afraid of using complete words when an abbreviation seems unclear.

Some constants' names are also driven by the underlying technology. For instance, the `os` module uses some constants that are defined on C side, such as the `EX_XXX` series, that defines exception numbers.

```
>>> import os
>>> try:
...     os._exit(0)
... except os.EX_SOFTWARE:
...     print 'internal software error'
...     raise
```

A good practice when using constants is to gather them at the top of a module that uses them, and combine them under new variables when they are intended for such operations:

```
>>> import doctest
>>> TEST_OPTIONS = (doctest.ELLIPSIS |
...                  doctest.NORMALIZE_WHITESPACE |
...                  doctest.REPORT_ONLY_FIRST_FAILURE)
```

Naming and Usage

Constants are used to define a set of values the program relies on, such as the default configuration file name.

A good practice is to gather all the constants in a single file in the package. That is how Django, for instance, works. A module named `config.py` provides all the constants:

```
# config.py
SQL_USER = 'tarek'
SQL_PASSWORD = 'secret'
SQL_URI = 'postgres://%s:%s@localhost/db' % \
          (SQL_USER, SQL_PASSWORD)
MAX_THREADS = 4
```

Another approach is to use a configuration file that can be parsed with the `ConfigParser` module, or an advanced tool such as `ZConfig`, which is the parser used in Zope to describe its configuration files. But some people argue that it is rather an overkill to use another file format in a language such as Python, where a file can be edited and changed as easily as a text file.

For options that act like flags, a good practice is to combine them with Boolean operations, as the `doctest` and `re` modules do. The pattern taken from `doctest` is quite simple:

```
>>> OPTIONS = {}
>>> def register_option(name):
...     return OPTIONS.setdefault(name, 1 << len(OPTIONS))
>>> def has_option(options, name):
...     return bool(options & name)
>>> # now defining options
>>> BLUE = register_option('BLUE')
>>> RED = register_option('RED')
>>> WHITE = register_option('WHITE')
>>>
>>> # let's try them
>>> SET = BLUE | RED
>>> has_option(SET, BLUE)
True
>>> has_option(SET, WHITE)
False
```

When such a new set of constants is created, avoid using a common prefix for them, unless the module has several sets. The module name itself is a common prefix.

Using binary bit-wise operations to combine options is common in Python. The inclusive OR (|) operator will let you combine several options in a single integer, and the AND (&) operator will let you check that the option is present in the integer. (See the `has_option` function)

This works if the integer can be shifted with the << operator, to stay distinct from one another in the combined integer. In other words, it is a power of two (see `register_options`).

Beware that this technique has one important pitfall: constants' values change if their definitions change order in source file. So you will need to append new constants at the end of the list and not change their ordering.

Public and Private Variables

For global variables that are mutable and public, a lower case with an underscore should be used when they need to be protected. But these kinds of variables are not used frequently, since the module usually provides getters and setters to work with them when they need to be protected. A leading underscore, in that case, can mark the variable as a private element of the package:

```
>>> _observers = []
>>> def add_observer(observer):
...      _observers.append(observer)
>>> def get_observers():
...      """Makes sure _observers cannot be modified."""
...      return tuple(_observers)
```

Variables that are located in functions and methods follow the same rules, and are never marked as private since they are local to the context.

For class or instance variables, using the private marker (the leading underscore) should be done only if making the variable a part of the public signature does not bring any useful information, or is redundant.

In other words, if the variable is used internally in the method to provide a public feature, and is dedicated to this role, it is better to make it private.

For instance, the attributes that power a property are good private citizens:

```
>>> class Citizen(object):
...      def __init__(self):
...          self._message = 'Go boys'
...      def _get_message(self):
...          return self._message
...      kane = property(_get_message)
>>> Citizen().kane
'Go boys'
```

Another example would be a variable that keeps an internal state. This value is not useful for the rest of the code, but participates in the behavior of the class:

```
>>> class MeanElephant(object):
...      def __init__(self):
...          self._people_to_kill = []
...      def is_slapped_on_the_butt_by(self, name):
...          self._people_to_kill.append(name)
...          print 'Ouch!'
...      def revenge(self):
```

```
...             print '10 years later...'
...             for person in self._people_to_kill:
...                 print 'Me kill %s' % person
>>> joe = MeanElephant()
>>> joe.is_slapped_on_the_butt_by('Tarek')
Ouch!
>>> joe.is_slapped_on_the_butt_by('Bill')
Ouch!
>>> joe.revenge()
10 years later...
Me kill Tarek
Me kill Bill
```

[Never bet on how your class might be subclassed.]

Functions and Methods

Function and methods should be in lower case with underscores. This rule is not always true in the standard library though, and you can find some modules with mixedCase such as currentThread in the threading module (which will probably change in Python 3000).

This way of writing methods was common before the lower case norm became the standard, and some frameworks such as Zope also use mixedCase for methods. The community of developers working with it is quite large. So the choice between mixedCase and lower case with an underscore is definitely driven by the library you are using.

As a Zope developer, it is not easy to stay consistent because building an application that mixes pure Python modules and modules that import Zope code is difficult. In Zope, some classes mix both conventions because the code base is evolving to an egg-based framework, where each module is closer to pure Python than before.

A decent practice in this kind of library environment is to use mixedCase only for elements that are exposed in the framework, and to keep the rest of the code in PEP 8 style.

The Private Controversy

For private methods and functions, a leading underscore is conventionally added. This rule was quite controversial because of the name mangling feature in Python. When a method has two leading underscores, it is renamed on the fly by the interpreter to prevent a name collision with a method from any subclass.

So some people tend to use a double leading underscore for their private attributes to avoid name collision in the subclasses:

```
>>> class Base(object):
...        def __secret(self):
...            print "don't tell"
...        def public(self):
...            self.__secret()
>>> Base.__secret
Traceback (most recent call last):
  File "<stdin>", line 1, in <module>
AttributeError: type object 'Base' has no attribute '__secret'
>>> dir(Base)
['_Base__secret', ..., 'public']
>>> class Derived(Base):
...        def __secret(self):
...            print "never ever"
>>> Derived().public()
don't tell
```

The original motivation for name mangling in Python was not to provide a private gimmick like in C++, but to make sure that some base classes implicitly avoid collisions in subclasses, especially in multiple inheritance contexts. But using it for every attribute obfuscates the code in private, which is not Pythonic at all.

Therefore, some people opined that explicit name mangling should always be used:

```
>>> class Base(object):
...        def _Base_secret(self):        # don't do this !!!
...            print "you told it ?"
```

This duplicates the class name all over the code and so __ should be preferred.

But the best practice, as the **BDFL** (Guido, the **Benevolent Dictator For Life**, see http://en.wikipedia.org/wiki/BDFL) said, is to avoid using name mangling by looking at the __mro__ (method resolution order) value of a class before writing a method in a subclass. Changing the base class private methods has to be done carefully.

For more information on this topic, an interesting thread occurred in the "python-dev" list a few years ago, where people argued the utility of name mangling and its fate in the language. It can be found at: `http://mail.python.org/pipermail/python-dev/2005-December/058555.html`.

Special Methods

Special methods (`http://docs.python.org/ref/specialnames.html`) start and end with a double underscore, and no normal method should use this convention. They are used for operator overloading, container definitions, and so on. For the sake of readability, they should be gathered at the beginning of class definitions:

```
>>> class weirdint(int):
...     def __add__(self, other):
...         return int.__add__(self, other) + 1
...     def __repr__(self):
...         return '<weirdo %d>' % self
...     #
...     # public API
...     #
...     def do_this(self):
...         print 'this'
...     def do_that(self):
...         print 'that'
```

For a normal method, you should never use these kinds of names. So don't invent a name for a method such as this:

```
>>> class BadHabits(object):
...     def __my_method__(self):
...         print 'ok'
```

Arguments

Arguments are in lower case, with underscores if needed. They follow the same naming rules as variables.

Properties

The names of properties are in lower case, or in lower case with underscores. Most of the time, they represent an object's state, which can be a noun or an adjective, or a small phrase when needed:

```
>>> class Connection(object):
...     _connected = []
...     def connect(self, user):
...         self._connected.append(user)
...     def _connected_people(self):
...         return '\n'.join(self._connected)
...     connected_people = property(_connected_people)
>>> my = Connection()
>>> my.connect('Tarek')
>>> my.connect('Shannon')
>>> print my.connected_people
Tarek
Shannon
```

Classes

The names of classes are always in CamelCase, and may have a leading underscore when they are private to a module.

The class and instance variables are often noun phrases, and form a usage logic with the method names that are verb phrases:

```
>>> class Database(object):
...     def open(self):
...         pass
>>> class User(object):
...     pass
>>> user = User()
>>> db = Database()
>>> db.open()
```

Modules and Packages

Besides the special module __init__, the module names are in lower case with no underscores.

The following are some examples from the standard library:

* os
* sys
* shutil

When the module is private to the package, a leading underscore is added. Compiled C or C++ modules are usually named with an underscore and imported in pure Python modules.

Packages follow the same rules, since they act like modules in the namespace.

Naming Guide

A common set of naming rules can be applied on variables, methods, functions, and properties. The names of classes and modules also play an important role in namespace construction, and in turn in code readability. This mini-guide provides common patterns and anti-patterns for picking their names.

Use "has" or "is" Prefix for Boolean Elements

When an element holds a Boolean value, the "is" and "has" prefixes provide a natural way to make it more readable in its namespace:

```
>>> class DB(object):
...     is_connected = False
...     has_cache = False
>>> database = DB()
>>> database.has_cache
False
>>> if database.is_connected:
...     print "That's a powerful class"
... else:
...     print "No wonder..."
No wonder...
```

Use Plural for Elements That Are Sequences

When an element is holding a sequence, it is a good idea to use a plural form. Some mappings can also benefit from this when they are exposed like sequences:

```
>>> class DB(object):
...     connected_users = ['Tarek']
...     tables = {'Customer': ['id', 'first_name',
...                            'last_name']}
```

Use Explicit Names for Dictionaries

When a variable holds a mapping, you should use an explicit name when possible. For example, if a `dict` holds some persons' addresses, it can be named `person_address`:

```
>>> person_address = {'Bill': '6565 Monty Road',
...                    'Pamela': '45 Python street'}
>>> person_address['Pamela']
'45 Python street'
```

Avoid Generic Names

Using terms such as `list`, `dict`, `sequence`, or `elements`, even for local variables, is evil if your code is not building a new abstract data type. It makes the code hard to read, understand, and use. Using a built-in name has to be avoided as well, to avoid shadowing it in the current namespace. Generic verbs should also be avoided, unless they have a meaning in the namespace.

Instead, domain-specific terms should be used:

```
>>> def compute(data):          # too generic
...     for element in data:
...         yield element * 12
>>> def display_numbers(numbers):    # better
...     for number in numbers:
...         yield number * 12
```

Avoid Existing Names

It is a bad practice to use names that already exist in the context because it makes reading and, more specifically, debugging very confusing:

```
>>> def bad_citizen():
...     os = 1
...     import pdb; pdb.set_trace()
...     return os
>>> bad_citizen()
> <stdin>(4)bad_citizen()
(Pdb) os
1
(Pdb) import os
(Pdb) c
<module 'os' from '/Library/Frameworks/Python.framework/Versions/2.5/
lib/python2.5/os.
pyc'>
```

In this example, the `os` name was shadowed by the code. Both built-ins and module names from the standard library should be avoided.

Try to create original names, even if they are local to the context. For keywords, a trailing underscore is a way to avoid a collision:

```
>>> def xapian_query(terms, or_=True):
...     """if or_ is true, terms are combined
...     with the OR clause"""
...     pass
```

Note that `class` is often replaced by `klass` or `cls`:

```
>>> def factory(klass, *args, **kw):
...     return klass(*args, **kw)
```

Best Practices for Arguments

The signatures of functions and methods are the guardians of code integrity. They drive its usage and build its API. Besides the naming rules that we have seen previously, special care has to be taken for arguments. This can be done through three simple rules:

- Build arguments by Iterative Design.
- Trust the arguments and your tests.
- Use `*args` and `**kw` magic arguments carefully.

Build Arguments by Iterative Design

Having a fixed and well-defined list of arguments for each function makes the code more robust. But this can't be done in the first version, so arguments have to be built by iterative design. They should reflect the precise use cases the element was created for, and evolve accordingly.

For instance, when some arguments are appended, they should have default values wherever possible to avoid any regression:

```
>>> class BD(object): # version 1
...     def _query(self, query, type):
...         print 'done'
...     def execute(self, query):
...         self._query(query, 'EXECUTE')
>>> BD().execute('my query')
done
```

```
>>> import logging
>>> class BD(object): # version 2
...     def _query(self, query, type, logger):
...         logger('done')
...     def execute(self, query, logger=logging.info):
...         self._query(query, 'EXECUTE', logger)
>>> BD().execute('my query')    # old-style call
>>> BD().execute('my query', logging.warning)
WARNING:root:done
```

When the argument of a public element has to be changed, a deprecation process is to be used, which is presented later in this section.

Trust the Arguments and Your Tests

Given the dynamic typing nature of Python, some developers use assertions at the top of their functions and methods to make sure the arguments have a proper content:

```
>>> def division(dividend, divisor):
...     assert type(dividend) in (long, int, float)
...     assert type(divisor) in (long, int, float)
...     return dividend / divisor
>>> division(2, 4)
0
>>> division(2, 'okok')
Traceback (most recent call last):
  File "<stdin>", line 1, in <module>
  File "<stdin>", line 3, in division
AssertionError
```

This is often done by developers who are used to static typing and feel that something is missing in Python.

This way of checking arguments is a part of the **Design by Contract** (**DbC**, see http://en.wikipedia.org/wiki/Design_By_Contract) programming style, where pre-conditions are checked before the code is actually run.

The two main problems in this approach are:

1. DbC's code explains how it should be used, making it less readable.
2. This can make it slower, since the assertions are made on each call.

The latter can be avoided with the "-O" option of the interpreter. In that case, all assertions are removed from the code before the byte code is created, so that the checking is lost.

In any case, assertions have to be done carefully, and should not be used to bend Python to a statically typed language. The only use case for this is to protect the code from being called nonsensically.

A healthy Test-Driven Development style provides a robust base code in most cases. Here, the functional and unit tests validate all the use cases the code is created for.

When code in a library is used by external elements, making assertions can be useful, as the incoming data might break things up or even create damage. This happens for code that deals with databases or the file system.

Another approach towards this is "fuzz testing" (http://en.wikipedia.org/wiki/Fuzz_testing), where random pieces of data are sent to the program to detect its weaknesses. When a new defect is found, the code can be fixed to take care of that, together with a new test.

Let's take care that a code base, which follows the TDD approach, evolves in the right direction, and gets increasingly robust, since it is tuned every time a new failure occurs. When it is done in the right way, the list of assertions in the tests becomes similar in some way to the list of pre-conditions.

Anyhow, many DbC libraries exist in Python for people that are fond of it. You can have a look at *Contracts for Python* (http://www.wayforward.net/pycontract/).

Use *args and **kw Magic Arguments Carefully

*args and **kw arguments can break the robustness of a function or method. They make the signature fuzzy, and the code often starts to build a small argument parser where it should not:

```
>>> def fuzzy_thing(**kw):
...     if 'do_this' in kw:
...         print 'ok i did'
...     if 'do_that' in kw:
...         print 'that is done'
...     print 'errr... ok'
>>> fuzzy_thing()
errr... ok
>>> fuzzy_thing(do_this=1)
```

```
ok i did
errr... ok
>>> fuzzy_thing(do_that=1)
that is done
errr... ok
>>> fuzzy_thing(hahahahaha=1)
errr... ok
```

If the argument list gets long and complex, it is tempting to add magic arguments. But this is more a sign of a weak function or method that should be broken into pieces or refactored.

When *args is used to deal with a sequence of elements that are treated the same way in the function, asking for a unique container argument such as an iterator is better:

```
>>> def sum(*args):        # okay
...        total = 0
...        for arg in args:
...            total += arg
...        return total
>>> def sum(sequence):     # better !
...        total = 0
...        for arg in sequence:
...            total += arg
...        return total
...
```

For **kw, the same rule applies. It is better to fix the named arguments to make the method's signature meaningful:

```
>>> def make_sentence(**kw):
...        noun = kw.get('noun', 'Bill')
...        verb = kw.get('verb', 'is')
...        adj = kw.get('adjective', 'happy')
...        return '%s %s %s' % (noun, verb, adj)
>>> def make_sentence(noun='Bill', verb='is', adjective='happy'):
...        return '%s %s %s' % (noun, verb, adjective)
```

Another interesting approach is to create a container class that groups several related arguments to provide an execution context. This structure differs from *args or **kw because it can provide internals that work over the values and can evolve independently. The code that uses it as an argument will not have to deal with its internals.

For instance, a web request passed on to a function is often represented by an instance of a class. This class is in charge of holding the data passed by the web server:

```
>>> def log_request(request):      # version 1
...     print request.get('HTTP_REFERER', 'No referer')
>>> def log_request(request):      # version 2
...     print request.get('HTTP_REFERER', 'No referer')
...     print request.get('HTTP_HOST', 'No host')
```

Magic arguments cannot be avoided sometimes, especially in meta-programming, for example, decorators that work on functions with any kind of signature. More globally, when working with unknown data that just traverses the function, magic arguments are great:

```
>>> import logging
>>> def log(**context):
...     logging.info('Context is:\n%s\n' % str(context))
```

Class Names

The name of a class has to be concise, precise, so that it sufficient to understand from it what the class does. A common practice is to use a suffix that informs about its type or nature, for example:

- SQL**Engine**
- Mime**Types**
- String**Widget**
- Test**Case**

For base classes, a Base or Abstract prefix can be used as follows:

- **Base**Cookie
- **Abstract**Formatter

The most important thing is to be consistent with the class attributes. For example, try to avoid redundancy between the class and its attributes' names:

```
>>> SMTP.smtp_send()   # redundant information in the namespace
>>> SMTP.send()        # more readable and mnemonic
```

Module and Package Names

Module and package names inform about the purpose of their content. The names are short, in lower case, and without underscores.

- `sqlite`
- `postgres`
- `sha1`

They are often suffixed with `lib` if they implement a protocol:

```
>>> import smtplib
>>> import urllib
>>> import telnetlib
```

They also need to be consistent within the namespace, so their usage is easier:

```
>>> from widgets.stringwidgets import TextWidget     # bad
>>> from widgets.strings import TextWidget    # better
```

Again, always avoid using the same name as that of one of the modules from the standard library.

When a module gets complex, and contains a lot of classes, it is a good practice to create a package and split the module's elements in other modules.

The __init__ module can also be used to put back some APIs at the top level, as it will not impact its usage but will help re-organizing the code in smaller parts. For example, a module in a `foo` package

```
from module1 import feature1, feature2
from module2 import feature3
```

will allow users to import features directly:

```
>>> from foo import feature1
>>> from foo import feature2, feature3
```

But beware that this can increase your chances of getting circular dependencies, and that the code added in the __init__ module will be instantiated. So use it with care.

Working on APIs

We have seen in the previous section that packages and modules are first-class citizens to ease the usage of a library or an application. They should be organized carefully, since together they create an API.

This section provides some insights on how to work through this matter:

- Tracking verbosity
- Building the namespace tree
- Splitting the code
- Using a deprecation process
- Using eggs

Tracking Verbosity

A common mistake when creating a library is "API verbosity". This happens when a feature is provided through a set of calls instead of a single call to the package.

Let's take an example of a `script_engine` package that will let you execute some code:

```
>>> from script_engine import make_context
>>> from script_engine import compile
>>> from script_engine import execute
>>> context = make_context({'a': 1, 'b':3})
>>> byte_code = compile('a + b')
>>> print execute(byte_code, context)
4
```

This use case should be provided within the package under a new function:

```
>>> from script_engine import run
>>> print run('a + b', context={'a': 1, 'b':3})
4
```

Both low-level and high-level functions will then be available for high-level calls and other combinations of low-level functions.

 This principle is described in Chapter 14 through the Facade design pattern.

Building the Namespace Tree

A simple technique to organize an application API is to build a namespace tree through use cases and see how the code can be organized.

Let's take an example. An application called `acme` provides an engine that knows how to create PDF files. It is based on a list of template files and on a query made on a MySQL database.

The three parts of the `acme` application are:

- A PDF generator
- An SQL engine
- A template collection

From there, a first draft of the namespace tree that comes in mind could be:

- `acme`
  - `pdfgen.py`
    - class `PDFGen`
  - `sqlengine.py`
    - class `SQLEngine`
  - `templates.py`
    - class `Template`

Let's now try the namespace in a code sample and see how a PDF could be created from this application. We will guess how the classes and functions could be named and called in a glue function that resembles the feature of `acme`:

```
>>> from acme.templates import Template
>>> from acme.sqlengine import SQLEngine
>>> from acme.pdfgen import PDFGen
>>> SQL_URI = 'sqlite:///:memory:'
>>> def generate_pdf(query, template_name):
...     data = SQLEngine(SQL_URI).execute(query)
...     template = Template(template_name)
...     return PDFGen().create(data, template)
```

This first version gives us some feedback on the usability of the namespace and can be refactored to simplify things with API verbosity tracking and common sense.

For instance, the `PDFGen` class does not need to be created within the caller, since any instance of the class can generate any PDF instance. Therefore, it can stay private. The `templates` usage can also be simplified in the following manner:

```
>>> from acme import templates
>>> from acme.sqlengine import SQLEngine
>>> from acme.pdf import generate
>>> SQL_URI = 'sqlite:///:memory:'
>>> def generate_pdf(query, template_name):
...     data = SQLEngine(SQL_URI).execute(query)
...     template = templates.generate(template_name)
...     return generate(data, template)
```

A second draft of the namespace will then be:

- `acme`
  - `config.py`
    - `SQL_URI`
  - `utils.py`
    - function `generate_pdf`
  - `pdf.py`
    - function `generate`
    - class `_Generator`
  - `sqlengine.py`
    - class `SQLEngine`
  - `templates.py`
    - function `generate`
    - class `_Template`

The changes made are as follows:

- `config.py` contains the configuration element.
- `utils.py` provides the high-level API.
- `pdf.py` provides a unique function.
- `templates.py` provides a factory.

For each new use case, such structural changes help in designing a usable API. This has to be done before the package is released and used. For released packages, a deprecation process has to be set, which will be explained later in this chapter.

 The namespace tree should be carefully designed through real uses cases. We will see in Chapter 11 how to build it through tests.

Splitting the Code

Small is beautiful! And this should be applied to the code as well, at all levels. When a function, class, or a module gets too big, it should be split.

A function or a method should not be bigger than a screen, which is around 25 to 30 lines. Otherwise it is hard to follow and understand.

See the related chapter, in the *Art of Unix Programming* by Eric Raymond (http://www.faqs.org/docs/artu/ch13s01.html) for more information about code complexity.

A class should have a limited number of methods. When there are more than ten methods, even the creator can have a hard time to get the whole picture. A common practice is to isolate the functionalities and create several classes out of it.

A module should also be limited in its size. When it is more than 500 lines, it should be split into several modules.

This work will impact the API and will imply some extra work at the package level to ensure that the way the code is split and organized won't make it difficult to use.

In other words, the API should always be tested from the user's point of view to make sure it is usable, mnemonic, and concise.

Using Eggs

When an application grows, the number of packages under the main folder can get quite big. For instance, a framework such as Zope has more than 50 packages under the `zope` namespace, which is the root package.

To avoid having the whole code base within the same folder, and to be able to release each package separately, "Python eggs" (http://peak.telecommunity.com/DevCenter/PythonEggs) can be used. They provide a simple way to build "namespaced packages", such as JARs provide in Java.

For instance, if you want to distribute `acme.templates` as a separate package, you can build an egg-based package with `setuptools` (the library for creating Python Eggs), using a special `__init__.py` file in the `acme` folder, containing (http://peak.telecommunity.com/DevCenter/setuptools#namespace-packages):

```
try:
    __import__('pkg_resources').declare_namespace(__name__)
except ImportError:
    from pkgutil import import extend_path
    __path__ = extend_path(__path__, __name__)
```

The `acme` folder will then be able to hold a `templates` folder and be available under the `acme.templates` namespace. `acme.pdf` can even be separated in a separated `acme` folder.

Following the same rule, the packages from the same organization can be gathered in the same namespace using eggs, even if they are not related to each other. For example, all packages from Ingeniweb are using the `iw` namespace and can be found on the Cheeseshop using the following prefix: `http://pypi.python.org/pypi?%3A action=search&term=iw.&submit=search`.

Besides the namespace, distributing the applications in eggs helps the modularization of your work, since each egg can be seen as a separated component.

 Chapter 6 will cover how to build, release, and deploy an egg-based application.

Using a Deprecation Process

Changing the API has to be done carefully when the package is already released and used by third-party code. The simplest way to deal with such changes is to follow a deprecation process where an intermediate release contains both versions.

For example, if a class has a `run_script` method that is replaced by a simplified `run` command, the `DeprecationWarning` built-in exception can be used in the intermediate result along with the `warnings` module as follows:

```
>>> class SomeClass(object):               # version 1
...     def run_script(self, script, context):
...         print 'doing the work'
>>> import warnings
>>> class SomeClass(object):               # version 1.5
...     def run_script(self, script, context):
...         warnings.warn(("'run_script' will be replaced "
...                        "by 'run' in version 2"),
...                       DeprecationWarning)
...         return self.run(script, context)
...     def run(self, script, context=None):
...         print 'doing the work'
>>> SomeClass().run_script('a script', {})
__main__:4: DeprecationWarning: 'run_script' will be replaced by 'run'
in version 2
doing the work
>>> SomeClass().run_script('a script', {})
doing the work
>>> class SomeClass(object):               # version 2
...     def run(self, script, context=None):
...         print 'doing the work'
```

The `warnings` module will warn the user on the first call and will ignore the next calls. Another nice feature about this module is that filters can be created to manage warnings that are impacting the application. For example, warnings can be automatically ignored or turned into exceptions to make the changes mandatory. See `http://docs.python.org/lib/warning-filter.html`.

Useful Tools

Part of the previous conventions and practices can be controlled and worked out with the following tools:

- **Pylint**, a very flexible source code analyzer
- **CloneDigger**, a duplicate code detection tool

Pylint

Besides some quality assurance metrics, Pylint allows checking whether a given source code follow a naming convention. Its default settings correspond to PEP 8 and a Pylint script provides a shell report output.

To install Pylint, you can use the `logilab.installer` egg, with `easy_install`:

```
$ easy_install logilab.pylintinstaller
```

After this step, the command is available and can be run against a module, or several modules using wild cards:

```
$ pylint bootstrap.py
No config file found, using default configuration
************* Module bootstrap
C: 25: Invalid name "tmpeggs" (should match (([A-Z_][A-Z1-9_]*)|(__.*__
))$)
C: 27: Invalid name "ez" (should match (([A-Z_][A-Z1-9_]*)|(__.*__))$)
W: 28: Use of the exec statement
C: 34: Invalid name "cmd" (should match (([A-Z_][A-Z1-9_]*)|(__.*__))$)
C: 36: Invalid name "cmd" (should match (([A-Z_][A-Z1-9_]*)|(__.*__))$)
C: 38: Invalid name "ws" (should match (([A-Z_][A-Z1-9_]*)|(__.*__))$)

...

Global evaluation
-----------------

Your code has been rated at 6.25/10
```

Notice that there will always be some cases where Pylint will give you bad rates or complaints. For instance an import statement that is not used by the code of the module itself is perfectly fine in some cases (having it available in the namespace).

Making calls to libraries that use mixedCase for methods can also lower your rating. In any case, the global evaluation is not as important as "lint" is in C. Pylint is just a tool that points the possible improvements.

The first thing to do to fine-tune Pylint is to create a .pylinrc configuration file in your home directory, with the -generate-rcfile option:

```
$ pylint --generate-rcfile > ~/.pylintrc
```

Under Windows, the "~" folder has to be replaced with the user folder, which is usually in the **Documents and Settings** folder. (See the USERPROFILE environment variable.)

The first thing to change in the configuration file is to set the reports variable to **no** in the **REPORTS** section, in order to avoid a verbose report. In our case, we just want to use the tool to detect the names. After that change, the tool will only display the warnings:

```
$ pylint boostrap.py
************ Module bootstrap
C: 25: Invalid name "tmpeggs" (should match (([A-Z_][A-Z1-9_]*)|(__.*__
))$)
C: 27: Invalid name "ez" (should match (([A-Z_][A-Z1-9_]*)|(__.*__))$)
W: 28: Use of the exec statement
C: 34: Invalid name "cmd" (should match (([A-Z_][A-Z1-9_]*)|(__.*__))$)
C: 36: Invalid name "cmd" (should match (([A-Z_][A-Z1-9_]*)|(__.*__))$)
C: 38: Invalid name "ws" (should match (([A-Z_][A-Z1-9_]*)|(__.*__))$)
```

CloneDigger

CloneDigger (`http://clonedigger.sourceforge.net`) is a nice tool that tries to detect similarities in the code by visiting the code tree. It is based on a rather complex algorithm explained on the website, and complements Pylint.

To install it, use `easy_install`:

```
$ easy_install CloneDigger
```

You will get a `clonedigger` command that can be used to detect a duplicate. The options are described here: `http://clonedigger.sourceforge.net/documentation.html`.

```
$ clonedigger html_report.py ast_suppliers.py
Parsing  html_report.py ... done
Parsing  ast_suppliers.py ... done
40 sequences
average sequence length: 3.250000
maximum sequence length: 14
Number of statements:  130
Calculating size for each statement... done
Building statement hash... done
Number of different hash values:  52
Building patterns... 66 patterns were discovered
Choosing pattern for each statement... done
Finding similar sequences of statements... 0  sequences were found
Refining candidates... 0 clones were found
Removing dominated clones... 0 clones were removed
```

An HTML output is generated in `output.html` that contains a report on CloneDigger's work.

Summary

This chapter explained the following:

- PEP 8 is the absolute reference for naming convention.
- A few rules should be followed when choosing names:
  - Use "has" or "is" prefix for Boolean elements.
  - Use plural for elements that are sequences.
  - Avoid generic names.
  - Avoid shadowing existing names, especially built-ins.
- A set of good practices for arguments is:
  - Build arguments by design.
  - Don't try to implement static-type checking using assertions.
  - Don't misuse *args and **kw.
- Some common practices when working on APIs are:
  - Track verbosity.
  - Build the namespace tree by design.
  - Split the code into small pieces.
  - Use eggs for your libraries, under a common namespace.
  - Use a deprecation process.
- Use Pylint and CloneDigger to control the code.

The next chapter explains how to write a package.

5
Writing a Package

This chapter focuses on a repeatable process to write and release Python packages. Its intents are:

- To shorten the time needed to set up everything before starting the real work, in other words the boiler-plate code
- To provide a standardized way to write packages
- To ease the use of a test-driven development approach
- To facilitate the releasing process

It is organized in the following four parts:

- A **common pattern** for all packages that describes the similarities between all Python packages, and how distutils and setuptools play a central role
- How **generative programming** (http://en.wikipedia.org/wiki/Generative_programming) can help this through the template-based approach
- The **package template creation**, where everything needed to work is set
- Setting up a development cycle

A Common Pattern for All Packages

We have seen in the last chapter that the easiest way to organize the code of an application is to split it into several packages using eggs. This makes the code simpler, and easier to understand, maintain, and change. It also maximizes the reusability of each package. They act like components.

Applications for a given company can have a set of eggs glued together with a master egg.

Therefore, all packages can be built using egg structures.

This section presents how a **namespaced package** is organized, released, and distributed to the world through `distutils` and `setuptools`.

Writing an egg, as we have seen in the previous chapter, is done by layering the code in a nested folder that provides a common prefix namespace. For instance, for the Acme company, the common namespace can be `acme`. The result is a namespaced package.

For example, a package whose code relates to SQL can be called `acme.sql`. The best way to work with such a package is to create an `acme.sql` folder that contains the `acme` and then the `sql` folder:

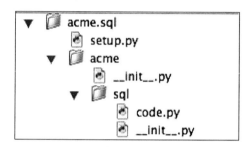

setup.py, the Script That Controls Everything

The root folder contains a `setup.py` script, which defines all metadata as described in the `distutils` module, combined as arguments in a call to the standard `setup` function. This function was extended by the third-party library `setuptools` that provides most of the egg infrastructure.

 The boundary between `distutils` and `setuptools` is getting fuzzy, and they might merge one day.

Therefore, the minimum content for this file is:

```
from setuptools import setup
setup(name='acme.sql')
```

`name` gives the full name of the egg. From there, the script provides several commands that can be listed with the `--help-commands` option.

```
$ python setup.py --help-commands
Standard commands:
  build          build everything needed to install
  ...
  install        install everything from build directory
```

```
sdist                 create a source distribution
register              register the distribution
bdist                 create a built (binary) distribution
Extra commands:
develop               install package in 'development mode'
...
test                  run unit tests after in-place build
alias                 define a shortcut
bdist_egg             create an "egg" distribution
```

The most important commands are the ones left in the preceding listing. **Standard commands** are the built-in commands provided by distutils, whereas **Extra commands** are the ones created by third-party packages such as setuptools or any other package that defines and registers a new command.

sdist

The sdist command is the simplest command available. It creates a release tree where everything needed to run the package is copied. This tree is then archived in one or many archived files (often, it just creates one tar ball). The archive is basically a copy of the source tree.

This command is the easiest way to distribute a package from the target system independently. It creates a dist folder with the archives in it that can be distributed. To be able to use it, an extra argument has to be passed to setup to provide a version number. If you don't give it a version value, it will use version = 0.0.0:

```
from setuptools import setup
setup(name='acme.sql', version='0.1.1')
```

This number is useful to upgrade an installation. Every time a package is released, the number is raised so that the target system knows it has changed.

Let's run the sdist command with this extra argument:

```
$ python setup.py sdist
running sdist
...
creating dist
tar -cf dist/acme.sql-0.1.1.tar acme.sql-0.1.1
gzip -f9 dist/acme.sql-0.1.1.tar
removing 'acme.sql-0.1.1' (and everything under it)
$ ls dist/
acme.sql-0.1.1.tar.gz
```

[Under Windows, the archive will be a ZIP file.]

The version is used to mark the name of the archive, which can be distributed and installed on any system having Python. In the `sdist` distribution, if the package contains C libraries or extensions, the target system is responsible for compiling them. This is very common for Linux-based systems or Mac OS because they commonly provide a compiler. But it is less usual to have it under Windows. That's why a package should always be distributed with a pre-built distribution as well, when it is intended to run under several platforms.

The MANIFEST.in File

When building a distribution with `sdist`, `distutils` browses the package directory looking for files to include in the archive.

`distutils` will include:

- All Python source files implied by the `py_modules`, `packages` and `scripts` option
- All C source files listed in the `ext_modules` option
- Files that match the glob pattern `test/test*.py`
- `README`, `README.txt`, `setup.py`, and `setup.cfg` files

Besides, if your package is under Subversion or CVS, `sdist` will browse folders such as `.svn` to look for files to include. `sdist` builds a `MANIFEST` file that lists all files and includes them into the archive.

Let's say you are not using these version control systems, and need to include more files. Now, you can define a template called `MANIFEST.in` in the same directory as that of `setup.py` for the `MANIFEST` file, where you indicate to `sdist` which files to include.

This template defines one inclusion or exclusion rule per line, for example:

```
include HISTORY.txt
include README.txt
include CHANGES.txt
include CONTRIBUTORS.txt
include LICENSE
recursive-include *.txt *.py
```

The full list of commands is available at `http://docs.python.org/dist/sdist-cmd.html#sdist-cmd`.

build and bdist

To be able to distribute a pre-built distribution, distutils provide the build command, which compiles the package in four steps:

- build_py: Builds pure Python modules by byte-compiling them and copying them into the build folder.
- build_clib: Builds C libraries, when the package contains any, using Python compiler and creating a static library in the build folder.
- build_ext: Builds C extensions and puts the result in the build folder like build_clib.
- build_scripts: Builds the modules that are marked as scripts. It also changes the interpreter path when the first line was set (!#) and fixes the file mode so that it is executable.

Each of these steps is a command that can be called independently. The result of the compilation process is a build folder that contains everything needed for the package to be installed. There's no cross-compiler option yet in the distutils package. This means that the result of the command is always specific to the system it was build on.

 Some people have recently proposed patches in the Python tracker to make distutils able to cross-compile the C parts. So this feature might be available in the future.

When some C extensions have to be created, the build process uses the system compiler and the Python header file (Python.h). This **include** file is available from the time Python was built from the sources. For a packaged distribution, an extra package called python-dev often contains it, and has to be installed as well.

The C compiler used is the system compiler. For Linux-based system or Mac OS X, this would be **gcc**. For Windows, Microsoft Visual C++ can be used (there's a free command-line version available) and the open-source project MinGW as well. This can be configured in distutils, as explained in Chapter 1.

The build command is used by the bdist command to build a binary distribution. It calls build and all dependent commands, and then creates an archive in the same way as sdist does.

Let's create a binary distribution for acme.sql under Mac OS X:

```
$ python setup.py bdist
running bdist
running bdist_dumb
```

```
running build

...

running install_scripts
tar -cf dist/acme.sql-0.1.1.macosx-10.3-fat.tar .
gzip -f9 acme.sql-0.1.1.macosx-10.3-fat.tar
removing 'build/bdist.macosx-10.3-fat/dumb' (and everything under it)
$ ls dist/
acme.sql-0.1.1.macosx-10.3-fat.tar.gz    acme.sql-0.1.1.tar.gz
```

Notice that the newly created archive's name contains the name of the system and the distribution it was built under (*Mac OS X 10.3*).

The same command called under Windows will create a specific distribution archive:

```
C:\acme.sql> python.exe setup.py bdist

...

C:\acme.sql> dir dist
25/02/2008  08:18    <DIR>          .
25/02/2008  08:18    <DIR>          ..
25/02/2008  08:24          16 055 acme.sql-0.1.win32.zip
              1 File(s)         16 055 bytes
              2 Dir(s)  22 239 752 192 bytes free
```

If a package contains C code, apart from a source distribution, it's important to release as many different binary distributions as possible. At the very least, a Windows binary distribution is important for those who don't have a C compiler installed.

A binary release contains a tree that can be copied directly into the Python tree. It mainly contains a folder that is copied into Python's `site-packages` folder.

bdist_egg

The `bdist_egg` command is an extra command provided by `setuptools`. It basically creates a binary distribution like `bdist`, but with a tree comparable to the one found in the source distribution. In other words, the archive can be downloaded, uncompressed, and used as it is by adding the folder to the Python search path (`sys.path`).

These days, this distribution mode should be used instead of the `bdist`-generated one.

install

The `install` command installs the package into Python. It will try to build the package if no previous build was made and then inject the result into the Python tree. When a source distribution is provided, it can be uncompressed in a temporary folder and then installed with this command. The `install` command will also install dependencies that are defined in the `install_requires` metadata.

This is done by looking at the packages in the Python Package Index (PyPI). For instance, to install `pysqlite` and `SQLAlchemy` together with `acme.sql`, the setup call can be changed to:

```
from setuptools import setup
setup(name='acme.sql', version='0.1.1',
      install_requires=['pysqlite', 'SQLAlchemy'])
```

When we run the command, both dependencies will be installed.

How to Uninstall a Package

The command to uninstall a previously installed package is missing in `setup.py`. This feature was proposed earlier too. This is not trivial at all because an installer might change files that are used by other elements of the system.

The best way would be to create a snapshot of all elements that are being changed, and a record of all files and directories created.

A `record` option exists in `install` to record all files that have been created in a text file:

```
$ python setup.py install --record installation.txt

running install

...

writing list of installed files to 'installation.txt'
```

This will not create any backup on any existing file, so removing the file mentioned might break the system. There are platform-specific solutions to deal with this. For example, `distutils` allow you to distribute the package as an RPM package. But there's no universal way to handle it as yet.

The simplest way to remove a package at this time is to erase the files created, and then remove any reference in the `easy-install.pth` file that is located in the `site-packages` folder.

develop

`setuptools` added a useful command to work with the package. The `develop` command builds and installs the package in place, and then adds a simple link into the Python `site-packages` folder. This allows the user to work with a local copy of the code, even though it's available within Python's `site-packages` folder. We will see in the next chapter that this is a great feature when building an egg-based application. All packages that are being created are linked with the `develop` command to the interpreter.

When a package is installed this way, it can be removed specifically with the `-u` option, unlike the regular install:

```
$ sudo python setup.py develop
running develop
...
Adding iw.recipe.fss 0.1.3dev-r7606 to easy-install.pth file

Installed /Users/repos/ingeniweb.sourceforge.net/iw.recipe.fss/trunk
Processing dependencies ...
$ sudo python setup.py develop -u
running develop
Removing
...
Removing iw.recipe.fss 0.1.3dev-r7606 from easy-install.pth file
```

Notice that a package installed with `develop` will always prevail over other versions of the same package installed.

test

Another useful command is `test`. It provides a way to run all tests contained in the package. It scans the folder and aggregates the test suites it finds. The test runner tries to collect tests in the package but is quite limited. A good practice is to hook an extended test runner such as zope.testing or Nose that provides more options.

To hook Nose transparently to the test command, the test_suite metadata can be set to 'nose.collector' and Nose added in the test_requires list:

```
setup(
...
test_suite='nose.collector',
test_requires=['Nose'],
...
)
```

[Chapter 11 presents a few test runners, and explains how to use Nose.]

register and upload

To distribute a package to the world, two commands are available:

- `register`: This will upload all metadata to a server.
- `upload`: This will upload to the server all archives previously built in the `dist` folder.

The main PyPI server, previously named the Cheeseshop, is located at `http://pypi.python.org/pypi` and contains over 3000 packages from the community. It is a default server used by the `distutils` package, and an initial call to the `register` command will generate a `.pypirc` file in your home directory.

Since the PyPI server authenticates people, when changes are made to a package, you will be asked to create a user over there. This can also be done at the prompt:

```
$ python setup.py register
running register
...
We need to know who you are, so please choose either:
 1. use your existing login,
 2. register as a new user,
 3. have the server generate a new password for you (and email it to
you), or
 4. quit
Your selection [default 1]:
```

Now, a `.pypirc` file will appear in your home directory containing the user and password you have entered. These will be used every time `register` or `upload` is called:

```
[server-index]
username: tarek
password: secret
```

 There is a bug on Windows with Python 2.4 and 2.5. The home directory is not found by `distutils` unless a HOME environment variable is added. But, this has been fixed in 2.6. To add it, use the technique described in Chapter 1 where we modified the PATH variable. Then add a HOME variable for your user that points to the directory returned by `os.path.expanduser('~')`.

When the `download_url` metadata or the `url` is specified, and is a valid URL, the PyPI server will make it available to the users on the project web page as well.

Using the `upload` command will make the archive directly available at PyPI, so the `download_url` can be omitted:

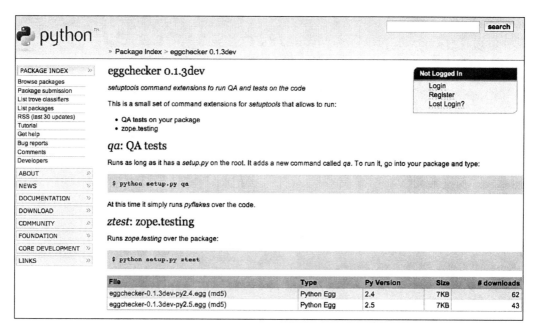

Distutils defines a Trove categorization (see *PEP 301*: `http://www.python.org/dev/peps/pep-0301/#distutils-trove-classification`) to classify the packages, such as the one defined at Sourceforge. The trove is a static list that can be found at `http://pypi.python.org/pypi?%3Aaction=list_classifiers`, and that is augmented from time to time with a new entry.

Each line is composed of levels separated by "`::`":

```
...
Topic :: Terminals
Topic :: Terminals :: Serial
Topic :: Terminals :: Telnet
Topic :: Terminals :: Terminal Emulators/X Terminals
Topic :: Text Editors Topic :: Text Editors :: Documentation
Topic :: Text Editors :: Emacs
...
```

A package can be classified in several categories, which can be listed in the classifiers `meta-data`. A GPL package that deals with low-level Python code (for instance) can use:

```
Programming Language :: Python
Topic :: Software Development :: Libraries :: Python Modules
License :: OSI Approved :: GNU General Public License (GPL)
```

Python 2.6 .pypirc Format

The `.pypirc` file has evolved under Python 2.6, so several users and their passwords can be managed along with several PyPI-like servers. A Python 2.6 configuration file will look somewhat like this:

```
[distutils]
index-servers =
    pypi
    alternative-server
    alternative-account-on-pypi

[pypi]
username:tarek
password:secret

[alternative-server]
username:tarek
password:secret
repository:http://example.com/pypi
```

The `register` and `upload` commands can pick a server with the help of the `-r` option, using the repository full URL or the section name:

```
# upload to http://example.com/pypi
$ python setup.py sdist upload -r  alternative-server

#  registers with default account (tarek at pypi)
$ python setup.py register

#  registers to http://example.com
$ python setup.py register -r http://example.com/pypi
```

This feature allows interaction with servers other than PyPI. When dealing with a lot of packages that are not to be published at PyPI, a good practice is to run your own PyPI-like server. The Plone Software Center (see `http://plone.org/products/plonesoftwarecenter`) can be used, for example, to deploy a web server that can interact with `distutils` upload and `register` commands.

Creating a New Command

`distutils` allows you to create new commands, as described in `http://docs.python.org/dist/node84.html`. A new command can be registered with an entry point, which was introduced by `setuptools` as a simple way to define packages as plug-ins.

An entry point is a named link to a class or a function that is made available through some APIs in `setuptools`. Any application can scan for all registered packages and use the linked code as a plug-in.

To link the new command, the `entry_points` metadata can be used in the setup call:

```
setup(name="my.command",
        entry_points="""
          [distutils.commands]
          my_command  = my.command.module.Class
        """)
```

All named links are gathered in named sections. When `distutils` is loaded, it scans for links that were registered under `distutils.commands`.

This mechanism is used by numerous Python applications that provide extensibility.

setup.py Usage Summary

There are three main actions to take with `setup.py`:

- Build a package.
- Install it, possibly in develop mode.
- Register and upload it to PyPI.

Since all the commands can be combined in the same call, some typical usage patterns are:

```
# register the package with PyPI, creates a source and
# an egg distribution, then upload them
$ python setup.py register sdist bdist_egg upload

# installs it in-place, for development purpose
$ python setup.py develop

# installs it
$ python setup.py install
```

The alias Command

To make the command line work easily, a new command has been introduced by `setuptools` called `alias`. In a file called `setup.cfg`, it creates an alias for a given combination of commands. For instance, a release command can be created to perform all actions needed to upload a source and a binary distribution to PyPI:

```
$ python setup.py alias release register sdist bdist_egg upload
running alias
Writing setup.cfg
$ python setup.py release
...
```

Other Important Metadata

Besides the name and the version of the package being distributed, the most important arguments `setup` can receive are:

- `description`: A few sentences to describe the package
- `long_description`: A full description that can be in reStructuredText
- `keywords`: A list of keywords that define the package
- `author`: The author's name or organization

- author_email: The contact email address
- url: The URL of the project
- license: The license (GPL, LGPL, and so on)
- packages: A list of all names in the package; setuptools provides a small function called find_packages that calculates this
- namespace_packages: A list of namespaced packages

A completed setup.py file for acme.sql would be:

```python
import os
from setuptools import setup, find_packages

version = '0.1.0'

README = os.path.join(os.path.dirname(__file__), 'README.txt')
long_description = open(README).read() + '\n\n'

setup(name='acme.sql',
      version=version,
      description=("A package that deals with SQL, "
                  "from ACME inc"),
      long_description=long_description,
      classifiers=[
        "Programming Language :: Python",
        ("Topic :: Software Development :: Libraries ::
         "Python Modules"),
        ],
      keywords='acme sql',
      author='Tarek',
      author_email='tarek@ziade.org',
      url='http://ziade.org',
      license='GPL',
      packages=find_packages(),
      namespace_packages=['acme'],
      install_requires=['pysqlite','SQLAchemy']
      )
```

The two comprehensive guides to keep under your pillow are:

The distutils guide at http://docs.python.org/dist/dist.html

The setuptools guide at http://peak.telecommunity.com/DevCenter/setuptools

The Template-Based Approach

The boiler-plate code in `acme.sql` is composed of a tree of folders that create the namespace of a few files in the root folder. To make all packages follow the same structure, a generic code template can be extracted and provided through a code-generation tool. This approach, called generative programming, is very useful at the organization level. It standardizes the way the code is written and makes developers more productive, as they focus on the code they really need to create. This approach is also a good opportunity to prepare a few things in the package such as complex test fixtures that are common to several packages.

There are numerous generative tools available in the community, but the most used is probably Python Paste (`http://pythonpaste.org`).

Python Paste

The Python Paste project was partly responsible for the success of frameworks such as Pylons (`http://pylonshq.com`). Developers are driven by an extensive suite of templates that lets them create applications' skeletons within minutes.

From the official tutorial, this is a three-liner to create a web application and run it:

```
$ paster create -t pylons helloworld
$ cd helloworld
$ paster serve --reload development.ini
```

The Plone and Zope communities followed this philosophy, and now provide Python Paste templates to generated skeletons as well. ZopeSkel (`http://pypi.python.org/pypi/ZopeSkel`) is one of them.

Python Paste contains several tools, and the template engine we are interested in is PasteScript. It can be installed with `easy_install`. It will get all dependencies from the Paste project:

```
$ easy_install PasteScript
Searching for PasteScript
Reading http://pypi.python.org/simple/PasteScript/
Reading http://pythonpaste.org/script/
Best match: PasteScript 1.6.2
Downloading

...
```

```
Processing dependencies for PasteScript
Searching for PasteDeploy
...
Searching for Paste>=1.3
...
Finished processing dependencies for PasteScript
```

The `paster` command will be available with a few default templates that can be listed with the `-list-templates` option of the `create` command:

```
$ paster create --list-templates
Available templates:
  basic_package:  A basic setuptools-enabled package
  paste_deploy:   A web application deployed through paste.deploy
```

The `basic_package` is almost what `acme.sql` would have needed to build a namespaced package with a `setup.py` file. When run, the command line asks a few questions and the corresponding answers will be used to fill the templates:

```
$ paster create -t basic_package mypackage
Selected and implied templates:
  PasteScript#basic_package  A basic setuptools-enabled package
...
Enter version (Version (like 0.1)) ['']: 0.1
Enter description ['']: My package
Enter long_description ['']: this is the package
Enter keywords ['']: package is mine
Enter author (Author name) ['']: Tarek
Enter author_email (Author email) ['']: tarek@ziade.org
Enter url (URL of homepage) ['']: http://ziade.org
Enter license_name (License name) ['']: GPL
Enter zip_safe [False]:
Creating template basic_package
...
```

The resulting structure is a valid, setuptools-compliant, one-level structure:

```
$ find mypackage
mypackage
mypackage/mypackage
mypackage/mypackage/__init__.py
mypackage/setup.cfg
mypackage/setup.py
```

Creating Templates

Python Paste, let's call it **the paster**, can work with the Cheetah template engine for instance (`http://cheetahtemplate.org`), and feed it with the user input.

To create a new template for the paster, three elements have to be provided:

- A class derived from `paste.script.templates.Template`
- The structure to be created that contains folder and files (Cheetah templates or static files)
- A `setuptools` entry point to `paste.paster_create_template`, to register the class

Creating the Package Template

Let's create the template that would have been used for `acme.sql`.

All templates created in this book, including the `package` are gathered in `pbp.skels` that is available for your convenience at PyPI. So if you don't want to create your own from scratch, install it:

```
$ easy_install pbp.skels
```

This section has step-by-step instructions explaining how `pbp.skels` was created.

To create the `package` template, the first thing to do is to create a structure for this new package:

```
$ mkdir -p pbp.skels/pbp/skels
$ find pbp.skels
pbp.skels
pbp.skels/pbp
pbp.skels/pbp/skels
```

Then, an __init__.py file with the following code is created in the pbp folder. It tells distutils to make it a namespaced package:

```
try:
    __import__('pkg_resources').declare_namespace(__name__)
except ImportError:
    from pkgutil import extend_path
    __path__ = extend_path(__path__, __name__)
```

Next, create a setup.py file in the root folder (path_to_pbp_package/pbp.skels/__init__.py) with the right metadata. The correct code for this is shown here:

```
from setuptools import setup, find_packages

version = '0.1.0'
classifiers = [
    "Programming Language :: Python",
    ("Topic :: Software Development :: "
     "Libraries :: Python Modules")]

setup(name='pbp.skels',
      version=version,
      description=("PasteScript templates for the Expert "
                   "Python programming Book."),
      classifiers=classifiers,
      keywords='paste templates',
      author='Tarek Ziade',
      author_email='tarek@ziade.org',
      url='http://atomisator.ziade.org',
      license='GPL',
      packages=find_packages(exclude=['ez_setup']),
      namespace_packages=['pbp'],
      include_package_data=True,
      install_requires=['setuptools',
                        'PasteScript'],
      entry_points="""
      # -*- Entry points: -*-
      [paste.paster_create_template]
      pbp_package = pbp.skels.package:Package
      """)
```

The entry point adds a new template that will be available in the paster.

The next step is to write the `Package` class in the `pbp/skels` folder, in a module called `package`:

```python
from paste.script.templates import var
from paste.script.templates import Template

class Package(Template):
    """Package template"""
    _template_dir = 'tmpl/package'
    summary = "A namespaced package with a test environment"
    use_cheetah = True

    vars = [
        var('namespace_package', 'Namespace package',
            default='pbp'),
        var('package', 'The package contained',
            default='example'),
        var('version', 'Version', default='0.1.0'),
        var('description',
            'One-line description of the package'),
        var('author', 'Author name'),
        var('author_email', 'Author email'),
        var('keywords', 'Space-separated keywords/tags'),
        var('url', 'URL of homepage'),
        var('license_name', 'License name', default='GPL')
        ]

    def check_vars(self, vars, command):
        if not command.options.no_interactive and \
           not hasattr(command, '_deleted_once'):
            del vars['package']
            command._deleted_once = True
        return Template.check_vars(self, vars, command)
```

This class defines:

- The folder containing the template structure (`_template_dir`)
- A summary of the template that will appear in the paster
- A flag to indicate if Cheetah is used in the template structure
- A list of variables, where each variable is composed of a name, a label, and a default value (if needed), which is used by the paster to ask the user at the prompt to enter his or her values
- A `check_vars` method that makes sure the package variable will be requested at the prompt

The last thing to do is to create the `tmpl/package` directory content by copying the one created for `acme.sql`. All files that contain values to be changed, such as the namespace, have to be suffixed by `_tmpl`. The values are replaced by `${variable}`, where `variable` is the name of the variable listed in the `Package` class.

The `setup.py` file (for instance) becomes `setup.py_tmpl` and contains:

```
from setuptools import setup, find_packages
import os
version = ${repr($version) or "0.0"}
long_description = open("README.txt").read()
classifiers = [
    "Programming Language :: Python",
    ("Topic :: Software Development :: "
     "Libraries :: Python Modules")]
setup(name=${repr($project)},
      version=version,
      description=${repr($description) or $empty},
      long_description=long_description,
      classifiers=classifiers,
      keywords=${repr($keywords) or $empty},
      author=${repr($author) or $empty},
      author_email=${repr($author_email) or $empty},
      url=${repr($url) or $empty},
      license=${repr($license_name) or $empty},
      packages=find_packages(exclude=['ez_setup']),
      namespace_packages=[${repr($namespace_package)}],
      include_package_data=True,
      install_requires=[
          'setuptools',
          # -*- Extra requirements: -*-
      ],
      test_suite='nose.collector',
      test_requires=['Nose'],
      entry_points="""
      # -*- Entry points: -*-
      """,
      )
```

The `repr` function will tell Cheetah to add quotes around the string values.

You can use the same technique for all files located in `acme.sql` to make a template. For instance, the `README.txt` file is copied to `README.txt_tmpl`. Then all references to `acme.sql` are replaced by values defined in the `Package` class in the `vars` list.

For instance, getting the full package name is done by:

```
${namespace_package}.${package}
```

Last, to use a variable value for a folder name it has to be named with a "+" prefix and suffix. For instance, the namespaced package folder will be called +namespace_package+ and the package folder +package+.

The final structure of `pbp.skels`, after the `acme.sql` has been generalized, will look like this:

```
$ cd pbp.skels
$ find .
setup.py
pbp
pbp/__init__.py
pbp/skels
pbp/skels/__init__.py
pbp/skels/package.py
pbp/skels/tmpl
pbp/skels/tmpl/package
pbp/skels/tmpl/package/README.txt_tmpl
pbp/skels/tmpl/package/setup.py_tmpl
pbp/skels/tmpl/package/+namespace_package+
pbp/skels/tmpl/package/+namespace_package+/__init__.py_tmpl
pbp/skels/tmpl/package/+namespace_package+/+package+
pbp/skels/tmpl/package/+namespace_package+/+package+/__init__.py
---
```

From there, the package can be symlinked to Python's `site-packages` directory with a `develop` command, and made available to the paster:

```
$ python setup.py develop
...
Finished processing dependencies for pbp.skels==0.1.0dev
```

After the develop command is run, you should find the template listed in `paster`:

```
$ paster create --list-templates
Available templates:
  basic_package:  A basic setuptools-enabled package
  pbp_package:    A namespaced package with a test environment
  paste_deploy:   A web application ... paste.deploy
$ paster create -t pbp_package trying.it
Selected and implied templates:
  pbp.skels#package  A namespaced package with a test environment

Variables:
```

```
   egg:         trying.it
   package:     tryingit
   project:     trying.it
Enter namespace_package (Namespace package) ['pbp']: trying
Enter package (The package contained) ['example']: it
...
Creating template package
...
```

The generated tree will then contain the structure ready to work with right away.

Development Cycle

The development cycle of a package is composed of iterations, where the code is moved forward from an initial state to a new state. This phase lasts mostly for a few weeks and ends with a release. This does not happen in small packages that are very simple to work with, but can be found in all packages that have enough modules to make it worthwhile.

At the end of the iteration, a release is created with the commands we have previously seen. The package moves at this moment from a development state to a releasable state, and the delivered code can be seen as an official release.

Then a new cycle starts with an incremented version for the package.

What Version Numbers Should be Used?

There are no fixed conventions for incrementing a package's version number, and when developers feel the software has grown a lot, they often jump to a higher number that does not follow the previous series.

Most software usually start with a very small value and uses two or three digits. Sometimes an alphabet letter is appended to it when they are trying to finalize a version. **rc** suffixes are also used to mark a **release candidate**. That is a version in test phase where some fixes might be done:

- 0.1, 0.2, 0.3
- 0.1.0, 0.1.1, 0.1.2a, 0.1.2b
- 0.1, 0.2rc1, 0.2rc2

You should decide of your own convention as long as the versions stay consistent all the way. In companies, there are usually standards followed by all applications; whereas open-source applications have their own conventions.

The only rule that should be applied is to make sure that the number of digits is always the same, and avoid the "-" sign in the version, because it is used as a separator by many tools to extract a version number from a package name.

For instance, these should be avoided:

- 0.1, 0.1.1-alpha, 0.1.1-b, 0.2
- 0.1, 0.1-a, 0.1-b

Nightly Builds

If the package is still releasable anytime during the iteration, **development** releases can be made. Those are also called nightly builds. This continuous releasing process allows developers to get live feedback on their work, and save beta users some work. They don't need to get the code from a version repository, for instance, and can install the development release like a regular one.

To differentiate a development release from a regular release, the user has to append the dev suffix to the version number. For instance, the 0.1.2 version that is being developed and not yet released, will be known as the 0.1.2dev release.

distutils provide a way to mark this, by adding in a setup.cfg file a section that informs the build command about the development state:

```
[egg_info]
tag_build = dev
```

This will automatically add the dev prefix added to the version:

```
$ python setup.py bdist_egg
running bdist_egg
running egg_info
...
creating 'dist/iw.selenium-0.1.0dev-py2.4.egg'
```

Another useful tag can be the revision number when the package is living in Subversion repository. It can be appended with the tag_svn_revision flag:

```
[egg_info]
tag_build = dev
tag_svn_revision = true
```

The revision number will appear in the version as well in that case.

```
$ python setup.py bdist_egg
running bdist_egg
running egg_info
...
creating 'dist/iw.selenium-0.1.0dev_r38360-py2.4.egg'
```

The simplest way is to always keep this file in the trunk and remove it right before making a regular release. In other words, a releasing process with Subversion can be:

- Make a tag copy of the trunk.
- Check out the tag branch.
- Remove the setup.cfg (or the egg_info-specific section) in this branch and commit the change.
- Build the release from there.
- Raise the version number in the trunk.

This looks as follows:

```
svn cp http://example.com/my.package/trunk http://example.com/my.package/
branches/0.1
svn co http://example.com/my.package/branches/0.1 0.1
cd 0.1
svn rm setup.cfg
svn ci -m "removing the dev flag"
svn cp http://example.com/my.package/branches/0.1 http://example.com/
my.package/tags/0.1
python setup.py register sdist bdist_egg upload
```

 Chapter 8 explains what Version Control Systems, such as Subversion, are and how they work.

Summary

In this chapter we have seen:

- How a namespaced package is created
- The central role of `setup.py`, and how to use it to build and release the package
- The template-based approach to generated package skeletons
- How The Paster works and how to create a package skeleton
- How to release the package and provide nightly builds

The next chapter will focus on the same topics, but at the application level.

Writing an Application

6

We have seen in the last chapter a repeatable way to write packages and to gather code in namespaces. We can write a Python application by gathering a series of packages and making them interact by writing a package that ties everything together.

This chapter presents a small case study to demonstrate how to build, release, and distribute such an application.

Atomisator: An Introduction

Let's implement an application called **Atomisator**.

Atomisator is a small command-line tool that is able to generate an RSS XML file that is a combination of various news feeds:

```
$ atomisator
Reading source http://feeds.feedburner.com/dirtsimple Phillip Eby
10 entries read.
Reading source http://blog.ianbicking.org/feed/ Ian Bicking
10 entries read.
20 total.
Writing feed in atomisator.xml
Feed ready.
```

When the tool is invoked, all sources listed in a configuration file are read from the Web and stored into a database. An XML file is then generated out of the database, with the latest entries. This program is similar to **Planet** (http://www.planetplanet.org), except that it stores all fetched data in a database instead of doing a live merge.

This allows applying smart filters on the entries. For instance, every time an entry is read, it can be compared to the existing entries to make sure there are no duplicates. We will present in this chapter a light version of the application in order to focus on our goal, which is seeing how it is built.

> This chapter presents a simplified implementation, which does not correspond to the real Atomisator project.
>
> If you want to get the full version, check the project page at `http://atomisator.ziade.org`.

Overall Picture

The first thing to do is to list the packages that will compose our application. Atomisator could be written in one single package. But for the sake of maintainability, it is better to componentize it in separated pieces that can evolve independently.

By applying the rules explained in the previous chapter, Atomisator can be split in four packages:

- `atomisator.parser`: A feed parser that knows how to read a feed and return a list of entries
- `atomisator.db`: A package that provides read and write access to the database where entries will be stored
- `atomisator.feed`: A package that knows how to build an RSS 2.0-compliant XML file using the entries from the database
- `atomisator.main`: The main package, which uses a configuration file and provides three command-line utilities:
  - `load_feeds`: Fetches the data from the various sources
  - `generate_feed`: Builds the XML file
  - `atomisator`: Gathers previous commands in a single call

The process of interaction between the packages is shown in the following figure:

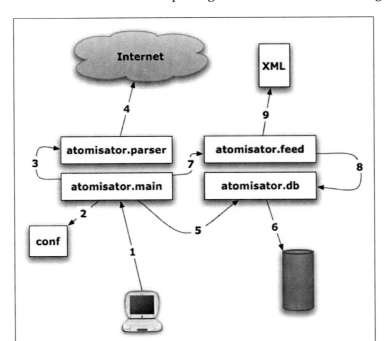

1. The user calls `atomisator.main` through the command line to ask for the feed generation.

2. `atomisator.main` reads the configuration file to list all sources to be fetched and for the database configuration.

3. `atomisator.main` asks `atomisator.parser` to read and return entries from various sources.

4. `atomisator.parser` reads the feeds and returns them as simple data structures.

5 and 6. `atomisator.main` updates the database through `atomisator.db`. It performs smart filtering to avoid adding duplicates.

7. `atomisator.main` asks `atomisator.feed` to generate a feed with the database.

8 and 9. `atomisator.feed` reads the database through `atomisator.db` and creates a file.

Given this process, the dependency between the packages is defined in the following illustration:

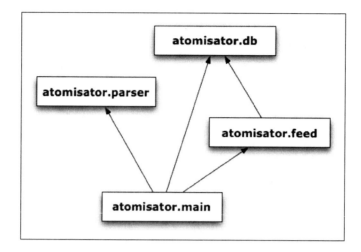

atomisator.parser and atomisator.db are independent packages, which should be written first. atomisator.feed should be written next, followed by the main package, which makes everything interact.

But first of all, let's set up a working environment for Atomisator.

Working Environment

Some packages in an application depend on other ones, and we have seen that these dependencies could be defined in the install_requires metadata. From there, a call to python setup.py develop fetches and installs all the dependencies needed to work on the code. But this requires those dependencies to be either available as eggs at PyPI or already installed in the same Python. And this is not the case, since all atomisator.* packages we will create for the Atomisator applications will be built altogether and are not released yet.

Of course, all packages can be installed with the develop command in the right order of dependency, but this would pollute the Python installation and make things really hard to track if some dependencies conflict with some packages that are already installed.

A working environment at the application level should, therefore, be able to isolate all dependencies for our application.

A nice solution is provided by the **virtualenv** project (`http://pypi.python.org/pypi/virtualenv`), that which the creation of a new isolated Python interpreter, on the top of an existing Python installation.

The result is a local execution context where libraries can be freely installed and developed to build a specific environment:

```
mkdir my_env
cd my_env/
$ easy_install -U virtualenv
Searching for virtualenv
Reading http://pypi.python.org/simple/virtualenv/
Best match: virtualenv 1.0
Processing virtualenv-1.0-py2.5.egg
Adding virtualenv 1.0 to easy-install.pth file
...
Finished processing dependencies for virtualenv
$ virtualenv --no-site-packages .
New python executable in ./bin/python
Installing setuptools...........done.
$ ls bin/
activate                easy_install           easy_install-2.5
python                  python2.5
```

> If you are under Windows, the scripts will be generated into a directory called `Scripts`. This is the case for all the following examples in this section.

The `virtualenv` command generates a folder with a new isolated interpreter, together with an `easy_install` script and an `activate` script. This last script is just a convenience script that lets you switch the environment variable to make the isolated Python the one that is called system-wide. The `--no-site-packages` option can be used to cut all dependencies from packages installed in the main Python. This option is great when you need to have a nude Python environment.

> PEP 370 (see `http://www.python.org/dev/peps/pep-0370`), which has been accepted recently, adds into Python a per-user site-packages folder and allows building the same kind of isolation that `virtualenv` does. It will probably be available in Python 2.7, which will make it easier to build custom environments.

Let's create such an environment for Atomisator in a new dedicated folder:

```
$ mkdir Atomisator
$ cd Atomisator
$ virtualenv --no-site-packages .
New python executable in ./bin/python
Installing setuptools...........done.
```

The great thing about `virtualenv` is that all packages installed using the local Python interpreter or the local `easy_install` will be installed locally as well.

Adding a Test Runner

To build our application, we will need a test runner. Nose was defined in the previous chapter as the default test runner in our package template, but let's also add it globally in our environment.

```
$ bin/easy_install nose
```

This will add a `nosetests` command within the local `bin` folder using the local Python interpreter. By doing this, all packages added in the environment will be seen by this test runner. Notice that the package template has been designed in order to use automatically the Nose test runner using the `test` command.

You can add a symbolic link in your system or add the `bin` folder in the `PATH` environment variable for your users' convenience.

If you have several environments, the best pick is to create specific names and make them available globally. Under Linux or Mac OS X this can be:

```
$ sudo ln -s bin/nosetests /usr/bin/atomisator-nosetests
$ sudo ln -s bin/python /usr/bin/atomisator-python
```

> Chapter 11 explains what a test runner is and compares a few.

Adding a packages Structure

So far, our Atomisator folder has a `bin` folder with a Python interpreter and a test runner. The packages we are going to build should be gathered in a subfolder called `packages` to make its tracking in a versioning system easier, and to facilitate its deployment: All folders in `packages` will be custom Python packages for the Atomisator application.

This initial structure is enough to start writing the packages code.

Writing the Packages

Following the previous diagram, packages will be built in the order of their dependencies, which are:

1. `atomisator.parser`

2. `atomisator.db`

3. `atomisator.feed`

4. `atomisator.main`

atomisator.parser

The standard tool in the Python community to read RSS 2.0 feeds is the Universal Feed Parser (`http://www.feedparser.org`). It is used by many programs that need to extract entries from feeds, no matter if they are provided as RSS 1.0, RSS 2.0, or in **Atom** format. For our needs, it is the perfect tool.

It could be used directly without having a specific package around it, but it is a good practice to control how external libraries are used in a program. Making sure all calls of an external package are made from the same custom package or module makes refactoring easier when things evolve. The work only has to be done in a single place in the code base and the dependencies with the rest of the application are therefore easier to control.

There are two types of package wrappers:

- **Leaky wrappers**: They provide a package on top of the external package, just to publish it. It can be simple imports or a few helpers around the external library API (see the Facade design pattern in Chapter 14).

- **Full wrappers**: They act like a black box around the library, and provide a full-featured API.

The latter is probably the best way to go to ensure there are no dependencies between the external library and the rest of the program. But it often means that a lot of extra code has to be written to mask it. It is also difficult to do it the right way when a project starts. A smart leaky wrapper API is often simpler and better to avoid reinventing the wheel.

For our feed parser, the choice is quite simple: A wrapper with a single facade function can be created since the **Universal Feed Parser** returns base types.

The process to write such a package is:

1. Creating the initial package with the appropriate template
2. Creating the initial `doctest` that describes how it works through examples
3. Building the test environment
4. Writing the code and adapting the initial `doctest`

Creating the Initial Package

The package is created with the `pbp_package` template inside the `packages` folder:

```
$ cd Atomisator/packages
$ paster create -t pbp_package atomisator.parser
```

This command generates the package structure. From there, the package can be linked into the interpreter by calling the `develop` command:

```
$ cd atomisator.parser
$ atomisator-python setup.py develop
running develop

...

Finished processing dependencies for atomisator.parser==0.1.0
```

Since our template has a default doctest located in atomisator/parser/README.txt, running nosetest in the empty package runs it, with the --doctest-extension=.txt option:

```
$ atomisator-nosetests --doctest-extension=.txt --with-doctest
----------------------------------------------------------------
Ran 1 test in 0.162s

OK
```

The tests could have been launched with `python setup.py test` but using the global nosetests script is easier to add some options, and to run tests over several packages if needed.

Notice that the 'doctest-extension' option can be omited if a .noserc file is added in the home directory. This is explained in Chapter 11.

Next, a dependency to `feedparser` (Universal Feed Parser name on PyPI) is added in the `atomisator.parser/setup.py` file:

```
...
setup(name='atomisator.parser',
      version=version,
      description=("A thin layer on the top of "
                  "the Universal Feed Parser"),
      long_description=long_description,
      classifiers=classifiers,
      keywords='python best practices',
      author='Tarek Ziade',
      author_email='tarek@ziade.org',
      url='http://atomisator.ziade.org',
      license='GPL',
      packages=find_packages(exclude=['ez_setup']),
      namespace_packages=['atomisator'],
      include_package_data=True,
      zip_safe=False,
      install_requires=[
          'setuptools',
          'feedparser'
          # -*- Extra requirements: -*-
      ],
      entry_points="""
      # -*- Entry points: -*-
      """,
      )
...
```

Running `atomisator-python setup.py develop` again will get `feedparser` from PyPI and link it to our environment. The initial package is then ready to be written.

Creating the Initial doctest

The `README.txt` file located in `atomisator.parser/atomisator/parser/` is the document people will refer to when they use the package. It has to contain a small text explaining the purpose of the package and a usage example.

Since it is a `doctest`, it will help us build the actual code using the right Test-Driven Development approach using `reStructuredText`.

 Chapter 11 explains in detail how to write tests, and the `reStructuredText` format is described in Chapter 10.

A first draft of this file can be:

```
==================
atomisator.parser
==================

The parser knows how to return a feed content, with
the 'parse' function, available as a top-level function::

    >>> from atomisator.parser import parse

This function takes the feed url and returns an iterator
over its content. A second parameter can specify a maximum
number of entries to return. If not given, it is fixed to 10::

    >>> res = parse('http://example.com/feed.xml')
    >>> res
    <generator ...>

Each item is a dictionary that contain the entry::

    >>> res.next()
```

This text specifies enough elements to start building the package. Let's make sure a call to the `bin/test` script will execute it and raise an error as expected, since there's no code at all yet:

```
$ atomisator-nosetests --doctest-extension=.txt
...
File "atomisator.parser/atomisator/parser/docs/README.txt", line 8, in
README.txt
Failed example:
    from atomisator.parser import parse
Exception raised:
    Traceback (most recent call last):
      ...
      File "<doctest README.txt[0]>", line 1, in ?
        from atomisator.parser import parse
    ImportError: cannot import name parse

----------------------------------------------------------------
Ran 1 test in 0.170s

FAILED (failures=1)
```

From there, it is easy to work in Test-Driven Development mode by changing the code until this test passes.

Building the Test Environment

When a package is created, a golden rule is to make sure all tests it contains can be launched without any external dependencies. Fake functions are to be created in the test fixture to simulate any call to external elements. This is sometimes hard to do. For instance, a package that depends on an LDAP server should get realistic data to be properly built and tested. A good practice in that case is to start working with a real server and record its output. A fake server can then serve back this collected data.

> When a fake is complex to create, mock objects can be used. See Chapter 11 for detailed information on this practice.

For `atomisator.parser` the simplest way to avoid calling a URL is to use a plain XML file since `feedparser` also supports it, thus making the package depend on a web connection. Let's get a feed and save it within the tests folder, in a file named `sample.xml`:

```
cd atomisator/parser/tests
wget http://ziade.org/atomisator/sample.xml
```

> This is a sample feed made for this book. So the upcoming examples will look similar in your tests, but any other feed would also fill the need.

The `README.txt` can be changed accordingly to use it:

```
...
>>> res = parse(os.path.join(test_dir, 'sample.xml'))
...
```

The package can now be tested independently from a web connection.

Writing the Code

From there, a `parse` function can be added in the package, and built until the test passes. The final form is:

```
from feedparser import parse as feedparse
from itertools import islice
from itertools import imap

def _filter_entry(entry):
    """Filters entry fields."""
```

```
        entry['links'] = [link['href'] for link in entry['links']]

        return entry
    def parse(url, size=10):
        """Returns entries of the feed."""
        result = feedparse(url)
        return islice(imap(_filter_entry,
                            result['entries']), size)
```

And the adapted doctest is:

```
    ...
    Each item is a dictionary that contains the entry::
        >>> entry = res.next()
        >>> entry['title']
        u'CSSEdit 2.0 Released'
    The keys available are:
        >>> keys = sorted(entry.keys())
        >>> list(keys)
        ['id', 'link', 'links', 'summary', 'summary_detail',
         'tags', 'title', 'title_detail']
```

atomisator.db

We follow the same principles to build atomisator.db. A new package named atomisator.db is added and linked to the local interpreter.

Notice that using Nose as a test runner, when you have several packages in the same namespace, will qualify all tests. So you will run atomisator.parser tests as well from here when working in atomisator.db. While this is often not a problem, you might want to use filtering options when focusing on a particular package.

For the rest of this section, we will focus on SQL-specific elements to describe a common way to work with databases.

SQLAlchemy

The most convenient way to work with relational databases in Python is to use **SQLAlchemy** (http://www.sqlalchemy.org), which is an object-relational mapper (see http://en.wikipedia.org/wiki/Object-relational_mapping). This tool provides a mapping system that allows synchronizing Python objects with SQL table rows, without having to write any line of SQL.

SQLAlchemy has several database back ends available that make many database systems usable, such as PostgreSQL, SQLite, MySQL, or even Oracle. The great thing about this philosophy is that it is possible to switch to any back end with the same code. This means, for instance, that a SQLite flat file can be used in the test environment to build the connector, while PostgreSQL will be used in production:

```
>>> if big_daddy_server:
...     sqluri = 'postgres://tarek@localhost/database'
... else:
...     sqluri = 'sqlite://relative/path/to/database.db'
```

This feature is limited, of course, to operations that are common to all database systems and covered by SQLAlchemy. But as long as the provided API is used to interact with the database, the switch remains possible. This can be hard to keep to when specific calls have to be made, such as stored procedure calls for the sake of optimization. But most things in a database Python package can be built using SQLite as a test database.

Therefore, SQLAlchemy can be seen as a universal database utility for Python. Many Python projects in the community rely on this tool, and it is now considered as one of the best ways to work with databases. Another similar project might also be considered, which is **Storm** (https://storm.canonical.com) from the Ubuntu makers, Canonical. This tool uses an implicit mapping system, whereas SQLAlchemy relies on an explicit mapping system that has to be defined on the Python side to describe how Python objects are linked to SQL tables.

Creating the Mappings

The `atomisator.db` database model is quite simple to build since it just keeps one table of entries, together with a table of links and a table of tags. The following figure provides a simplified view of the database. The main table, `atomisator_entry`, is filled with the feed entries provided by `atomisator.parser`, together with the current date. `atomisator_link` and `atomisator_tag` are secondary tables that keep a list of unique values and let an entry point to them (`links` and `tags` fields):

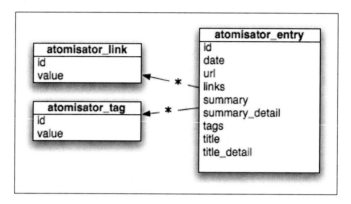

SQLAlchemy automatically provides these one-to-many relations, and such a structure can be described like this:

```
from sqlalchemy import *

from sqlalchemy.orm import *
from sqlalchemy.orm import mapper

metadata = MetaData()
link = Table('atomisator_link', metadata,
            Column('id', Integer, primary_key=True),
            Column('url', String(300)),
            Column('atomisator_entry_id', Integer,
                ForeignKey('atomisator_entry.id')))
class Link(object):
    def __init__(self, url):
        self.url = url

    def __repr__(self):
        return "<Link('%s')>" % self.url

mapper(Link, link)

tag = Table('atomisator_tag', metadata,
            Column('id', Integer, primary_key=True),
```

```
                    Column('value', String(100)),
                    Column('atomisator_entry_id', Integer,
                        ForeignKey('atomisator_entry.id'))))
class Tag(object):
    def __init__(self, value):
        self.value = value

    def __repr__(self):
        return "<Tag('%s')>" % self.value

mapper(Tag, tag)

entry = Table('atomisator_entry', metadata,
              Column('id', Integer, primary_key=True),
              Column('url', String(300)),
              Column('date', DateTime()),
              Column('summary', Text()),
              Column('summary_detail', Text()),
              Column('title', Text()),
              Column('title_detail', Text()))

class Entry(object):
    def __init__(self, title, url, summary, summary_detail='',
                 title_detail=''):
        self.title = title
        self.url = url
        self.summary = summary
        self.summary_detail = summary_detail
        self.title_detail = title_detail

    def add_links(self, links):
        for link in links:
            self.links.append(Link(link))

    def add_tags(self, tags):
        for tag in tags:
            self.tags.append(Tag(tag))

    def __repr__(self):
        return "<Entry(%r)>" % self.title

mapper(Entry, entry, properties={
        'links':relation(Link, backref='atomisator_entry'),
        'tags':relation(Tag, backref='atomisator_entry'),
        })
```

We will not go into greater detail on this code, and it can be understood by taking the official tutorial here: `http://www.sqlalchemy.org/docs/04/ormtutorial.html`. Furthermore, SQLAlchemy is a very active framework. So, the code presented might not be the best way to do things by the time the book is printed.

The important point is to understand that each table on the database is wired with a class on the Python side. Each instance of this class represents a row of the table.

 atomisator.db, like all packages created for this book, is available at PyPI. Although the latest version is complete, there is an evolving version that differs from this one.

Providing the APIs

On the top of these mappings, the APIs have to provide a way to add entries, and to query them. The main doctest built together with the code will look like this at the end:

```
=============
atomisator.db
=============

This package provides a few mappers to store feed entries
in a SQL database.

The SQL uri is provided in the config module::

    >>> from atomisator.db import config
    >>> config.SQLURI = 'sqlite://:memory:'

Let's create an entry::

    >>> from atomisator.db import create_entry
    >>> entry = {'url': 'http://www.python.org/news',
    ...     'summary': 'Summary goes here',
    ...     'title': 'Python 2.6alpha1 and 3.0alpha3 released',
    ...     'links': ['http://www.python.org'],
    ...     'tags': ['cool', 'fun']}
    >>> id_ = create_entry(entry)
    >>> type(id_)
    <type 'int'>

We get the database id back. Now let's look for entries::

    >>> from atomisator.db import get_entries
    >>> entries = get_entries()  # returns a generator object
    >>> entries.next()
    <Entry('Python 2.6alpha1 and 3.0alpha3 released')>

Some filtering can be done ::

    >>> entries = \
    ...     get_entries(url='http://www.python.org/news')
    >>> entries.next()
    <Entry('Python 2.6alpha1 and 3.0alpha3 released')>
```

When no entry is found, the generator is empty::

```
>>> entries = get_entries(url='xxxx')
>>> entries.next()
Traceback (most recent call last):
...
StopIteration
```

Two global functions are provided by this package to work with the database:

- `get_entries`: Returns entries that can be filtered.
- `create_entry`: Adds an entry.

atomisator.feed

`atomisator.feed` uses `atomisator.db` to read the latest entries and generate an XML file that presents them in RSS. This is done with the `Cheetah` template engine that was used to create a code skeleton in the previous chapter. The RSS template file implements the RSS 2.0 structure:

```
<?xml version="1.0" encoding="utf-8"?>
<rss version="2.0" xmlns:rdf="http://www.w3.org/1999/02/22-rdf-syntax-
ns#">
<channel>
<title><![CDATA[${channel.title}]]></title>
<description><![CDATA[${channel.description}]]></description>
<link>${channel.link}</link>
<language>en</language>
<copyright>Copyright 2008, Atomisator</copyright>
<pubDate>${publication_date}</pubDate>
<lastBuildDate>${build_date}</lastBuildDate>
#for $entry in $entries
  <item>
    <title><![CDATA[${entry.title}]]></title>
    <description><![CDATA[${entry.summary}]]></description>
    <link><![CDATA[${entry.url}]]></link>
    <pubDate>${entry.date}</pubDate>
  </item>
#end for
</channel>
</rss>
```

The entries are provided by the database and the extra information such as the channel title is given by the configuration. The `doctest` for this package looks like this:

```
===============
atomisator.feed
===============

Generates a feed using a template::
    >>> from atomisator.feed import generate
    >>> print generate('feed', 'the feed', 'http://link')
    <?xml version="1.0" encoding="utf-8"?>
    <rss version="2.0" xmlns:rdf="...">
    <channel>
    <title><![CDATA[feed]]></title>
    <description><![CDATA[the feed]]></description>
    <link>http://link</link>
    <language>en</language>
    ...
    <item>
      <title><![CDATA[Python 2.6alpha1 and
                      3.0alpha3 released]]></title>
      <description><![CDATA[Summary goes here]]></description>
      <link><![CDATA[http://www.python.org/news]]></link>
      <pubDate>...</pubDate>
    </item>
    ...
    </channel>
    </rss>
```

This package can be used by the main package that feeds fresh entries to it.

atomisator.main

The main package combines everything together by reading a configuration file called `atomisator.cfg` that provides a list of the feeds and a few global variables:

```
[atomisator]
# feeds to read
sites =
    sample1.xml
    sample2.xml

# database location
database = sqlite:///atomisator.db
```

```
# fields used for the channel
title = My Feed
description = The feed
link = the link
# name of the generated file
file = atomisator.xml
```

This file is read by a dedicated module called `config`. From there, three methods are provided in the main module to join all the pieces of the puzzle:

```
from atomisator.main.config import parser
from atomisator.parser import parse
from atomisator.db import config
from atomisator.db import create_entry
from atomisator.feed import generate

config.SQLURI = parser.database

def _log(msg):
    print msg

def load_feeds():
    """Fetches feeds."""
    for count, feed in enumerate(parser.feeds):
        _log('Parsing feed %s' % feed)
        for entry in parse(feed):
            count += 1
            create_entry(entry)
    _log('%d entries read.' % count+1)

def generate_feed():
    """Creates the meta-feed."""
    _log('Writing feed in %s' % parser.file)
    feed = generate(parser.title,
                    parser.description, parser.link)
    f = open(parser.file, 'w')
    try:
        f.write(feed)
    finally:
        f.close()
    _log('Feed ready.')

def atomisator():
    """Calling both."""
    load_feeds()
    generate_feed()
```

They are then hooked as console scripts in `setup.py`:

```
...
entry_points = {
    "console_scripts": [
        "load_feeds = atomisator.main:load_feeds",
        "generate_feed = atomisator.main:generate_feed",
        "atomisator = atomisator.main:atomisator"
    ]
}
...
```

This will add three new executable scripts in the system that point to the three functions.

This package also defines the other `atomisator` packages as dependencies in `setup.py`, in order to install them when `atomisator.main` is installed:

```
...
    install_requires=[
        'atomisator.db',
        'atomisator.feed',
        'atomisator.parser'
    ],
...
```

Distributing Atomisator

The application is now ready to be distributed by pushing eggs in PyPI.

Each package can be released as an egg using the `sdist`, `bdist`, or `bdist_egg` command. For our application, since there is no code to compile, a source distribution is enough for all platforms.

For each egg, the `register` and `upload` commands can be invoked together with `sdist`, but only if you have created an account as described in the previous chapter. The `register sdist upload` sequence will register the package at PyPI, build a source distribution, and then upload it:

```
$ cd atomisator.main
$ python setup.py register sdist upload
Using PyPI login from /Users/tarek/.pypirc
Registering atomisator.parser to http://pypi.python.org/pypi
Server response (200): OK
```

```
running sdist

...

running upload

Using PyPI login from /Users/tarek/.pypirc

Submitting dist/atomisator.parser-0.1.0.tar.gz to http://pypi.python.org/
pypi

Server response (200): OK
```

The package will then be available at PyPI.

A good practice is to create a `release` alias into each package by invoking the `alias` command:

```
$ python setup.py alias release register sdist upload

running alias

Writing setup.cfg

$ more setup.cfg

[aliases]

release = register sdist upload
```

The `release` command can then be used to push the package. Let's do it in `atomisator.db` and for the others:

```
$ cd atomisator.db

$ python setup.py alias release register sdist upload

running alias

Writing setup.cfg

$ python setup.py release

running register

Using PyPI login from /Users/tarek/.pypirc

Registering atomisator.db to http://pypi.python.org/pypi

Server response (200): OK

...

running upload

Using PyPI login from /Users/tarek/.pypirc

Submitting dist/atomisator.db-0.1.0.tar.gz to http://pypi.python.org/pypi

Server response (200): OK

$ cd ../atomisator.feed/

$ python setup.py alias release register sdist upload

...
```

```
$ python setup.py release
...
$ cd ../atomisator.parser
...
```

The four packages will then be available at PyPI. If you try to search for "atomisator" in PyPI (try: http://pypi.python.org/pypi?%3Aaction=search&term=atomisator&submit=search), you should find them all.

Now from any computer that has setuptools installed, Atomisator can be installed with this command:

```
$ easy_install atomisator.main
```

This command will take care of installing all packages and their dependencies, and make the three commands created in atomisator.main available at the prompt.

Dependencies between Packages

Distributing an application in several packages creates some overhead when it comes to releasing it.

For example, if you make some changes in atomisator.db that impact atomisator.main, you will have to:

- Upgrade the versions of each package
- Make sure the new atomisator.main package gets the right atomisator.db version
- Release both packages again

Version dependency can be configured directly in the install_requires metadata in setup.py. For instance, if the 1.4.6 version of atomisator.main needs at least the 1.4.4 version of atomisator.db to run, its setup.py file will look like this:

```
version = '1.4.6'
...
    install_requires=[
        'atomisator.db>=1.4.4',
        'atomisator.feed',
        'atomisator.parser'
    ],
...
```

This overhead can be reduced by writing a few scripts to automate the releasing of your application. In any case, it is better to split your application into several packages than rely on a single package. If each package represents a logical part of your application, each one of them will evolve at its own pace. In the meantime, if two packages are always modified together, it probably means that they should be merged in a single package.

Don't worry too much about how your application is split when you start coding it. If the split is not correct, the problem will appear on the road and you will always be able to re-factor the code in order to fix it.

Summary

In this chapter, we have seen a toy implementation of an application that is distributed in several packages at PyPI under the same namespace.

We have set up a working environment using `virtualenv` and have also discussed setting up a test runner to play with the packages being developed.

While working on bigger applications, some extra packaging work has to be done around the packages for installers that go beyond a Python installation.

The next chapter goes a bit further and presents `zc.buildout`, which is the tool used to build an application environment.

7
Working with zc.buildout

We have seen in the last chapter how to write an application based on several eggs. When distributing such an application, the user gets the package and its dependencies installed in the `site-packages` directory of Python, and gets some entry points such as command-line utilities.

But for bigger applications than Atomisator, this approach is limited: If you need to deploy some configuration files or write log files, it is not practical to make them live inside the code packages.

The best approach is to integrate them seamlessly in the target system by creating specific installers. On Linux-based systems for instance, the log files should be in `/var/log` and the configuration files in `/etc`. But creating such installers requires a lot of system-specific work.

Another approach, a bit similar to what `virtualenv` provides, is to work on a self-contained directory that has everything needed to run the application and then distribute it. This directory can also contain the required packages, and an installer that takes care of bootstrapping everything on the target system.

`zc.buildout` (see `http://pypi.python.org/pypi/zc.buildout`) is a tool that can be used to create such an environment and this chapter presents how to:

- Organize an application through a descriptive language where all packages needed to run the application can be defined
- Deploy such applications as a source release

Alternative tools to `zc.buildout` are `Paver` and `AutomateIt`. See `http://www.blueskyonmars.com/projects/paver` and `http://automateit.org`.

This chapter is organized in three parts:

- `zc.buildout` philosophy
- How to distribute `zc.buildout`-based applications
- The application template that creates a `zc.buildout` application environment using the `paster` tool

zc.buildout Philosophy

`virtualenv` is pretty convenient to isolate a Python environment. It works locally, as we saw in the previous chapter, but still requires a lot of manual work at the prompt to set up and maintain a project environment.

`zc.buildout` offers the same isolation feature, but goes further by providing:

- A simple description language to define these dependencies in a **configuration** file
- A plug-in system that provides entry points to chain a combination of code calls
- A way to deploy and release the application sources together with their execution environment

The configuration file describes which eggs are needed in the environment, their states (being developed locally, or available at PyPI, or anywhere else), and all other elements needed to build an application.

The plug-in system registers packages and chains them in a sequence it executes.

Last, the whole environment is independent and isolated and can be, therefore, used in the same way as it is to be released and deployed.

`zc.buildout` has great documentation on its PyPI page (`http://pypi.python.org/pypi/zc.buildout`). This section will just summarize the most important elements one needs to know in order to build and work at the application level. The elements are as follows:

- The configuration file structure
- The `buildout` command
- Recipes

Configuration File Structure

`zc.buildout` relies on a configuration file that uses a structure compatible with the `ConfigParser` module. These INI-like files have sections delimited by `[headers]` with lines that contain `name:value` or `name=value`.

Minimum Configuration File

The minimum `buildout` configuration file contains a `[buildout]` section and has a variable called `parts` in it. This variable contains a multi-line value that provides a list of sections:

```
[buildout]
parts =
    part1
    part2
[part1]
recipe = my.recipe1
[part2]
recipe = my.recipe2
```

Each section specified in `parts` has at least one `recipe` value that provides the name of a package. This package can be any Python package as long as it defines a `zc.buildout` entry point.

With this file, `buildout` will play this sequence:

- It will check if the package `my.recipe1` is installed. If it's not installed, it fetches it and installs it locally.
- It will execute the code pointed to by `my.recipe1`'s entry point.
- Then, it will do the same thing for `part2`.

A `buildout` is, therefore, a plug-in-based script that chains the execution of independent packages called `recipes`. Building an environment with this tool consists of defining the right sequence of recipes.

[buildout] Section Options

Besides `parts`, the `[buildout]` section has several options available. The most important ones are:

- **develop**: Multi-line value that lists the eggs to be installed with the `python setup.py develop` command in the environment. Each of these values is a path to the package folder where `setup.py` is located.
- **find-links**: Multi-line value that provides a list of locations (URL or file) provided to `easy_install` to find the eggs defined in `eggs` or in any dependency when installing an egg.

From there, a `buildout` can list a series of eggs to be installed in the environment. For each value specified in `develop`, the tool runs the `setuptools develop` command and fetches PyPI when dependencies are defined.

The web location used to find the package is the same as that used by `easy_install` is `http://pypi.python.org/simple`, which is a web page not intended for humans that contains a list of package links that can be browsed automatically.

Last, the `find-links` option provides a way to point to alternative sources when the packages are available in other places.

Let's take an example:

```
[buildout]
parts =
develop =
    /home/tarek/dev/atomisator.feed
find-links =
    http://acme.com/packages/index
```

With this configuration, `buildout` will install the `atomisator.feed` package as `python setup.py develop` would, and use the extra link from `http://acme.com/packages/index` to find any dependencies when they are not available at PyPI.

This environment can be built using the `buildout` command.

The buildout Command

The `buildout` command is installed by `zc.buildout` with the usual `easy_install` call and can be used to interpret configuration files:

```
$ easy_install zc.buildout
...
$ buildout
While:
  Initializing.
Error: Couldn't open /Users/tarek/buildout.cfg
```

An initial call with the `init` option in an empty directory will create a default `buildout.cfg` file and a few other elements:

```
$ cd /tmp
$ mkdir tests
$ cd tests
$ buildout init
Creating '/tmp/tests/buildout.cfg'.
Creating directory '/tmp/tests/bin'.
Creating directory '/tmp/tests/parts'.
```

```
Creating directory '/tmp/tests/eggs'.
Creating directory '/tmp/tests/develop-eggs'.
Generated script '/tmp/tests/bin/buildout'.
$ find .
.
./bin
./bin/buildout
./buildout.cfg
./develop-eggs
./eggs/setuptools-0.6c7-py2.5.egg
./eggs/zc.buildout-1.0.0b30-py2.5.egg
./parts
$ more buildout.cfg
[buildout]
parts =
```

The bin folder contains a local buildout script, in which three other folders
are created:

- parts corresponds to the sections defined in the configuration file. It is a
  standard place where each called recipe can write elements.
- develop-eggs will hold information to link the environment to the packages
  defined in develop.
- eggs contains eggs used by the environment. It is filled already with
  zc.buildout and setuptools eggs.

Let's change the cfg file by adding a develop section:

```
[buildout]
parts =
develop =
    /home/tarek/dev/atomisator.feed
```

The specified folder will be installed by zc.buildout as a develop egg by calling the
buildout command again:

```
$ bin/buildout
Develop: '/home/tarek/dev/atomisator.feed'
$ ls develop-eggs/
atomisator.feed.egg-link
$ more develop-eggs/atomisator.feed.egg-link
/home/tarek/dev/atomisator.feed
```

The `develop-eggs` folder now contains a link to the `atomisator.feed` package located in `/home/tarek/dev/atomisator.feed`. Of course, any folder containing a package can be tied into the `buildout` script with the `develop` option.

Recipes

We have seen that each section specifies a package as a recipe. The `zc.recipe.egg` one, for instance, is used to specify one or several eggs to install in the `buildout`. This recipe will pull the package as `easy_install` would, by calling PyPI, and will eventually look into the links provided in `find-links` if PyPI does not have it.

For example, if we want to install `Nose` into the `buildout`, this can be done by adding a dedicated section into the configuration file and pointing to it in the `parts` variable of the `buildout` section:

```
[buildout]
parts =
    test
develop =
    /home/tarek/dev/atomisator.feed
[test]
recipe = zc.recipe.egg
eggs =
    nose
```

Running the `buildout` script again will play the `test` section and pull the `Nose` egg as `easy_install` would:

```
$ bin/buildout
Develop: '/home/tarek/dev/atomisator.feed'
Installing test.
Getting distribution for nose
Got nose 0.10.3.
```

The `nosetest` script will be installed into the `bin` folder, and the `Nose` egg in the `eggs` folder.

Let's add a new section in the `cfg` file called `other` using `zc.recipe.egg` again:

```
[buildout]
parts =
    test
    other
develop =
    /home/tarek/dev/atomisator.feed
```

```
[test]
recipe = zc.recipe.egg
eggs =
    nose
[other]
recipe = zc.recipe.egg

eggs =
    elementtree
    PIL

...
```

This new section defines two new packages. Let's run the buildout script again:

```
$ bin/buildout
Develop: '/home/tarek/dev/atomisator.feed'
Updating test.
Installing other.
Getting distribution for elementtree
Got elementtree 1.2.7-20070827-preview.
Getting distribution for 'PIL'.
Got PIL 1.1.6.
```

The sections pointed to in parts are run in the order they are defined. When run again, zc.buildout checks the already installed parts, to see if they need to be updated, and if so installs new ones. From the other section, the eggs folder gets populated with two new eggs.

Recipes are simple Python packages, usually dedicated to this sole role. They are conventionally nested namespaced packages, where the first part is the name of the organization, the second one is the recipe, and the third one the name of the recipe.

The recipe we have used so far is provided by the Zope Corporation (zc), but many recipes are available at PyPI to handle many needs in a buildout environment.

Since frameworks such as Zope or Plone rely on this tool, a quick search on http://pypi.python.org with buildout or recipe in the query will return hundreds of packages that can be used to compose any kind of buildout.

Notable Recipes

Here's a small list of useful recipes found on PyPI :

- `collective.recipe.ant`: Builds Ant (Java) projects.
- `iw.recipe.cmd`: Executes a command line.
- `iw.recipe.fetcher`: Downloads a file pointed by a URL.
- `iw.recipe.pound`: Compiles and installs Pound (a load balancer).
- `iw.recipe.squid`: Configures and runs Squid (a cache server).
- `z3c.recipe.ldap`: Deploys OpenLDAP.

Creating Recipes

A recipe is a simple class with two methods, namely, `install` and `update`. They return a list of installed files. Coding a new recipe is, therefore, dead simple and can be done using a template.

The `ZopeSkel` project, which is used in the Zope community to build new recipes, can be installed to have a new template called `recipe` among a few others:

```
$ easy_install ZopeSkel
Searching for ZopeSkel
Best match: ZopeSkel 2.1
...
Finished processing dependencies for ZopeSkel
$ paster create --list-templates
Available templates:
  ...
  recipe:            A recipe project for zc.buildout
  ...
```

`recipe` generates a nested namespace package structure with a `Recipe` class skeleton that has to be completed:

```
$ paster create -t recipe atomisator.recipe.here
Selected and implied templates:
  ZopeSkel#recipe  A recipe project for zc.buildout
  ...
Enter namespace_package ['plone']: atomisator
Enter namespace_package2 ['recipe']:
Enter package ['example']: here
```

```
Enter version (Version) ['1.0']:
Enter description ['']: description is here.
Enter long_description ['']:
Enter author (Author name) ['']: Tarek
Enter author_email (Author email) ['']: tarek@ziade.org

...

Creating template recipe
Creating directory ./atomisator.recipe.here

...

$ more atomisator.recipe.here/atomisator/recipe/here/__init__.py
# -*- coding: utf-8 -*-
"""Recipe here"""

class Recipe(object):
    """zc.buildout recipe"""

    def __init__(self, buildout, name, options):
        self.buildout, self.name, self.options = \
                buildout, name, options

    def install(self):
        """Installer"""
        # XXX Implement recipe functionality here

        # Return files that were created by the recipe.
        # The buildout will remove all returned files
        # upon reinstall.
        return tuple()

    def update(self):
        """Updater"""
        pass
```

Atomisator buildout Environment

The Atomisator project can benefit from zc.buildout by creating a dedicated buildout configuration together with the packages, and defining an environment in it.

The buildout environment can be built in two steps:

1. Creating a buildout folder structure
2. Initializing the buildout

buildout Folder Structure

Since `buildout` allows us to link any folder of the system as a `develop` package, the application environment can be separated from it. The cleanest layout is to use a folder for the `buildout` and a folder for the packages being developed.

Let's revisit the Atomisator folder we created in the previous chapter. So far, it contains a `bin` folder with a local interpreter and a `packages` folder. Let's add a `buildout` folder to it:

```
$ cd Atomisator
$ mkdir buildout
```

A new `buildout` environment is then built in the `buildout` folder:

```
$ cd buildout
$ buildout init
Creating 'Atomisator/buildout/buildout.cfg'.
Creating directory 'Atomisator/buildout/bin'.
Creating directory 'Atomisator/buildout/parts'.
Creating directory 'Atomisator/buildout/eggs'.
Creating directory 'Atomisator/buildout/develop-eggs'.
Generated script 'Atomisator/buildout/bin/buildout'.
```

`buildout.cfg` is changed in order to generate a local `nosetest` script, and to install the Atomisator eggs as `develop` eggs:

```
[buildout]
develop =
    ../packages/atomisator.main
    ../packages/atomisator.db
    ../packages/atomisator.feed
    ../packages/atomisator.parser

parts =
    test

[test]
recipe = pbp.recipe.noserunner
eggs =
    atomisator.main
    atomisator.db
    atomisator.feed
    atomisator.parser
```

This configuration file will generate a complete Atomisator environment located in the `buildout` folder.

In the last chapter, we installed `Nose` in the same local interpreter where the packages were being developed, thanks to `virtualenv`. When working in a `buildout`, having the same feature requires more work: Installing `Nose` as an egg in the `buildout` will not make other eggs directly visible to the test runner. To get a similar environment, the `pbp.recipe.noserunner` is a small recipe that generates a local `nosetests` runner with a specific environment. All eggs defined in its `eggs` variable will be added in the test runner execution environment.

The recipe uses the section name for the name of the generated script. So a `test` script will be available in our case, which can be used to test all `atomisator` packages:

```
$ bin/test atomisator
........
------------------------------------------------------------------
Ran 8 tests in 0.015s


OK
```

Going Further

Another step could be performed to create and use the `atomisator.cfg` file in the `etc` folder, which is in the `buildout` folder. This would be needed to create a new recipe that reads the values in the `buildout.cfg` file and generates `atomisator.cfg`.

A new section would then be created like this:

```
...
[atomisator-configuration]
recipe = atomisator.recipe.installer
sites =
    sample1.xml
    sample2.xml
database = sqlite:///${buildout:directory}/var/atomisator.db
title = My Feed
description = The feed
link = the link
file = ${buildout:directory}/var/atomisator.xml
...
```

The `${buildout:directory}` is replaced with the `buildout` path.

Releasing and Distributing

We have seen in the previous section that a `buildout` is a standalone folder that is able to include everything needed to run the application. All needed eggs are installed in it, and the console scripts are created in the `bin` folder.

As a matter of fact, the top `Atomisator` folder could be archived in an archive as it is, and then unpacked on some other computer that has Python. By running `buildout` again on this new target, everything would get bootstrapped correctly and the application could run from there.

Distributing the source this way is universal compared to the other packaging systems that every operating system provides, such as `apt` or `RPM`. Everything is isolated in a self-contained folder and will work on every system. Therefore, it will not integrate smoothly in the target system and will use its own specific standards. This is fine for many applications, but purists will want it to be installable with the package system used on the target system to ease system maintenance.

If this is required, extra platform-specific integration work is needed. It will not be covered by this book because it is a very wide topic that is out of scope, but the source release that is covered here is the first step toward a target-specific release.

So let's focus on distributing the `buildout` folder as it is.

However having the `packages` folder shipped together with the `buildout` one along with its sub-folders linked as `develop eggs` is not the best option, since we would like to release tagged versions for each egg. `buildout` can interpret any configuration file. So the best practice is to create a dedicated configuration file that does not use the `develop` option together with a set of built eggs for each package we have created.

So releasing a `buildout` is done in three steps:

1. Releasing the packages
2. Creating the release configuration
3. Building and preparing the release

Releasing the Packages

Each package can be released as eggs using the `sdist`, `bdist`, or `bdist_egg` command. For our application, since there is no code to compile, a source distribution is enough for all platforms.

For each package, a source distribution is built in the same way as we have seen in the last chapter:

```
$ python setup.py sdist
running sdist
...
Writing atomisator.db-0.1.0/setup.cfg
tar -cf dist/atomisator.db-0.1.0.tar atomisator.db-0.1.0
gzip -f9 dist/atomisator.db-0.1.0.tar
removing 'atomisator.db-0.1.0' (and everything under it)
$ ls dist/
atomisator.db-0.1.0.tar.gz
```

The result is an archive that is either pushed to PyPI or stored in a folder.

Adding a Release Configuration File

zc.buildout provides an extension mechanism that will let you create configuration files in layers. Using the extends option that specifies another configuration file, a file can inherit all its values and then add new ones, or override some of them.

A new configuration file dedicated to the releases can be created in the following manner to set specific things in it:

- We need to point to the buildout released packages.
- We need to get rid of the develop option.

The result is:

```
[buildout]
extends = buildout.cfg
develop =
parts =
    atomisator
    eggs

download-cache = downloads

[atomisator]
recipe = zc.recipe.eggs
eggs =
    atomisator.main
    atomisator.db
    atomisator.feed
    atomisator.parser
```

Here, `download-cache` is a system folder where the `buildout` stores eggs downloaded from PyPI. The `downloads` folder is best created inside the `buildout` folder:

```
$ mkdir downloads
```

The `eggs` part is inherited from `buildout.cfg` and does not need to be copied in this new file. The `atomisator` part will pull released eggs from PyPI and store them in `downloads`.

Building and Releasing the Application

The `buildout` can then be built using this specific configuration, using the `-c` option to point to a specific configuration file, together with the `-v` option to get more details:

```
$ bin/buildout -c release.cfg -v
Installing 'zc.buildout', 'setuptools'.
...
Installing atomisator.
Installing 'atomisator.db', 'atomisator.feed', 'atomisator.parser',
'atomisator.main'.
...
Picked: setuptools = 0.6c8
```

When this step is finished, the packages will be downloaded and stored in the `downloads` folder:

```
$ ls downloads/dist/
```

atomisator.feed-0.1.0.tar.gz

atomisator.main-0.1.0.tar.gz

atomisator.db-0.1.0.tar.gz

atomisator.parser-0.1.0.tar.gz

This means that the packages will not get pulled from PyPI on the next run. In other words, the `buildout` can be built in an offline mode at this point.

The released version is ready to be shipped by distributing the `buildout` folder in an archived version, for example.

The last thing to do is to add a `bootstrap.py` file in the folder to automate the installation of `zc.buildout`, and the creation of the `bin/buildout` script on the target system in the same way `buildout init` does:

```
$ wget http://ziade.org/bootstrap.py
```

Some tools in the community provide some scripts to prepare those archived versions with extra options, for instance `collective.releaser` and `zc.sourcerelease`.

Summary

We have seen in this chapter that `zc.buildout`:

- Can be used to build egg-based applications
- Knows how to gather eggs together to build an isolated environment
- Chains recipes, which are small Python packages, to build a script for building the environment
- Can be used to make source distributions of Python applications

To summarize, working with `zc.buildout` is done by:

- Creating a `buildout` with a list of eggs and using it to develop
- Creating a configuration file dedicated to releases and using it to build a distributable `buildout` folder

The next chapter will go further with this tool to explain how projects can be managed with it, together with other tools.

8
Managing Code

Working on a software project that involves more than one person is tough. Everything slows down and gets harder. This happens for several reasons. The chapter will expose these reasons, and will try to provide some ways to fight against them.

This chapter is organized in two parts, which explain:

- How to work with a version control system
- How to set up continuous integration

First of all, a code base evolves so much that it is important to track all the changes that are made, even more so when many developers work on it. That is the role of a **version control system**.

Next, several brains that are not directly wired together can still work on the same project. They have different roles and work on different aspects. Therefore, a lack of global visibility generates a lot of confusion about what is going on, and what is being done by others. This is unavoidable, and some tools have to be used to provide continuous visibility and mitigate the problem. This is done by setting up a series of tools for **continuous integration**.

Now, we will discuss these two aspects in detail.

Version Control Systems

Version control systems (VCS) provide a way to share, synchronize, and back up any kind of files. They are categorized in two families:

1. Centralized systems
2. Distributed systems

Centralized Systems

A centralized version control system is based on a single server that holds the files and lets people check in and check out the changes that are made to those files. The principle is quite simple: Everyone can get a copy of the files on his/her system and work on them. From there, every user can *commit* his/her changes to the server. They will be applied and the *revision* number will be raised. Other users will then be able to get those changes by synchronizing their *repository* copy through an *update*.

The repository evolves through all the commits, and the system archives all revisions into a database to undo any change, or provide information on what has been done:

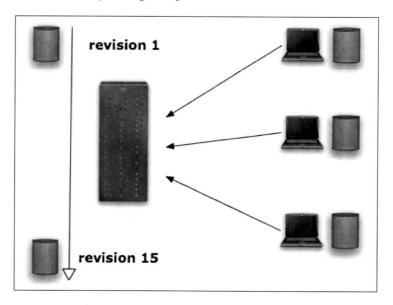

Every user in this centralized configuration is responsible for synchronizing his/her local repository with the main one, in order to get the other users changes. This means that some conflicts can occur when a locally-changed file has been changed, and is checked in by someone else. A conflict resolution mechanism is carried out, in this case, on the user system as shown in the following figure:

1. Joe checks in a change.
2. Pamela attempts to check in a change on the same file.
3. The server complains that her copy of the file is out of date.
4. Pamela updates her local copy. The version control software may or may not be able to merge the two versions seamlessly (that is, without a conflict).
5. Pamela commits a new version that contains the latest changes made by Joe and her own.

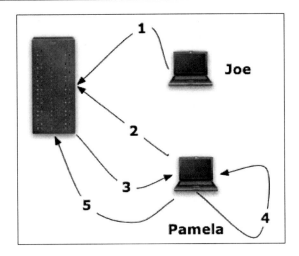

This process is perfectly fine on small-sized projects that involve a few developers and a small number of files. But it becomes problematic for bigger projects. For instance, a complex change involves a lot of files, which is time consuming, and keeping everything local before the whole work is done is unfeasible.

- It is dangerous because the user may keep on his/her computer changes that are not necessarily backed up.
- It is hard to share with others until it is checked in and sharing it before it is done would leave the repository in an unstable state, and so the other users would not want to share.

Centralized VCS have resolved this problem by providing "branches" and "merges". It is possible to fork from the main stream of revisions to work on a separated line, and then to get back to the main stream.

In the figure that follows overleaf, Joe starts a new branch from revision 2, to work on a new feature. The revisions are incremented in the main stream and in his branch, every time a change is checked in. At revision 7, Joe has finished his work and commits his changes into trunk (the main branch). This requires, most of the time, some conflict resolution.

But in spite of their advantages, centralized VCS have several pitfalls:

- Branching and merging is quite hard to deal with. It can become a nightmare.
- Since the system is centralized, it is impossible to commit changes offline. This can lead to a huge, single commit to the server when the user gets back online. Last of all, it doesn't work very well for projects such as Linux, where many companies permanently maintain their own "branch" of the software, and there is no central repository that everyone has an account on.

For the latter, some tools are making it possible to work offline, such as SVK (http://svk.bestpractical.com/view/HomePage), but a more fundamental problem is how the centralized VCS work.

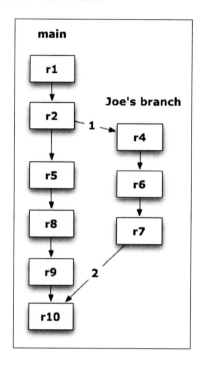

Despite these pitfalls, VCS are really popular amongst open-source developers.

In the open-source world, **CVS (Concurrent Version System**, see http://cvs.org) has made centralized version control systems very popular in the last fifteen years, and forges such as Sourceforge (http://sourceforge.net) or Gna! (http://gna.org) made them available to any public project. Almost all open-source projects use a VCS. Subversion (http://subversion.tigris.org) is currently the most popular and is used by thousands of projects.

But another kind of VCS has evolved in the last few years, which tries to make things better: **Distributed VCS (DVCS)**.

Distributed Systems

Distributed VCS is the answer to the centralized VCS. It does not rely on a main server that people work with, but on peer-to-peer principles. Everyone can hold and manage his/her own independent repository for a project, and synchronize it with other repositories:

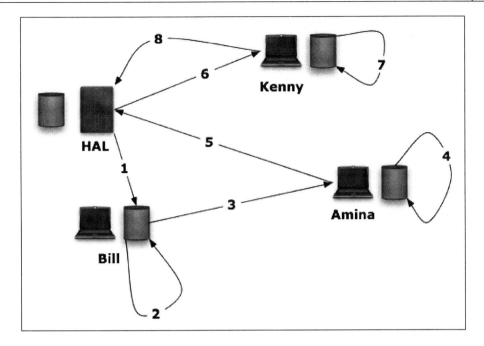

In the last figure, we can see an example of such a system in use:

1. Bill *pulls* the files from HAL's repository.
2. Bill makes some changes on the files.
3. Amina *pulls* the files from Bill's repository.
4. Amina changes the files too.
5. Amina *pushes* the changes to HAL.
6. Kenny *pulls* the files from HAL.
7. Kenny makes changes.
8. Kenny regularly *pushes* his changes to HAL.

The key concept is that people *push* and *pull* the files with other repositories, and this behavior changes according to the way people work and the way the project is managed. Since there is no main repository anymore, the maintainer of the project needs to define a strategy for people to *push* and *pull* the changes.

Furthermore, people have to be a bit smarter when they work with several repositories. Since the revision numbers are local to each repository, there are no global revision IDs anyone can refer to. Therefore, *tags* have to be used to make things clearer. They are labels that can be attached to a revision. Last, users are responsible for backing up their own repositories, which is not the case in a centralized infrastructure where the administrator usually sets back up strategies.

Distributed Strategies

A centralized server is, of course, still desirable with a DVCS, if you're working in a company setting with everyone working toward the same goal.

Different approaches can be applied. The simplest one is to set up a server that acts like a regular centralized server, where every member of the project can push his/her changes into a common stream. But this approach is a bit simplistic. It does not take full advantage of the distributed system, since people will use push and pull commands in the same way as they would do with a centralized system.

Another approach consists of providing several repositories on a server with different levels of access:

- An **unstable repository** is where everyone can push changes.
- A **stable repository** is read-only for all members, except the release managers. They are allowed to pull changes from the unstable repository and decide what should be merged.
- Various **release repositories** corresponds to the releases and are read-only, as we will see later in the chapter.

This allows people to contribute, and managers to review the changes before they make it to the stable repository.

Other strategies can be made up, since DVCS provides infinite combinations. For instance, the Linux Kernel, which is using Git (`http://git.or.cz`), is based on a star model, where Linus Torvalds is maintaining the official repository, and pulls the changes from a set of developers he trusts. In this model, people who wish to push changes to the kernel will try to push them to the trusted developers so that they reach Linus through them, hopefully.

Centralized or Distributed?

Choosing between a centralized and a distributed approach depends a lot on the nature of the project and the way the team works.

For instance, an application that is being developed by an isolated team will not need the features provided by a distributed system. Everything is *under control* in a development server, and the managers will not deal with outside contributors. There are no worries about backing up the work people do. Developers create branches when needed, and then go back to the trunk as soon as possible. They might have a hard time when they need to merge their changes, or when they are working away from an Internet connection, but they are still happy with what such a system provides. Branching and merging does not occur often in such a context anyway.

That's why most companies do not deal with a wider community of contributors. Their own employees are massively using centralized version control systems. Everyone is working together in the same place.

For projects with a broader list of contributors, the centralized approach is a bit rigid, and using a DVCS makes more sense. Many open-source projects are opting for this model now-a-days. For instance, adopting a DVCS for Python is currently being discussed, and this will probably occur soon, since it is mainly a matter of setting up a set of good practices and teaching the developers this new way of working with the code.

In this book, we will use a DVCS and explain how it can be used in project management, together with a set of good practices. The chosen software for this is Mercurial.

Mercurial

Mercurial (`http://www.selenic.com/mercurial/wiki`) is a DVCS written in Python that provides a simple, yet powerful, command-line utility to work with the code.

To install it, the simplest way is to call `easy_install`:

```
$ easy_install mercurial
```

> Under some versions of Windows, the script generated in Python's `Scripts` directory is wrong and `hg` is not available at the prompt. In that case, you might want to rename it to `hg.py` and run it as `hg.py` in the prompt.
>
> A specific binary installer can be used if you still encounter problems. See `http://mercurial.berkwood.com`.

If you are under systems such as Debian or Ubuntu, you can also use the package system provided:

```
$ apt-get install mercurial
```

A script called hg is then available at the prompt with an exhaustive list of options (truncated here):

```
$ hg -h
Mercurial Distributed SCM
list of commands:
 add           add the specified files on the next commit
 clone         make a copy of an existing repository
 commit        commit the specified files
 copy          mark files as copied for the next commit
 diff          diff repository (or selected files)
 incoming      show new changesets found in source
 init          create a new repository in the given directory
 pull          pull changes from the specified source
 push          push changes to the specified destination
 status        show changed files in the working directory
 update        update working directory
use "hg -v help" to show aliases and global options
```

Creating a repository is done with the init command in a folder that will contain the repository:

```
$ cd /tmp/
$ mkdir repo
$ hg init repo
```

From there, files can be added in the repository with the add command:

```
$ cd repo/
$ touch file.txt
$ hg add file.txt
```

The file is not checked in until the commit (ci) command is called:

```
$ hg status
A file.txt
$ hg commit -m "added file.txt"
No username found, using 'tziade@macziade' instead
$ hg log
changeset:    0:d557683c40bc
tag:          tip
user:         tziade@macziade
date:         Tue Apr 01 17:56:41 2008 +0200
summary:      added file.txt
```

The repository is self-contained in the directory it was created in, and can be copied in another directory with the `clone` command:

```
$ hg clone . /tmp/repo2
1 files updated, 0 files merged, 0 files removed, 0 files unresolved
```

This can also be done through SSH to another machine if it has an SSH server and Mercurial installed:

```
$ hg clone . ssh://tarek@ziade.org/repo
searching for changes
remote: adding changesets
remote: adding manifests
remote: adding file changes
remote: added 1 changeset with 1 change to 1 files
```

The distant repositories can then be synchronized using the `push` command:

```
$ echo more >> file.txt
$ hg diff
diff -r d557683c40bc file.txt
--- a/file.txt  Tue Apr 01 17:56:41 2008 +0200
+++ b/file.txt  Tue Apr 01 19:32:59 2008 +0200
@@ -0,0 +1,1 @@
+more
$ hg commit -m 'changing a file'
No username found, using 'tziade@macziade' instead
$ hg push ssh://tarek@ziade.org/repo
pushing to ssh://tarek@ziade.org/repo
searching for changes
remote: adding changesets
remote: adding manifests
remote: adding file changes
remote: added 1 changesets with 1 changes to 1 files
```

The `diff` command (`di`) is used here to display the changes made.

Another nice feature provided by the `hg` command is `serve`, which provides a small web server for the current repository:

```
$ hg serve
```

From here you can point your browser to `http://localhost:8000`. You will get a view of the repository, which will be similar to the following:.

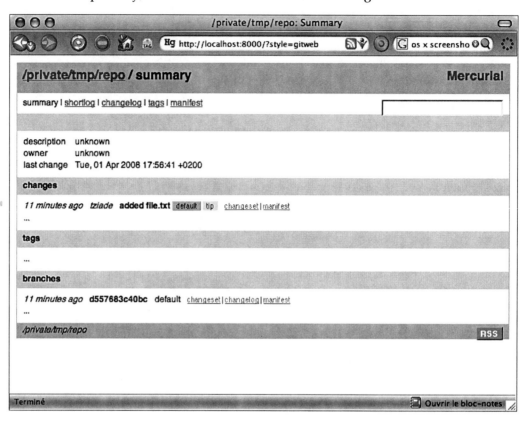

Beyond this view, `hg serve` will also provide access to other users who want to call the `clone` and `pull` commands:

```
$ hg clone http://localhost:8000 copy
requesting all changes
adding changesets
adding manifests
adding file changes
added 1 changesets with 1 changes to 1 files
1 files updated, 0 files merged, 0 files removed, 0 files unresolved
$ cd copy/
$ ls
file.txt
$ touch file2.txt
$ hg add file2.txt
$ hg ci -m "new file"
No username found, using 'tziade@macziade' instead
```

The `clone` command allows copying a repository to start working on it.

`hg serve` will not allow people to push changes, as this requires setting up a real web server to handle authentication, as we will see in the next section. But it can be useful in some situations where you want to temporarily share a repository for other people to pull it.

 To go deeper in Mercurial, an online book is available for free at `http://hgbook.red-bean.com`.

Project Management with Mercurial

The simplest way to manage repositories with Mercurial is to use the `hgwebdir.cgi` script provided with it. It is a **CGI (Common Gateway Interface)** script that can be used to publish the repository through a web server, and to provide the same features that `hg serve` provides. Furthermore, it allows `push` commands to be performed in a safe way, by configuring a password file to restrict this command usage.

 CGI is robust and simple to set up, but not the fastest way to publish a repository. Some other solutions based on `fastcgi` or `mod_wsgi` are available.

Configuring such a system is not hard, but can rely on platform-specific parts. So a generic installation tutorial is impossible to provide. This section will rather focus on how to set up everything on a Linux Debian Sarge and Apache 2 platform, which is quite common.

The steps to install such a server are:

- Setting up a dedicated folder
- Configuring `hgwebdir`
- Configuring Apache
- Setting up authorizations

Setting Up a Dedicated Folder

The multiple repository approach we described earlier is quite simple to set up with Mercurial, since one repository corresponds to one system folder. A `repositories` folder can be created to hold all repositories, and located in a folder dedicated to the project. This project folder can be located in a home folder. The user `mercurial` can be used for that matter.

Let's create a Mercurial environment for Atomisator:

```
$ sudo adduser mercurial
$ sudo su mercurial
$ cd
$ mkdir atomisator
$ mkdir atomisator/repositories
$ cd atomisator
```

From there, the `stable` and `unstable` repositories can be created with `hg`:

```
$ hg init repositories/stable
$ hg init repositories/unstable
$ ls repositories/
unstable  stable
```

 Some teams don't use separate repositories, but work on a single repository where they use a named branch to differentiate the stable version from the developments, and do the merges.

See `http://www.selenic.com/mercurial/wiki/index.cgi/Branch`.

Whenever a release is created, a new repository is added by cloning the `stable` one. For instance, if version `0.1` is released, it will be done like this:

```
$ hg clone repositories/stable repositories/release-0.1
```

Let's add the Atomisator code in the unstable repository, by copying the `buildout` and the `packages` folder that we created in the last chapter in the `unstable` folder, and checking them in. The `unstable` folder should look like this after it is done:

```
$ ls  repositories/unstable
buildout packages
```

 Releasing will be covered in the next chapter.

Configuring hgwebdir

To serve these repositories, the `hgwebdir.cgi` file has to be added in the `atomisator` folder. This script is provided with your installation. If you cannot find it, you can get it on the Mercurial website by downloading a source distribution. But make sure you get the file that strictly corresponds to the installed version:

```
$ hg --version
Mercurial Distributed SCM (version 0.9.4)
$ locate hgwebdir.cgi
/usr/share/doc/mercurial/examples/hgwebdir.cgi
$ cp /usr/share/doc/mercurial/examples/hgwebdir.cgi .
```

This script works with a configuration file called hgweb.config, which contains the path to the repositories folder:

```
[collections]
repositories/ = repositories/
[web]
style = gitweb
push_ssl = false
```

The collections section provides a generic way to point to a folder that contains several repositories. They are visited iteratively by the script.

The web section can be used to set a few options. In our case we can set two of them:

- style will set the look and feel of web pages, and gitweb is probably the best default. Notice that Mercurial uses templates to render all pages, and that they are all configurable.

- If push_ssl is true (its default value), users can only use the push command over HTTPS and not over HTTP.

Configuring Apache

The next step to configure is the web server layer that will execute the CGI script. The simplest way to do it is to provide a configuration file within the atomisator folder that defines a Directory, a ScriptAliasMatch and an AddHandler directive.

Let's add an apache.conf file with this content:

```
AddHandler cgi-script .cgi
ScriptAliasMatch        ^/hg(.*)          /home/mercurial/atomisator/
hgwebdir.cgi$1
<Directory /home/mercurial/atomisator>
  Options ExecCGI FollowSymLinks
  AllowOverride None
  AuthType Basic
  AuthName "Mercurial"
  AuthUserFile /home/mercurial/atomisator/passwords
  <LimitExcept GET>
    Require valid-user
  </LimitExcept>
</Directory>
```

Notice that:

- The `AddHandler` directive might not be necessary with some distributions, but has to be present in Debian Sarge.
- The `ScriptAliasMatch` needs `mod_alias` to be enabled.
- When a POST occurs, which means the user sends data to the server, an authentication is done using a password file.

 If you are not familiar with Apache, take a look at `http://httpd.apache.org/docs`.

The password file is generated with the `htpasswd` utility in the `atomisator` folder:

```
$ htpasswd -c passwords tarek
New password:
Re-type new password:
Adding password for user tarek
$ htpasswd passwords rob
New password:
Re-type new password:
Adding password for user rob
```

 Under Windows, you might need to add the `htpasswd` location into PATH manually if not available at the prompt.

Every time a user who is allowed to push into a repository needs to be added, this file can be upgraded with `htpasswd`.

Lastly, a few steps are required in order to allow the execution of the script, and to make sure that the data is available to the group that is used by the Apache process:

```
sudo chmod +x /home/mercurial/atomisator/hgwebdir.cgi
sudo chown -R mercurial:www-data /home/mercurial/atomisator
sudo chmod -R g+w /home/mercurial/atomisator
```

To hook the configuration, the file can be added into the `site-enabled` directory visited by Apache:

```
$ sudo ln -s /home/mercurial/atomisator/apache.conf /etc/apache2/sites-enabled/007-atomisator
$ sudo apache2ctl restart
```

After Apache is restarted, the page should be reachable at `http://localhost/hg`, as in the following screenshot:

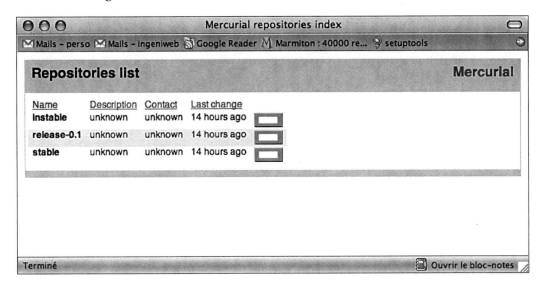

 Notice that each repository comes with an RSS feed that people can use to keep track of the changes. Every time someone pushes a file, a new entry is added in the RSS feed, with a link to the change log. This change log will display a detailed log together with a different view.

If you need to virtual-host your Mercurial repository, you will need to add a specific rewrite rule that will serve the static files used by `hgwebdir`, such as the style sheet.

This is the `apache.conf` file used to publish the book repository (that contains source code from examples) on the Web, which corresponds to `http://hg-atomisator.ziade.org/`:

```
<VirtualHost *:80>
  ServerName hg-atomisator.ziade.org
  CustomLog /home/mercurial/atomisator/access_log combined
  ErrorLog  /home/mercurial/atomisator/error.org.log
  AddHandler cgi-script .cgi
  RewriteEngine On
  DocumentRoot /home/mercurial/atomisator
  ScriptAliasMatch ^/(.*) /home/mercurial/atomisator/hgwebdir.cgi/$1
  <Directory /home/mercurial/atomisator>
    Options ExecCGI FollowSymLinks
    AllowOverride None
    AuthType Basic
```

```
      AuthName "Mercurial"
      AuthUserFile /home/mercurial/atomisator/passwords
      <LimitExcept GET>
        Require valid-user
      </LimitExcept>
    </Directory>
  </VirtualHost>
```

Each repository can be reached from this front page. To make all pages use the same style, an `hgrc` file has to be added in each repository, in the `.hg` configuration directory. This file can define a `web` section like the main `CGI` file uses:

```
$ more repositories/stable/.hg/hgrc
[web]
style = gitweb
description = Stable branch
contact = Tarek <tarek@ziade.org>
```

The `description` and `contact` fields will be used in the web pages as well.

Setting Up Authorizations

We have seen that a global access file filters the people that are allowed to push. This is a first level of authorization, as we need to define the `push` policy for each repository. The strategy we defined earlier was:

- Let all registered developers be allowed to `push` in the `unstable` repository.
- Leave the `stable` repository in read-only access for everyone, except the release manager.

This can be set with the `allow_push` parameter in the `hgrc` file for each repository. If the user `tarek` is the release manager, the `stable` hgrc file will look like this:

```
$ more repositories/stable/.hg/hgrc
[web]
style = gitweb
description = Stable branch
contact = Tarek <tarek@ziade.org>
push_ssl = false
allow_push = tarek
```

Notice that `push_ssl` has been added in order to push through HTTP. The `hgrc` file for the `unstable` repository will look like this:

```
$ more repositories/unstable/.hg/hgrc
[web]
style = gitweb
```

```
description = Unstable branch
contact = Tarek <tarek@ziade.org>
push_ssl = false
allow_push = *
```

This means that everyone is allowed to push in this repository, as long as they are added to the password file.

 In this book, an SSL configuration was not set for the sake of simplicity, but should be used in a real server for more secure transactions. For instance, in our configuration, HTTP allows sniffing.

Setting Up the Client Side

To avoid authentication prompts, and to provide a human-readable name in the commit logs, a .hgrc file can be added in the HOME directory on the client side:

```
[ui]
username = Tarek Ziade
[paths]
default  = http://tarek:secret@atomisator.ziade.org/hg/unstable
unstable = http://tarek:secret@atomisator .ziade.org/hg/unstable
stable = http://tarek:secret@atomisator.ziade.org/hg/stable
```

The ui part gives the server the full name of the committer, and the paths part a list of the repository URLs. Notice that here we put the user name and the password in the URL, which prevents prompting every time a push is done. This is not safe at all, and a password prompt would be safer. However, the safest way would be to work with the server through the SSH protocol instead of using a web server.

With this file, pushes can be done like this:

```
$ hg push    # will push to the default repository (unstable)
$ hg push stable # will push to stable
$ hg push unstable # will push to unstable
```

 If you need to install it on another platform, the steps will not differ a lot. This page will help you out on platform specifics: http://www.selenic.com/mercurial/wiki/index.cgi/ HgWebDirStepByStep.

Continuous Integration

Setting up a repository is the first step towards continuous integration, which is a set of software practices that have emerged from **eXtreme Programming (XP)**. The principles are clearly described on Wikipedia (`http://en.wikipedia.org/wiki/ Continuous_integration#The_Practices`), and define a way to make sure the software is easy to build, test, and deliver.

Let's summarize these practices in our egg-based application environment, using `zc.buildout` and Mercurial:

- **Maintain a code repository**: This is done by Mercurial.

- **Automate the build**: `zc.buildout` fulfills this need, as we have seen in the previous chapter.

- **Make your build self-testing**: `zc.buildout` provides a way to launch a test campaign over the whole software.

- **Everyone commits everyday**: Mercurial provides the tool for the developers to commit changes often. But this is more a developer behavior. People should commit as often as possible, as long as it doesn't break the build.

- **Every commit should be built**: Every time a change is made, the software should be built again and all tests run to make sure there are no regressions introduced. If such a problem occurs, a mail should be sent to warn the developers. This is not yet covered in this chapter.

- **Keep the build fast**: This is not a real problem for Python applications, since the compilation step is not needed most of the time. In any case, when the software is built two times in a row, the second pass should be way faster.

- **Test in a staging environment that is a clone of the production environment**: It is important to be able to test the software on all production environments. This is not yet covered in this chapter.

- **Make it easy to get the latest deliverables**: `zc.buildout` provides a simple way to bundle the deliverables in archives.

- **Everyone can see the result of the latest build**: The system should provide feedback on builds. This is not yet covered in this chapter.

Using these practices raises the code quality through early discovery of problems, even if those problems are related to the code or are specific to a target platform.

Furthermore, having an automated system to build and re-launch tests makes the developer's life easier, since they will not have to re-launch an exhaustive set of tests.

Finally, such rules will make the developers more responsible on what they commit. Checking in broken code will generate a feedback seen by everyone.

The only parts that are not yet covered in our environment are:

- Building the system on every commit
- Building the system on target systems
- Providing feedback on the latest builds

This can be covered with Buildbot, a software that automates builds.

Buildbot

Buildbot (`http://buildbot.net/trac`) is software written in Python that automates the compile and test cycles for any kind of software projects. It is configurable in a way that every change made on a source code repository generates some builds and launches some tests, and then provides some feedback:

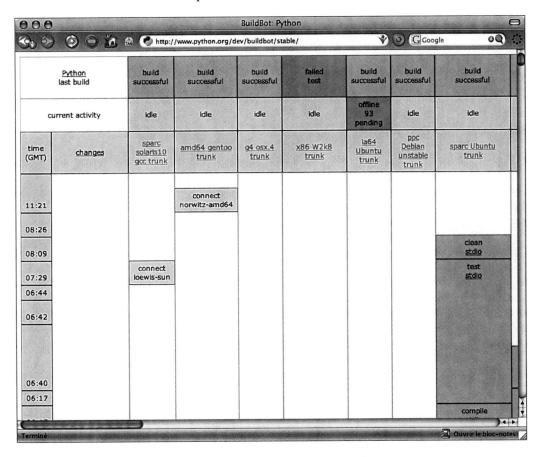

This tool is used, for instance, by Python for the core development, and can be seen at `http://www.python.org/dev/buildbot/stable/` (don't forget the last "/").

Each column corresponds to a **build** composed of **steps** and is associated with some **build slaves**. The whole system is driven by the build master:

- The build master centralizes and drives everything.
- A build is a sequence of steps used to build an application and run tests over it.
- A **step** is an atomic command, for example:
  - Check out the files of a project.
  - Build the application.
  - Run tests.

A build slave is a machine that is in charge of running a build. It can be located anywhere as long as it can reach the build master.

Installing Buildbot

Buildbot installation is mainly based on installing a series of required software, and on creating a Python script to configure Buildbot. This is described in the User Manual available online at `http://buildbot.net/trac/wiki/UserManual`.

Another option is to use the `collective.buildbot` project, which provides a `zc.buildout`-based configuration tool. In other words, it makes possible the defining of a Buildbot in a configuration file, without having to take care of either installing all required software, or writing any Python script.

Let's create such a buildout in our server environment, besides the repositories in a dedicated folder:

```
$ cd /home/mercurial/atomisator
$ mkdir buildbot
$ cd buildbot
$ wget http://ziade.org/bootstrap.py
```

A `buildout.cfg` file is then added in the `buildbot` folder with this content:

```
[buildout]
parts =
    buildmaster
    linux
    atomisator
[buildmaster]
```

```
recipe = collective.buildbot:master
project-name = Atomisator project buildbot
project-url = http://atomisator.ziade.org
port = 8999
wport = 9000
url = http://atomisator.ziade.org/buildbot
slaves =
    linux       ty54ddf32
[linux]
recipe = collective.buildbot:slave
host = localhost
port = ${buildmaster:port}
password = ty54ddf32
[atomisator]
recipe = collective.buildbot:project
slave-names = linux
repository=http://hg-atomisator.ziade.org/unstable
vcs = hg
build-sequence =
    ./build
test-sequence =
    buildout/bin/nosetests
email-notification-sender = tarek@ziade.org
email-notification-recipient = tarek@ziade.org
[poller]
recipe = collective.buildbot:poller
repository=http://hg-atomisator.ziade.org/unstable
vcs = hg
user=anonymous
```

This defines a build master, together with a build slave and an Atomisator project. The project defines a build script to be called and a test sequence that runs the test runner located in the project buildout.

 Complementary information on options can be found at PyPI: http://pypi.python.org/pypi/collective.buildbot

The build script referenced in the build-sequence is a script that has to be added in the root of the repository, with this content:

```
#!/bin/sh
cd buildout
python bootstrap.py
bin/buildout -v
```

Do not forget to set the execution flag before it is pushed:

```
$ chmod +x build
$ hg add build
$ hg commit -m "added build script"
```

From there let's run the buildout:

```
$ python bootstrap.py
$ bin/buildout -v
```

 `bootstrap.py` is a small script that makes sure your system meets the requirements to build the buildbot.

You should get two scripts in the `bin` folder: one that launches the build master and one for the build slave.

They are named with the buildout sections; and now let's run them:

```
$ bin/buildmaster.py start
Following twistd.log until startup finished..
2008-04-03 16:06:49+0200 [-] Log opened.
...
2008-04-03 16:06:50+0200 [-] configuration update complete
The buildmaster appears to have (re)started correctly.
$ bin/linux.py start
Following twistd.log until startup finished..
The buildslave appears to have (re)started correctly.
```

From there, you should be able to reach the Buildbot in your web browser at `http://localhost:9000`, and force a build by clicking on the `atomisator` link to control everything.

 There's a good Buildbot manual available online here: `http://buildbot.net/repos/release/docs/buildbot.html`

Hooking Buildbot and Mercurial

There's one more step to finish this setup: that is hooking the repository commit events with the Buildbot, so it is automatically rebuilt every time someone pushes a file. This is done by the `hgbuildbot.py` script that comes with Buildbot.

To make it available as a command, simply run an `easy_install` over pbp. `buildbotenv`. That will install the script and make sure Buildbot and Twisted are installed as well:

$ easy_install pbp.buildbotenv

The hook is added in the `unstable hgrc` file in the `.hg` folder at `/path/to/ unstable/.hg/hgrc`:

```
[web]
style = gitweb
description = Unstable branch
contact = Tarek <tarek@ziade.org>
push_ssl = false
allow_push = *
[hooks]
changegroup.buildbot = python:buildbot.changes.hgbuildbot.hook
[hgbuildbot]
master = atomisator.ziade.org:8999
```

The `hooks` section links the `hgbuildbot` script, and the `hgbuildbot` section defines where the master server and the slave port are located.

Hooking Apache and Buildbot

From there, a rewrite rule can be added in Apache, to make the Buildbot available without calling the specific `9000` port.

The simplest way is to create a specific virtual host for it and add it into your Apache configuration file collection:

```
<VirtualHost *:80>
  ServerName atomisator-buildbot.ziade.org
  CustomLog /var/log/apache2/bot-access_log combined
  ErrorLog  /var/log/apache2/bot-error.org.log
  RewriteEngine On
  RewriteRule ^(.*) http://localhost:9000/$1
</VirtualHost>
```

Summary

We have learned the following things in this chapter:

- The difference between the centralized and distributed version control systems
- How to use Mercurial, which is a great distributed version control system
- How to set up and use a multiple repository strategy
- What continuous integration is
- How to set up Buildbot together with Mercurial, in order to provide continuous integration

The next chapter will explain how to manage the software life-cycle using an iterative and incremental approach.

9
Managing Life Cycle

Managing a software development is hard. Often, projects are delivered late; and in some cases, they are even dropped. Modern software management has created methods to reduce risks. And the most common approach that has proven its efficiency is using an **iterative development approach**. Many methodologies exist that use an iterative approach. They are commonly named **agile methodologies**.

This chapter will not provide a complete software management guide, as this would require an entire book. (You might want to read *Agile and Iterative Development: A Manager's Guide* from Addison-Wesley.)

It will rather give some tips and a summary on how to manage a software life cycle based on iterations, and how this can be done with a few tools.

Different Approaches

Before presenting how an iterative life cycle can be set, let's describe a few development models that exist in the software industry.

Waterfall Development Model

The waterfall development model treats software as a whole, where each phase is started only when the previous phase is over. In other words, the work is organized into a sequence of phases, which can be:

- Analyze the needs.
- Design the global architecture and how the software is organized in pieces.
- Design each piece.
- Code each piece with a TDD (Test-Driven Development) approach. (Some people don't use TDD in this method.)
- Reunite pieces and do global system tests.
- Deploy.

Therefore, the work organization looks like a waterfall, as shown in the illustration:

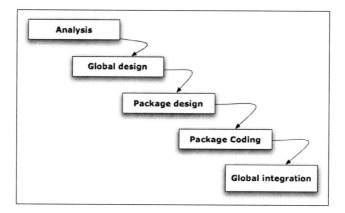

This model is used in many large companies, where each step is carefully done and reviewed before the next one is started. This means that after the designing is over, developers just have to implement that design. The final step is where all pieces are gathered and tested together.

This model is quite rigid, since it is almost impossible to think about all aspects of software before it is globally tested. In reality, the final step often reveals some inconsistency, or missing pieces, or even performance issues due to a design flaw.

Such a model is probably easier to apply with a really well-known target environment, and with an experienced team. But for most software, this is impossible.

Spiral Development Model

The spiral model is based on feedback over prototypes. A first version of the program is created based on the initial requirements, without any polishing. This prototype is then refined depending on the feedback it receives. Its weaknesses and strengths are pinpointed so that it can be refactored.

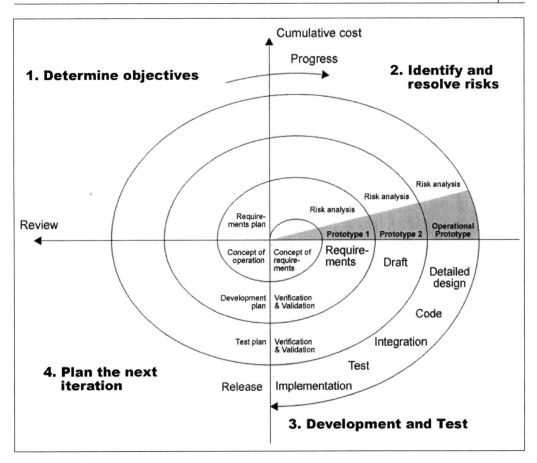

After a few cycles, when everyone agrees that the prototype meets the needs, it is polished and then delivered.

This model reduces the risk a lot as developers can start to code earlier on the software, without having to deal with a stone-set design, like that which the Waterfall model induces. Managers have a better overview of the time needed to finish the project after the first cycle is over.

Iterative Development Model

The Iterative model is similar to the Spiral model, but doesn't look at the application as a whole. Instead, it focuses on delivering some new features to the system, and reworking the existing ones through feedback.

This means that unlike the Spiral and Waterfall models, analysis, design, and coding occur during the whole project since they only concern a subset of functionalities on each cycle.

Therefore, a project is cut into several iterations that can be seen as independent projects, where the software is designed, built, and delivered. Every involved party focuses on the functionalities of the current iteration through cross-disciplined work.

Providing feedback at each iteration helps a lot in making all involved people work smoothly together. Each functionality can evolve a lot before it sticks to reality, and often differs from the initial thoughts people had. Everyone gets some food for thought, and can correct the analysis and design on the next iteration.

Since this gradual approach concerns smaller parts of the system, it raises the frequency of feedback. An iteration often lasts from one to four weeks, and a software requires several iterations before it can be delivered. Since the whole software grows after each iteration, it is built **incrementally**.

Many methodologies are based on iterative approaches, such as **Scrum** or **XP**. And this is a common base to all **agile methods**.

However, an iterative approach is not an excuse to be lazy about design. It has a cost. In order to maintain flexibility, agile programmers heavily emphasize testing. By writing tests, they ensure that they do not break their existing code when changing it.

A rule of thumb in such an iterative approach is to define a fixed length for each iteration, and to make something special at its end.

This chapter will propose a generic model that is a common base to many open-source projects, and will describe it through a set of tools that can be used for this purpose.

Defining a Life Cycle

Defining a life cycle for a project consists of planning regular releases and trying to keep up the pace. It is often better to postpone some elements that are not ready by the end of a cycle, and keep up with the promised calendar. This is called the **train approach**: When the train leaves, get in or stay there. However, some projects move the release date rather than removing some features. But this approach often seems less predictable.

After the project has started, through an initial **initiation** phase, a global **planning** is defined. Basically, people join at a kick-off meeting and define together when the software should be delivered, and then cut the remaining time into iterations.

Depending on the nature of the software, these iterations can last from a week to four or five weeks. Each iteration should have the same length in order to keep the same rhythm throughout the project, as displayed in the following figure:

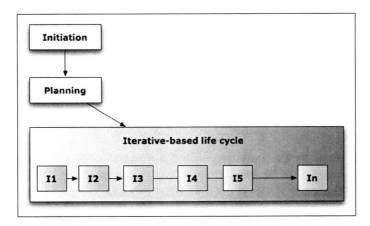

The iteration length might vary when the project reaches a stable state: It can last longer.

An iteration is a small independent project that can be composed of four phases:

- The **Planning** phase, where the work to be done is defined
- The **Analysis, Design, and Test-Driven Development** phase, where the work is done
- A **Cleaning** phase, where the work done is globally tested and debugged
- The **Release** phase, where the work is delivered

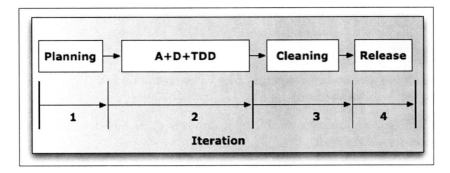

For an iteration that lasts for two weeks, which is ten working days, the duration for each phase can be:

- One day for **planning**
- Seven days for **development**
- A few days for **global cleaning**
- One day for **release**

Planning

The planning phase of an iteration consists of defining a series of tasks that have to be done. A task is an atomic operation over the code that can be done by a developer. Each task's duration is estimated to make sure the amount of work is realistic, given the remaining time and the number of developers involved.

This planning is done by the manager, with developers' feedback. Estimates must be validated to be accurate by the person who does the work. By the end of this step, the iteration should be clearly defined through a list of tasks to be achieved.

Development

The development phase consists of tasks for each developer to work on. This is done by:

- Accepting the task to be done, so everyone knows it is being processed
- Reviewing and correcting the estimated time, so the manager knows if it was not estimated correctly; this reviewing is also important to know if the workload for the iteration is realistic
- Coding
- Closing the task when it is done
- Taking another task and doing the same work on it

Global Debug

The global debug phase closes iteration. The whole software is tested and the remaining tasks are worked out.

The most efficient way to perform this final step is to gather all developers and managers in a special event.

The remaining tasks that could not be closed are postponed to the next release, and some showstoppers are often found during this final stage.

Release

The releasing phase consists of:

- Tagging the code and creating the release, as explained in the previous chapter
- Launching a new iteration

Setting Up a Tracking System

The planning phases define tasks to be done within an iteration. To keep track of these tasks, a tracking system can be used.

Such an application is used to keep relevant information for each task, such as:

- The person in charge
- The nature of the change: new feature, debug, refactoring, and so on
- The due date
- The iteration concerned
- The status: open, fixed, and so on
- The estimated charge

Each task can be put in an iteration, and the software needs to provide a global display of this iteration. During the development phase of an iteration, the status of each task is updated by developers, so that the global status can be followed.

Trac

Trac is a good candidate for such software. This wiki-based web application provides a complete issue-tracking system together with a lot of useful features:

- A user management system
- A fully editable wiki-based interface

- A plug-in system that allows adding new features to the software

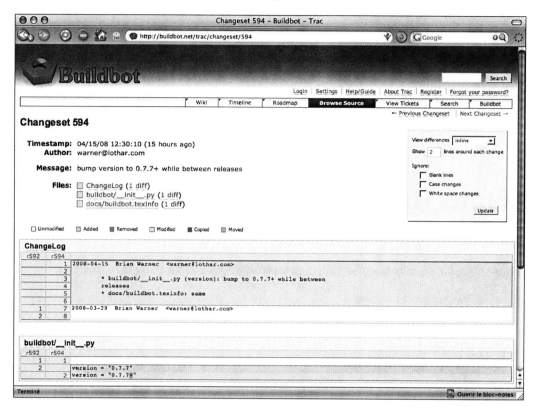

Trac interacts smoothly with most version control systems through plug-ins that wire the repository with the web interface. From there, the repository tree can be browsed through the Web and a live timeline displays the commit, together with readable `diff` reports.

This tool is often used in the open-source community as a project's website, and provides all needed features for developers to work with the code. Here are some examples of software that uses Trac:

- Plone: `http://dev.plone.org/plone`
- Buildbot: `http://buildbot.net/trac`
- Adium: `http://trac.adiumx.com/`

 Trac maintains a **Who Uses Trac?** page here: `http://trac.edgewall.org/wiki/TracUsers`. If your project uses it, you can add it there.

The minimalistic approach of its interface makes it simple to understand and use.

Installation

The `pbp.recipe.trac` recipe available at PyPI provides a fast way to set up a Trac instance together with the Mercurial server we have installed.

A new section `trac` can be added in the `buildout.cfg` file that we created in the previous chapter for Buildbot:

```
[buildout]
parts =
    buildmaster
    linux
    trac

[buildmaster]
...

[buildslave]
...

[trac]
recipe = pbp.recipe.trac

project-name = Atomisator
project-url = ${buildmaster:project-url}
repos-type = hg
repos-path = /home/mercurial/atomisator/repositories/unstable
buildbot-url = http://buildbot-atomisator.ziade.org/

components =
    atomisator.db       tarek
    atomisator.feed     tarek
    atomisator.main     tarek
    atomisator.parser   tarek
    pbp.recipe.trac     tarek
header-logo = atomisator.png
```

The new section defines:

- A `project name` that will be used as a title
- A `project url` that will be used in the Trac instance as the home page
- A `repository type`, `hg` in our case, that will be used to install the correct plug-in
- A `repository path` that points the repository, which has to be on the same server
- A `Buildbot url` that will be linked to a navigation button on the Trac navigation bar

- A `component list` with a component name and an owner, which will be used in the issue tracker
- A `header-logo`, which points to an image that will be used to replace the Trac logo in the header

The logo in our example is put in the buildout folder.

Let's run the buildout instance dedicated to Buildbot and Trac again:

```
$ bin/buildout -v
...
Project environment for 'Atomisator' created.
...
Try running the Trac standalone web server `tracd`:

  tracd --port 8000 /home/mercurial/atomisator/buildbot/parts/trac
...
Creating new milestone 'future'
Creating new component 'atomisator.db'
Creating new component 'atomisator.feed'
Creating new component 'atomisator.main'
Creating new component 'atomisator.parser'
```

A Trac environment is added in `parts/trac`, and two new scripts are added into the `bin` directory:

- `tracd`: A standalone web server that can be used to run the Trac instance
- `trac-admin`: A command-line shell that can be used to manage the instance

Try to run the `tracd` script from the buildout folder:

```
$ bin/tracd --port 8000 parts/trac
Server starting in PID 24971.
Serving on 0.0.0.0:8000 view at http://127.0.0.1:8000/
```

The Trac instance should be reachable in a browser at `http://127.0.0.1:8000/trac`, as shown in the figure that follows:

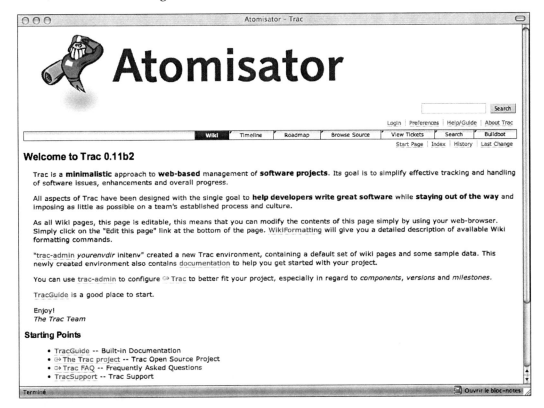

Notice that the Buildbot button allows the user to visit the Buildbot web page.

Apache Settings

Like Buildbot, Trac can be hooked to Apache through several handlers. The easiest way is to use the `mod_python` handler, which can be wired to the front end Trac provides.

`mod_python` can be installed on Debian Linux with:

```
$ sudo apt-get install libapache2-mod-python
```

For other platforms, refer to the project page: `http://www.modpython.org`.

From there, a new host can be added in the Apache configuration:

```
<VirtualHost *:80>
  ServerName atomisator.ziade.org

  <Location />
    SetHandler mod_python
    PythonHandler trac.web.modpython_frontend
    PythonOption TracEnv /home/mercurial/atomisator/buildbot/parts/
trac
    PythonOption TracUriRoot /
    PythonPath "sys.path + ['/home/mercurial/atomisator/buildbot/
parts/trac', '/home/mercurial/atomisator/buildbot/eggs']"
  </Location>

  <Location "/login">
    AuthType Basic
    AuthName "Trac login"
    AuthUserFile /home/mercurial/atomisator/passwords
    Require valid-user
  </Location>

</VirtualHost>
```

A few remarks on this configuration:

- The `PythonOption` defines a `TracEnv` value, so the Trac system knows where the instance is located.
- The `PythonPath` option points to the local buildout directories needed by the script to access Trac modules.
- The `/login` section's settings hook the `passwords` file we previously created for Mercurial, so users can log into the system with the same username.

Permission Settings

To work with the issue management system, we need to define a few groups:

- `manager`: A person who is able to fully manage Trac
- `developer`: A person who is able to modify the tickets and change the wiki's pages
- `authenticated`: A person who is able to create a ticket
- `anonymous`: A person who is able to view everything

These four roles are already set and available in Trac. This was either a default permission setting, or a setting automatically done by `pbp.recipe.trac` when the buildout was run.

The work that's left is to add some people in each group. Trac provides a command-line utility that can be used to set up a few elements in the instance:

```
$ bin/trac-admin parts/trac/
Welcome to trac-admin 0.11b2
Interactive Trac administration console.
Copyright (c) 2003-2007 Edgewall Software

Type:  '?' or 'help' for help on commands.


Trac [parts/trac]>
```

From there you can add a user to a group. Let's define tarek as a manager, and bill and bob as developers:

```
Trac [parts/trac]> permission add tarek manager
Trac [parts/trac]> permission add bob developer
Trac [parts/trac]> permission add bill developer
```

This will allow tarek to manage the project through the Web, and bill and bob to deal with the tickets and the wiki pages.

Project Life Cycle with Trac

These settings make Trac really easy to use when dealing with the life cycle, through the web interface and with the command-line tool.

Planning

The planning is done in Trac by creating a new milestone that corresponds to the iteration, and deciding when it should be delivered. The manager adds it either through the web interface or through trac-admin command line. The latter is more convenient, but it means you will have to connect to the server to perform those tasks.

Let's use the command line to add it:

```
Trac [parts/trac] > milestone add atomisator-0.1.0
Trac [parts/trac]> milestone due atomisator-0.1.0 2008-08-01
```

The same operation can be performed in the admin section of the web interface at /admin/ticket/milestones.

This milestone will then appear in the roadmap section. From there, tickets can be added to the milestone through the web interface by hitting the **New Ticket** button.

Let's create a ticket that defines a task in `atomisator.db`, defining a mapper to store the feed entries, as shown in this figure:

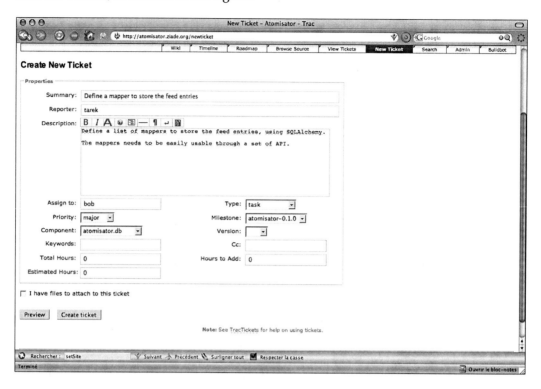

Besides the summary and description, the important information to be provided is:

- **Assign to**: The name of the developer (let's assign it to **Bob**)
- **Type**: **Task**, since this is a new feature
- **Component**: **atomisator.db**
- **Milestone**: **atomisator-0.1.0**
- **Estimated hours**: 8

The ticket will then appear in the milestone.

Bugs and enhancements are entered in the same way.

 The estimated hours are part of a Trac plug-in called `TimeAndEstimation`, automatically installed by `pbp.recipe.trac`. See `http://trac-hacks.org/wiki/TimingAndEstimationPlugin`.

Development

Each developer can view his or her tasks through the reports available under the /
`report` section, accessible through the **View Tickets** button. The **My Tickets** report
will display a list of tickets for the current user.

When Bob starts to work on the ticket we have entered previously, he performs the
`accept` action on it.

When the task is over, he fills the **Total Hours** field and performs the resolve action.

> This lightweight time management is not replacing a real management
> planning system, but will provide a useful indication on how the time
> was spent on tasks.
>
> Tracking time is an important part of improving estimates.

Cleaning

Often, when the team ends an iteration, some tasks are remaining. The cleaning
phase is a good opportunity to close a maximum number of small issues. Some
teams organize bug sprints, and work on bugs in a day or two.

At the end of the phase, the remaining tasks are postponed to the `future` milestone,
unless they are showstoppers. In that case they must be fixed, hopefully before the
end of the phase.

All these operations are done in the web interface by editing each task.

Release

Releasing consists of:

- Tagging the code
- Pulling the changes from the unstable repository to the stable repository
- Creating the release repository
- Preparing and shipping a release
- Closing the milestone by setting its state to `completed`
- Creating a new milestone and starting a new cycle: some teams create up
  to three future milestones, to be able to push tickets to future milestones
  with priorities

The tagging-and-pulling work occurs on the Mercurial side, as explained in the previous chapter, with the following set of commands:

```
$ cd /home/mercurial/atomisator/repositories/unstable
$ hg tag -f -m "tag for 0.1.0 release" 0.1.0
$ cd ../stable
$ hg pull ../unstable
$ hg clone . ../release-atomisator-0.1.0
```

Last, the milestone is closed by completing its due date:

```
Trac [parts/trac]> milestone completed atomisator-0.1.0 2008-08-01
```

Trac can be used as the central place of information, and the created releases can be added and announced on the wiki pages.

Summary

In this chapter we have:

- Described various ways to manage a software's development life cycle
- Explained why an iterative approach is great
- Described how to organize a project in iterations
- Explained how to install and use Trac

The next chapter will focus on how to document your software.

10
Documenting Your Project

Documentation is work that is often neglected by developers and sometimes by managers. This is often due to a lack of time towards the end of development cycles, and the fact that people think they are bad at writing. Some of them are bad, but the majority of them are able to produce fine documentation.

In any case, the result is a disorganized documentation made of documents that are written in a rush. Developers hate doing this kind of work most of the time. Things get even worse when existing documents need to be updated. Many projects out there are just providing poor, out-of-date documentation because the manager does not know how to deal with it.

But setting up a documentation process at the beginning of the project and treating documents as if they were modules of code makes documenting easier. Writing can even be fun when a few rules are followed.

This chapter provides a few tips to start documenting your project through:

- The seven rules of technical writing that summarize the best practices
- A reStructuredText primer, which is a plain text markup syntax used in most Python projects
- A guide for building good project documentation

The Seven Rules of Technical Writing

Writing good documentation is easier in many aspects than writing a code. Most developers think it is very hard, but by following a simple set of rules it becomes really easy.

We are not talking here about writing a book of poems but a comprehensive piece of text that can be used to understand a design, an API, or anything that makes up the code base.

Every developer is able to produce such material, and this section provides seven rules that can be applied in all cases.

- **Write in two steps**: Focus on ideas, and then on reviewing and shaping your text.
- **Target the readership**: Who is going to read it?
- **Use a simple style**: Keep it straight and simple. Use good grammar.
- **Limit the scope of the information**: Introduce one concept at a time.
- **Use realistic code examples**: Foos and bars should be dropped.
- **Use a light but sufficient approach**: You are not writing a book!
- **Use templates**: Help the readers to get habits.

These rules are mostly inspired and adapted from *Agile Documenting*, a book by Andreas Rüping that focuses on producing the best documentation in software projects.

Write in Two Steps

Peter Elbow, in *Writing with Power*, explains that it is almost impossible for any human being to produce a perfect text in one shot. The problem is that many developers write documentation and try to directly come up with a perfect text. The only way they succeed in this exercise is by stopping the writing after every two sentences to read them back, and do some corrections. This means that they are focusing both on the content and the style of the text.

This is too hard for the brain and the result is often not as good as it could be. A lot of time and energy is spent in polishing the style and shape of the text, before its meaning is completely thought through.

Another approach is to drop the style and organization of the text and focus on its content. All ideas are laid down on paper, no matter how they are written. The developer starts to write a continuous stream and does not pause when he or she makes grammatical mistakes, or for anything that is not about the content. For instance, it does not matter if the sentences are barely understandable as long as the ideas are written down. He or she just writes down what he wants to say, with a rough organization.

By doing this, the developer focuses on what he or she wants to say and will probably get more content out of his or her brain than he or she initially thought he or she would.

Another side-effect when doing free writing is that other ideas that are not directly related to the topic will easily go through the mind. A good practice is to write them down on a second paper or screen when they appear, so they are not lost, and then get back to the main writing.

The second step consists of reading back the whole text and polishing it so that it is comprehensible to everyone. Polishing a text means enhancing its style, correcting its faults, reorganizing it a bit, and removing any redundant information it has.

When the time dedicated to write documentation is limited, a good practice is to cut this time in two equal durations—one for writing the content, and one to clean and organize the text.

[Focus on the content, and then on style and cleanliness.]

Target the Readership

When starting a text, there is a simple question the writer should consider: *Who is going to read it?*

This is not always obvious, as a technical text explains how a piece of software works, and is often written for every person who might get and use the code. The reader can be a manager who is looking for an appropriate technical solution to a problem, or a developer who needs to implement a feature with it. A designer might also read it to know if the package fits his or her needs from an architectural point of view.

Let's apply a simple rule: Each text should have only one kind of readers.

This philosophy makes the writing easier. The writer precisely knows what kind of reader he or she is dealing with. He or she can provide a concise and precise documentation that is not vaguely intended for all kinds of readers.

A good practice is to provide a small introductory text that explains in one sentence what the documentation is about, and guides the reader to the appropriate part:

```
Atomisator is a product that fetches RSS feeds and saves them in a
database, with a filtering process.

If you are a developer, you might want to look at the API description
(api.txt)

If you are a manager, you can read the features list and the FAQ
(features.txt)

If you are a designer, you can read the architecture and
infrastructure notes (arch.txt)
```

By taking care of directing your readers in this way, you will probably produce better documentation.

 Know your readership before you start to write.

Use a Simple Style

Seth Godin is one of the best-selling writers on marketing topics. You might want to read *Unleashing the Ideavirus*, which is available for free on the Internet (http://en.wikipedia.org/wiki/Unleashing_the_Ideavirus).

Lately, he made an analysis on his blog to try to understand why his books sold so well. He made a list of all best sellers in the marketing area and compared the average number of words per sentences in each one of them.

He realized that his books had the lowest number of words per sentence (thirteen words). This simple fact, Seth explained, proved that readers prefer short and simple sentences, rather than long and stylish ones.

By keeping sentences short and simple, your writings will consume less brain power for their content to be extracted, processed, and then understood. Writing technical documentation aims to provide a software guide to readers. It is not a fiction story, and should be closer to your microwave notice than to the latest Stephen King novel.

A few tips to keep in mind are:

- Use simple sentences; they should not be longer than two lines.
- Each paragraph should be composed of three or four sentences, at the most, that express one main idea. Let your text breathe.
- Don't repeat yourself too much: Avoid journalistic styles where ideas are repeated again and again to make sure they are understood.
- Don't use several tenses. Present tense is enough most of the time.
- Do not make jokes in the text if you are not a really fine writer. Being funny in a technical book is really hard, and few writers master it. If you really want to distill some humor, keep it in code examples and you will be fine.

 You are not writing fiction, so keep the style as simple as possible.

Limit the Scope of the Information

There's a simple sign of bad documentation in a software: You are looking for some information that you know is present somewhere, but you cannot find it. After spending some time reading the table of contents, you are starting to grep the files trying several word combinations, but cannot get what you are looking for.

This happens when writers are not organizing their texts in topics. They might provide tons of information, but it is just gathered in a monolithic or non-logical way. For instance, if a reader is looking for a big picture of your application, he or she should not have to read the API documentation: that is a low-level matter.

To avoid this effect, paragraphs should be gathered under a meaningful title for a given section, and the global document title should synthesize the content in a short phrase.

A table of contents could be made of all the section's titles.

A simple practice to compose your titles is to ask yourself: What phrase would I type in Google to find this section?

Use Realistic Code Examples

Foo and bar are bad citizens. When a reader tries to understand how a piece of code works with a usage example, having an unrealistic example will make it harder to understand.

Why not use a real-world example? A common practice is to make sure that each code example can be cut and pasted in a real program.

An example of bad usage is:

We have a parse function:

```
>>> from atomisator.parser import parse
```

Let's use it:

```
>>> stuff = parse('some-feed.xml')
>>> stuff.next()
{'title': 'foo', 'content': 'blabla'}
```

A better example would be when the parser knows how to return a feed content with the parse function, available as a top-level function:

```
>>> from atomisator.parser import parse
```

Let's use it:

```
>>> my_feed = parse('http://tarekziade.wordpress.com/feed')
>>> my_feed.next()
{'title': 'eight tips to start with python',
 'content': 'The first tip is..., ...'}
```

This slight difference might sound overkill, but in fact it makes your documentation a lot more useful. A reader can copy those lines into a shell, understands that `parse` uses a URL as a parameter, and that it returns an iterator that contains blog entries.

 Code examples should be directly reusable in real programs.

Use a Light but Sufficient Approach

In most agile methodologies, documentation is not the first citizen. Making software that works is the most important thing, over detailed documentation. So a good practice, as Scott Ambler explains in his book *Agile Modeling: Effective Practices for Extreme Programming and the Unified Process*, is to define the real documentation needs, rather than creating an exhaustive set of documents.

For instance, a single document that explains how Atomisator works for administrators is sufficient. There is no other need for them than to know how to configure and run the tool. This document limits its scope to answer to one question: How do I run Atomisator on my server?

Besides readership and scope, limiting the size of each section written for the software to a few pages is a good idea. By making each section four pages long at the most, the writer will have to synthesize his or her thought. If it needs more, it probably means that the software is too complex to explain or use.

 Working software over comprehensive documentation
The Agile Manifesto.

Use Templates

Every page on Wikipedia is similar. There are boxes on the left side that are used to summarize dates or facts. At the beginning of the document is a table of contents with links that refer to anchors in the same text. There is always a reference section at the end.

Users get used to it. For instance, they know they can have a quick look at the table of contents, and if they do not find the info they are looking for, they will go directly to the reference section to see if they can find another website on the topic. This works for any page on Wikipedia. You learn the *Wikipedia way* to be more efficient.

So using templates forces a common pattern for documents, and therefore makes people more efficient in using them. They get used to the structure and know how to read it quickly.

Providing a template for each kind of document also provides a quick start for writers.

In this chapter, we will see the various kinds of documents a piece of software can have, and use Paster to provide skeletons for them. But the first thing to do is to describe the markup syntax that should be used in Python documentation.

A reStructuredText Primer

reStructuredText is also called reST (see `http://docutils.sourceforge.net/rst.html`). It is a plain text markup language widely used in the Python community to document packages. The great thing about reST is that the text is still readable since the markup syntax does not obfuscate the text like LaTeX would.

Here's a sample of such a document:

```
=====
Title
=====

Section 1
=========

This *word* has emphasis.

Section 2
=========

Subsection
::::::::::

Text.
```

reST comes in `docutils`, a package that provides a suite of scripts to transform a reST file to various formats, such as HTML, LaTeX, XML, or even S5, Eric Meyer's slide show system (see `http://meyerweb.com/eric/tools/s5`).

Writers can focus on the content and then decide how to render it, depending on the needs. For instance, Python itself is documented into reST, which is then rendered in HTML to build `http://docs.python.org`, and in various other formats.

The minimum elements one should know to start writing reST are:

- Section structure
- Lists
- Inline markup
- Literal block
- Links

This section is a really fast overview of the syntax. A quick reference is available for more information at: `http://docutils.sourceforge.net/docs/user/rst/quickref.html`, which is a good place to start working with reST.

To install reStructuredText, install `docutils`:

```
$ easy_install docutils
```

You will get a set of scripts starting with `rst2`, to be able to render reST in various formats.

For instance, the `rst2html` script will produce HTML output given an reST file:

```
$ more text.txt
Title
=====
content.
$ rst2html.py text.txt > text.html
$ more text.html
<?xml version="1.0" encoding="utf-8" ?>
...
<html ...>
<head>
...
</head>
<body>
<div class="document" id="title">
<h1 class="title">Title</h1>
<p>content.</p>
</div>
</body>
</html>
```

Section Structure

The document's title and its sections are underlined using non-alphanumeric characters. They can be overlined and underlined, and a common practice is to use this double markup for the title, and keep a simple underline for sections.

The most used characters to underline a section title are in the following order of precedence: =, -, _, :, #, +, ^.

When a character is used for a section, it is associated with its level and it has to be used consistently throughout the document.

For example:

```
=====
Title
=====
Section 1
=========
xxx
Subsection A
------------
xxx
Subsection B
------------
xxx
Section 2
=========
xxx
Subsection C
------------
xxx
```

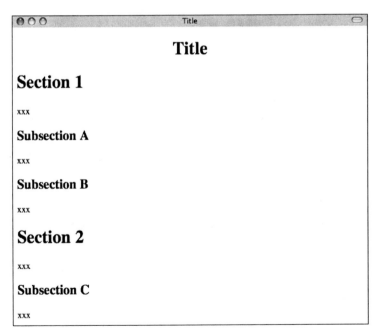

The HTML output of this file will look like the illustration shown above.

Lists

reST provides bullet, and enumerated and definition lists with auto-enumeration features:

```
Bullet list:

- one
- two
- three

Enumerated list:

1. one
2. two
#. auto-enumerated

Definition list:

one
    one is a number.

two
    two is also a number.
```

Inline Markup

Text can be styled using an inline markup:

- `*emphasis*`: Italics

- `**strong emphasis**`: Boldface

- `` ``inline literal`` ``: Inline preformatted text

- `` `a text with a link`_ ``: This will be replaced by a hyperlink as long as it is provided in the document (see in the Links section).

Literal Block

When you need to present some code examples, a literal block can be used. Two colons are used to mark the block, which is an indented paragraph:

```
This is a code example

::

    >>> 1 + 1
    2

Let's continue our text
```

Don't forget to add a blank line after : : and after the block, otherwise it will not be rendered.

Notice that the colon characters can be put in a text line. In that case, they will be replaced by a single colon in the various rendering formats:

```
This is a code example::

    >>> 1 + 1
    2

Let's continue our text
```

If you don't want to keep a single colon, you can insert a space between example and : :. In that case, : : will be interpreted and totally removed.

Links

A text can be changed into an external link with a special line starting with two dots, as long as it is provided in the document:

```
Try `Plone CMS`_, it is great ! It is based on Zope_.
.. _`Plone CMS`: http://plone.org
.. _Zope: http://zope.org
```

A usual practice is to group the external links at the end of the document. When the text to be linked contains spaces, it has to be surrounded with ` characters.

Internal links can also be used by adding a marker in the text:

```
This is a code example

.. _example:

::

    >>> 1 + 1
    2

Let's continue our text, or maybe go back to
the example_.
```

Sections are also targets that can be used:

```
=====
Title
=====

Section 1
=========

xxx
```

```
Subsection A
- - - - - - - - - - -
xxx
Subsection B
- - - - - - - - - - -
-> go back to `Subsection A`_
Section 2
=========
xxx
```

Building the Documentation

An easier way to guide your readers and your writers is to provide each one of them with helpers and guidelines, as we have learned in the previous section of this chapter.

From a writer's point of view, this is done by having a set of reusable templates together with a guide that describes how and when to use them in a project. It is called a **documentation portfolio**.

From a reader point of view, being able to browse the documentation with no pain, and getting used to finding the info efficiently, is done by building a **document landscape**.

Building the Portfolio

There are many kinds of documents a software project can have, from low-level documents that refer directly to the code, to design papers that provide a high-level overview of the application.

For instance, Scott Ambler defines an extensive list of document types in his book *Agile Modeling* (see `http://www.agilemodeling.com/essays/agileArchitecture.htm`). He builds a portfolio from early specifications to operations documents. Even the project management documents are covered, so the whole documenting needs are built with a standardized set of templates.

Since a complete portfolio is tightly related to the methodologies used to build the software, this chapter will only focus on a common subset that you can complete with your specific needs. Building an efficient portfolio takes a long time, as it captures your working habits.

Chapter 10

A common set of documents in software projects can be classified in three categories:

- **Design**: All documents that provide architectural information, and low-level design information, such as class diagrams, or database diagrams
- **Usage**: Documents on how to use the software; this can be in the shape of a cookbook and tutorials, or a module-level help
- **Operations**: Provide guidelines on how to deploy, upgrade, or operate the software

Design

The purpose of design documentation is to describe how the software works and how the code is organized. It is used by developers to understand the system but is also a good entry point for people who are trying to understand how the application works.

The different kinds of design documents a software can have are:

- Architecture overview
- Database models
- Class diagrams with dependencies and hierarchy relations
- User interface wireframes
- Infrastructure description

Mostly, these documents are composed of some diagrams and a minimum amount of text. The conventions used for the diagrams are very specific to the team and the project, and this is perfectly fine as long as it is consistent.

 UML provides thirteen diagrams that cover most aspects in a software design. The class diagram is probably the most used one, but it is possible to describe every aspect of software with it. See http://en.wikipedia.org/wiki/Unified_Modeling_Language#Diagrams.

Following a specific modeling language such as UML is not often fully done, and teams just make up their own way throughout their common experience. They pick up good practice from UML or other modeling languages, and create their own recipes.

For instance, for **architecture overview diagrams**, some designers just draw boxes and arrows on a whiteboard without following any particular design rules and take a picture of it. Others work with simple drawing programs such as Dia (`http://www.gnome.org/projects/dia`) or Microsoft Visio (not open source, so not free), since it is enough to understand the design. For example, all architecture diagrams presented in the *Chapter 6* of this book where made with OmniGraffle.

Database model diagrams depend on the kind of database you are using. There are complete data modeling software applications that provide drawing tools to automatically generate tables and their relations. But this is overkill in Python most of the time. If you are using an ORM such as SQLAlchemy (for instance), simple boxes with lists of fields, together with table relations as shown in *Chapter 6* are enough to describe your mappings before you start to write them.

Class diagrams are often simplified UML class diagrams: There is no need in Python to specify the protected members of a class, for instance. So the tools used for an architectural overview diagram fit this need too.

User interface diagrams depend on whether you are writing a web or a desktop application. Web applications often describe the center of the screen, since the header, footer, left, and right panels are common. Many web developers just handwrite those screens and capture them with a camera or a scanner. Others create prototypes in HTML and make screen snapshots. For desktop applications, snapshots on prototype screens, or annotated mock-ups made with tools such as Gimp or Photoshop are the most common way.

Infrastructure overview diagrams are like architecture diagrams, but they focus on how the software interacts with third-party elements, such as mail servers, databases, or any kind of data streams.

Common Template

The important point when creating such documents is to make sure the target readership is perfectly known, and the content scope is limited. So a generic template for design documents can provide a light structure with a little advice for the writer.

Such a structure can include:

- Title
- Author
- Tags (keywords)
- Description (abstract)
- Target (Who should read this?)
- Content (with diagrams)
- References to other documents

The content should be three or four screens (a 1024x768 average screen) at the most, to be sure to limit the scope. If it gets bigger, it should be split into several documents or summarized.

The template also provides the author's name and a list of tags to manage its evolutions and ease its classification. This will be covered later in the chapter.

Paster is the right tool to use to provide templates for documentation. `pbp.skels` implements the design template described, and can be used exactly like code generation. A target folder is provided and a few questions are answered:

```
$ paster create -t pbp_design_doc design
Selected and implied templates:
  pbp.skels#pbp_design_doc  A Design document

Variables:
  egg:      design
  package:  design
  project:  design
Enter title ['Title']: Database specifications for atomisator.db
Enter short_name ['recipe']: mappers
Enter author (Author name) ['John Doe']: Tarek
Enter keywords ['tag1 tag2']: database mapping sql
Creating template pbp_design_doc
Creating directory ./design
  Copying +short_name+.txt_tmpl to ./design/mappers.txt
```

The result can then be completed:

```
========================================
Database specifications for atomisator.db
========================================

:Author: Tarek
:Tags: database mapping sql

:abstract:
    Write here a small abstract about your design document.

.. contents ::

Who should read this ?
::::::::::::::::::::::::
Explain here who is the target readership.

Content
```

```
: : : : : : :
```

```
Write your document here. Do not hesitate to split it in several
sections.
```

```
References
```

```
: : : : : : : : : :
```

```
Put here references, and links to other documents.
```

Usage

Usage documentation describes how a particular part of the software works. This documentation can describe low-level parts such as how a function works, but also high-level parts such as command-line arguments for calling the program. This is the most important part of documentation in framework applications, since the target readership is mainly the developers that are going to reuse the code.

The three main kinds of documents are:

- **Recipe**: A short document that explains how to do something. This kind of document targets one readership and focuses on one specific topic.
- **Tutorial**: A step-by-step document that explains how to use a feature of the software. This document can refer to recipes, and each instance is intended to one readership.
- **Module helper**: A low-level document that explains what a module contains. This document could be shown (for instance) when you call the `help` built-in over a module.

Recipe

A recipe answers a very specific problem and provides a solution to resolve it.

For example, ActiveState provides a Python Cookbook online (a cookbook is a collection of recipes), where developers can describe how to do something in Python (see `http://aspn.activestate.com/ASPN/Python/Cookbook`).

These recipes must be short and are structured like this:

- Title
- Submitter
- Last updated
- Version
- Category
- Description

- Source (the source code)
- Discussion (the text explaining the code)
- Comments (from the web)

Often, they are one-screen long and do not go into great details. This structure perfectly fits a software's needs and can be adapted in a generic structure, where the target readership is added and the category replaced by tags:

- Title (short sentence)
- Author
- Tags (keywords)
- Who should read this?
- Prerequisites (other documents to read, for example)
- Problem (a short description)
- Solution (the main text, one or two screens)
- References (links to other documents)

The date and version are not useful here, since we will see later that the documentation is managed like source code in the project.

Like the `design` template, `pbp.skels` provide a `pbp_recipe_doc` template that can be used to generate this structure:

```
$ paster create -t pbp_recipe_doc recipes
Selected and implied templates:
  pbp.skels#pbp_recipe_doc  A recipe

Variables:
  egg:      recipes
  package:  recipes
  project:  recipes
Enter title (use a short question): How to use atomisator.db
Enter short_name ['recipe'] : atomisator-db
Enter author (Author name) ['John Doe']: Tarek
Enter keywords ['tag1 tag2']: atomisator db
Creating template pbp_recipe_doc
Creating directory ./recipes
  Copying +short_name+.txt_tmpl to ./recipes/atomisator-db.txt
```

The result can then be completed by the writer:

```
=========================
How to use atomisator.db
=========================
:Author: Tarek
:Tags: atomisator db
.. contents ::
Who should read this ?
::::::::::::::::::::::::
Explain here who is the target readership.

Prerequisites
::::::::::::::
Put here the prerequisites for people to follow this recipe.
Problem
:::::::
Explain here the problem resolved in a few sentences.
Solution
::::::::
Put here the solution.
References
::::::::::
Put here references, and links to other recipes.
```

Tutorial

A tutorial differs from a recipe in its purpose. It is not intended to resolve an isolated problem, but rather describes how to use a feature of the application step by step. This can be longer than a recipe and can concern many parts of the application. For example, Django provides a list of tutorials on its website. *Writing your first Django App, part 1* (see http://www.djangoproject.com/documentation/tutorial01) explains in ten screens how to build an application with Django.

A structure for such a document can be:

- Title (short sentence)
- Author
- Tags (words)
- Description (abstract)
- Who should read this?
- Prerequisites (other documents to read, for example)
- Tutorial (the main text)
- References (links to other documents)

The `pbp_tutorial_doc` template is provided in `pbp.skels` as well with this structure, which is similar to the design template.

Module Helper

The last template that can be added in our collection is the module helper template. A module helper refers to a single module and provides a description of its contents, together with usage examples.

Some tools can automatically build such documents by extracting the `docstrings` and computing module help using `pydoc`, like *Epydoc* (see `http://epydoc.sourceforge.net`). So it is possible to generate an extensive documentation based on API introspection. This kind of documentation is often provided in Python frameworks. For instance Plone provides an `http://api.plone.org` server that keeps an up-to-date collection of module helpers.

The main problems with this approach are:

- There is no smart selection performed over the modules that are really interesting to document.
- The code can be obfuscated by the documentation.

Furthermore, a module documentation provides examples that sometimes refer to several parts of the module, and are hard to split between the functions' and classes' docstrings. The module `docstring` could be used for that purpose by writing a text at the top of the module. But this ends in having a hybrid file composed of a block of text, then a block of code. This is rather obfuscating when the code represents less than 50% of the total length. If you are the author, this is perfectly fine. But when people try to read the code (not the documentation), they will have to jump the docstrings part.

Another approach is to separate the text in its own file. A manual selection can then be operated to decide which Python module will have its module helper file. The documents can then be separated from the code base and allowed to live their own life, as we will see in the next part. This is how Python is documented.

Many developers will disagree on the fact that doc and code separation is better than docstrings. This approach means that the documentation process is fully integrated in the development cycle; otherwise it will quickly become obsolete. The docstrings approach solves this problem by providing proximity between the code and its usage example, but doesn't bring it to a higher level: a document that can be used as part of a plain documentation.

The template for Module Helper is really simple, as it contains just a little metadata before the content is written. The target is not defined since it is the developers who wish to use the module:

- Title (module name)
- Author
- Tags (words)
- Content

 The next chapter will cover Test-Driven Development using doctests and module helpers.

Operations

Operation documents are used to describe how the software can be operated. For instance:

- Installation and deployment documents
- Administration documents
- "Frequently Asked Questions" documents that help the users when a failure occurs
- Documents that explain how people can ask for help or provide feedback

These documents are very specific, but they can probably use the tutorial template defined in the earlier section.

Make Your Own Portfolio

The templates that we discussed earlier are just a basis that you can use to document your software. From there, as explained in the chapter dedicated to Paster, you can tune it and add other templates to build your own document portfolio.

Keep in mind the light but sufficient approach for project documentation: Each document added should have a clearly defined target readership and should fill a real need. Documents that don't add a real value should not be written.

Building the Landscape

The document portfolio built in the previous section provides a structure at document level, but does not provide a way to group and organize it to build the documentation the readers will have. This is what Andreas Rüping calls a document landscape, referring to the mental map the readers use when they browse documentation. He came up with the conclusion that the best way to organize documents is to build a logical tree.

In other words, the different kinds of documents composing the portfolio need to find a place to live within a tree of directories. This place must be obvious to the writers when they create the document and to the readers when they are looking for it.

A great helper in browsing documentation is index pages at each level that can drive writers and readers.

Building a document landscape is done in two steps:

- Building a tree for the producers (the writers)
- Building a tree for the consumers (the readers), on the top of the producers' one

This distinction between producers and consumers is important since they access the documents in different places and different formats.

Producer's Layout

From a producer's point of view, each document is processed exactly like a Python module. It should be stored in the version control system and worked like code.

Writers do not care about the final appearance of their prose and where it is available. They just want to make sure that they are writing a document, so it is the single source of truth on the topic covered.

reStructuredText files stored in a folder tree are available in the version control system together with the software code, and are a convenient solution to build the documentation landscape for producers.

If we look back at the folder structure presented in Chapter 6 for Atomisator, the docs folder can be used as the root of this tree.

The simplest way to organize the tree is to group documents by nature:

```
$ cd atomisator
$ find docs
docs
docs/source
docs/source/design
docs/source/operations
docs/source/usage
docs/source/usage/cookbook
docs/source/usage/modules
docs/source/usage/tutorial
```

Notice that the tree is located in a `source` folder because the `docs` folder will be used as a root folder to set up a special tool in the next section.

From there, an `index.txt` file can be added at each level (besides the root), explaining what kind of documents the folder contains, or summarizing what each sub-folder contains. These index files can define a listing of the documents they contain. For instance, the operation folder can contain a list of operations documents available:

```
==========
Operations
==========

This section contains operations documents:

-   How to install and run Atomisator
-   How to install and manage a PostgreSQL database
for Atomisator
```

So that people do not forget to update them, we can have lists generated automatically.

Consumer's Layout

From a consumer's point of view, it is important to work out the index files and to present the whole documentation in a format that is easy to read and looks good. Web pages are the best pick and are easy to generate from reStructuredText files.

Sphinx (http://sphinx.pocoo.org) is a set of scripts and docutils extensions that can be used to generate an HTML structure from our text tree. This tool is used (for instance) to build the Python documentation, and many projects are now using it for their documentation. Among its built-in features, it produces a really nice browsing system, together with a light but sufficient client-side JavaScript search engine. It also uses pygments for rendering code examples, which produces really nice syntax highlights.

Sphinx can be easily configured to stick with the document landscape defined in the earlier section.

To install it, just call easy_install:

```
$ sudo easy_install-2.5 Sphinx
Searching for Sphinx
Reading http://cheeseshop.python.org/pypi/Sphinx/
...
Finished processing dependencies for Sphinx
```

This installs a few scripts such as sphinx-quickstart. This script will generate a script together with a Makefile, which can be used to generate the web documentation every time it is needed. Let's run this script in the docs folder and answer its questions:

```
$ sphinx-quickstart
Welcome to the Sphinx quickstart utility.

Enter the root path for documentation.
> Root path for the documentation [.]:
> Separate source and build directories (y/n) [n]: y
> Name prefix for templates and static dir [.]:
> Project name: Atomisator
> Author name(s): Tarek Ziadé
> Project version: 0.1.0
> Project release [0.1.0]:
> Source file suffix [.rst]: .txt
> Name of your master document (without suffix) [index]:
> Create Makefile? (y/n) [y]: y

Finished: An initial directory structure has been created.

You should now populate your master file ./source/index.txt and create
other documentation
source files. Use the sphinx-build.py script to build the docs, like so:

   make <builder>
```

This adds a `conf.py` file in the source folder that contains the configuration defined through the answers, and an `index.txt` file at the root, together with a `Makefile` in docs.

Running `make html` will then generate a tree in `build`:

```
$ make html
mkdir -p build/html build/doctrees
sphinx-build.py -b html -d build/doctrees -D latex_paper_size=  source
build/html
Sphinx v0.1.61611, building html
trying to load pickled env... done
building [html]: targets for 0 source files that are out of date
updating environment: 0 added, 0 changed, 0 removed
creating index...
writing output... index
finishing...
writing additional files...
copying static files...
dumping search index...
build succeeded.

Build finished. The HTML pages are in build/html.
```

The documentation will then be available in `build/html`, starting at `index.html`.

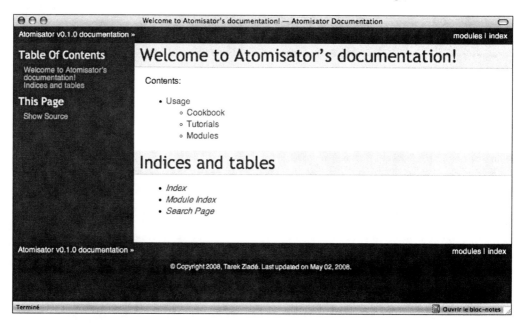

Besides the HTML versions of the documents, the tool also builds automatic pages such as a module list and an index. Sphinx provides a few `docutils` extensions to drive these features. The main ones are:

- A directive that builds a table of contents
- A marker that can be used to register a document as a module helper
- A marker to add an element in the index

Working on the Index Pages

Sphinx provides a `toctree` directive that can be used to inject a table of contents in a document, with links to other documents. Each line must be a file with its relative path, starting from the current document. Glob-style names can also be provided to add several files that match the expression.

For example, the index file in the `cookbook` folder, which we have previously defined in the producer's landscape, can look like this:

```
========
Cookbook
========

Welcome to the CookBook.

Available recipes:

.. toctree::
   :glob:

   *
```

With this syntax, the HTML page will display a list of all reStructuredText documents available in the cookbook folder. This directive can be used in all index files to build a browseable documentation.

Registering Module Helpers

For module helpers, a marker can be added so that it is automatically listed and available in the module's index page:

```
=======
session
=======

.. module:: db.session

The module session...
```

Notice that the db prefix here can be used to avoid module collision. Sphinx will use it as a module category and will group all modules that start with db. in this category.

For Atomisator db, feed, main, and parser can be used in order to group the entries, as shown in the figure:

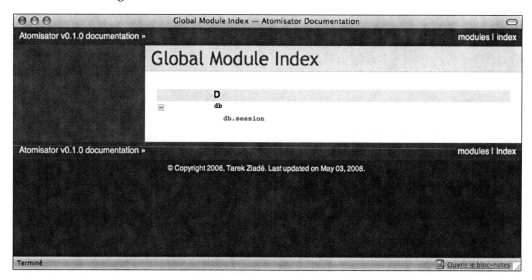

In your documentation, you can use this feature when you have a lot of modules.

 Notice that the module helper template that we created earlier (pbp_module_doc) can be changed to add the module directive by default.

Adding Index Markers

Another option can be used to fill the index page by linking the document to an entry:

```
=======
session
=======

.. module:: db.session

.. index::
   Database Access
   Session

The module session...
```

Two new entries, Database Access and Session will be added in the index page.

Cross-references

Finally, Sphinx provides an inline markup to set cross-references. For instance, a link to a module can be done like this:

```
:mod:`db.session`
```

Where `:mod:` is the module marker's prefix and `` `db.session` `` is the name of the module to be linked to (as registered previously), keep in mind that `:mod:` as well as the previous elements are the specific directives introduced in reSTructuredText by Sphinx.

> Sphinx provides a lot more features that you can discover in its website.
>
> For instance, the `autodoc` feature is a great option to automatically extract your doctests to build the documentation.
>
> See `http://sphinx.pocoo.org`.

Summary

This chapter explained in detail how to:

- Use a few rules for efficient writing
- Use reStructuredText, the Pythonistas LaTeX
- Build a document portfolio and landscape
- Use Sphinx to generate nice web documentation

The hardest thing to do when documenting a project is to keep it accurate and up to date. Making the documentation part of the code repository makes it a lot easier. From there, every time a developer changes a module, he or she should change the corresponding documentation as well.

This can be quite difficult in big projects, and adding a list of related documents in the header of the modules can help in that case.

A complementary approach to make sure the documentation is always accurate is to combine the documentation with tests through doctests.

This is covered in the next chapter, which presents Test-Driven Development principles, and then Document-Driven Development.

11
Test-Driven Development

Test-Driven Development (TDD) is a simple technique to produce quality software. It is widely used in the Python community, and probably more so than in communities that work with statically typed languages. This may be due to the fact that developers think that most tests are done by the compiler, which checks many things when it produces a binary.

Therefore, they might quit performing tests during the development phase. But this often leads to poor quality code and hours of debugging to make it work properly. Remember that most bugs are not related to bad syntax usage, but rather to logical errors and subtle misunderstandings that can lead to major breakages.

This chapter is split in two parts:

- **I don't test**, which advocates TDD and quickly describes how to do it with the standard library.
- **I do test**, which is intended for developers who practice tests and wish to get more out of them.

I Don't Test

If you are convinced by TDD, you should move to the next section. It focuses on advanced techniques, and on making your life easier when writing tests. This part is mainly intended for developers who are not using this approach, and tries to advocate its usage.

Test-Driven Development Principles

TDD consists of writing test cases that cover a desired feature, then writing the feature itself. In other words, the usage examples are written before the code even exists.

For example, a developer who is asked to write a function that provides the average value of a sequence of numbers will first write a few examples on how to use it, and the expected results:

```
assert average(1, 2, 3) == 2
assert average(1, -3) == -1
```

These examples can be provided by another person as well. From there, the function can be implemented until the two examples work:

```
>>> def average(*numbers):
...         return sum(numbers) / len(numbers)
...
>>> assert average(1, 2, 3) == 2
>>> assert average(1, -3) == -1
```

A bug or an unexpected result is a new example of usage the function should be able to deal with:

```
>>> assert average(0, 1) == 0.5
Traceback (most recent call last):
  File "<stdin>", line 1, in <module>
AssertionError
```

The code can be changed accordingly, until the new test passes:

```
>>> def average(*numbers):
...         # makes sure all numbers can be used as floats
...         numbers = [float(number) for number in numbers]
...         return sum(numbers) / float(len(numbers))
...
>>> assert average(0, 1) == 0.5
```

And more cases will make the code evolve:

```
>>> try:
...         average()
... except TypeError:
...         # we want an empty sequence to throw a type error
...         pass
...
Traceback (most recent call last):
  File "<stdin>", line 2, in <module>
  File "<stdin>", line 3, in average
ZeroDivisionError: integer division or modulo by zero
>>>
>>> def average(*numbers):
```

```
...         if numbers == ():
...             raise TypeError(('You need to provide at '
...                             'least one number'))
...         numbers = [float(number) for number in numbers]
...         return sum(numbers) / len(numbers)
...
>>> try:
...     average()
... except TypeError:
...     pass
...
```

From there all tests can be gathered in a test function, which is run every time the code evolves:

```
>>> def test_average():
...     assert average(1, 2, 3) == 2
...     assert average(1, -3) == -1
...     assert average(0, 1) == 0.5
...     try:
...         average()
...     except TypeError:
...         pass
...
>>> test_average()
```

Every time a change is made, test_average is changed together with average, then run again to make sure all cases still work. The usage is to gather all tests in the tests folder of the current package. Each module can have a corresponding test module there.

This approach provides a lot of benefits by:

- Preventing software regression
- Improving code quality
- Providing the best low-level documentation
- Producing robust code faster

Preventing Software Regression

We all face software regression issues in our developer lives. Software regression is a new bug introduced by a change. Regressions happen because of the simple fact that it is impossible at some point to guess what a single change in a codebase might lead to. Changing some code might break some other features, and sometimes lead to vicious side effects, such as silently corrupting data.

To avoid regression, the whole set of features software provides should be tested every time a change occurs.

Opening a codebase to several developers amplifies the problem, since each person will not be fully aware of all development activities. While having a version control system prevents conflicts, it does not prevent all unwanted interactions.

TDD helps reduce software regression. The whole software can be automatically tested after each change. This will work as long as each feature has the proper set of tests. When TDD is properly done, the test base grows together with the codebase.

Since a full test campaign can last for quite a long time, it is a good practice to delegate it to a `buildbot`, which can do the work in the background (this is described in Chapter 8). But local re-launching of the tests should be done manually by the user, at least for the concerned modules.

Improving Code Quality

When a new module, class, or a function is written, a developer focuses on how to write it and how to produce the best piece of code he or she can. But while he or she is concentrating on algorithms, he or she might lose the user's point of view: How and when will his or her function be used? Are the arguments easy and logical to use? Is the name of the API right?

This is done by applying the tips described in the previous chapters, such as **Choosing Good Names**. But the only way to do it efficiently is to write usage examples. This is when the developer realizes if the code he or she wrote is logical and easy to use. Often, the first refactoring occurs right after the module, class, or function is finished.

Writing tests, which are use cases for the code, helps in having this user point of view. Developers will, therefore, often produce a better code when they use TDD. It is difficult to test gigantic functions that both calculate things as well as have side effects. Code that is written with testing in mind tends to be architected more cleanly and modularly.

Providing the Best Developer Documentation

Tests are the best place for a developer to learn how software works. They are the use cases the code was primarily created for. Reading them provides a quick and deep insight into how the code works. Sometimes, an example is worth a thousand words.

The fact that these tests are always up to date with the codebase makes them the best developer documentation a piece of software can have. Tests don't go stale in the same way documentation does, otherwise they would fail.

Producing Robust Code Faster

Writing without tests leads to extensive debugging sessions. A bug in one part of the software might be felt in a distant part of that software. Since you don't know who to blame, you spend an inordinate amount of time debugging. It's better to fight small bugs one at a time when a test fails, because you'll have a better clue as to where the real problem is. And testing is often more fun than debugging because it is coding.

If you measure the time taken to fix the code together with the time taken to write it, it will usually be longer than the time a TDD approach would take. This is not obvious when you start a new piece of code. This is because the time taken to set up a test environment and write the first few tests is extremely long compared to the time taken just to write the first pieces of code.

But there are some test environments that are really hard to set up. For instance, when your code interacts with an LDAP or an SQL server, writing tests is not obvious at all. This is covered in the **Fakes and Mocks** section in this chapter.

What Kind of Tests?

There are several kinds of tests that can be made on any software. The main ones are **acceptance tests** (or **functional tests**) and **unit tests**.

Acceptance Tests

An acceptance test focuses on a feature, and deals with the software like a black box. It just makes sure that the software really does what it is supposed to do, using the same media as that of the users, and controlling the output. These tests are usually written out of the development cycle to validate that the application meets the requirements. They are usually run as a checklist over the software. Often, these tests are not done through TDD, and are built by managers or even customers. In that case, they are called **user acceptance tests**.

Still, they can and they should be done with TDD principles. Tests can be provided before the features are written. Developers get a pile of acceptance tests, usually made out of the functional specifications, and they make sure the code produced makes them pass.

The tools used to write those tests depend on the user interface the software provides. The most used tools by Python developers are:

Application type	Tool
Web application	Selenium (for Web UI with JavaScript (JS))
Web application	zope.testbrowser (doesn't test JS)
WSGI application	paste.test.fixture (doesn't test JS)
Gnome Desktop application	dogtail
Win32 Desktop application	pywinauto

 For an extensive list of functional testing tools, Grig Gheorghiu maintains a wiki page here: `http://www.pycheesecake.org/wiki/PythonTestingToolsTaxonomy`.

Unit Tests

Unit tests are low-level tests that perfectly fit the TDD approach. They focus on a single module (for example, one unit) and provide tests for it. No other modules are involved. The tests isolate the module from the rest of the application. When external dependencies are required, such as a database access, they are replaced by fake objects or mocks.

Python Standard Test Tools

Python provides two modules in the standard library to write tests:

- `unittest` (`http://docs.python.org/lib/module-unittest.html`), originally written by Steve Purcell (formely `PyUnit`)
- `doctest` (`http://docs.python.org/lib/module-doctest.html`), a literate testing tool

unittest

`unittest` basically provides what JUnit does for Java. It offers a base class called `TestCase`, which has an extensive set of methods to verify the output of a call.

This module was created to write unit tests, but acceptance tests can also be written with it as long as the test uses the user interface. For instance, some testing frameworks provide helpers to drive tools such as Selenium on the top of `unittest`.

Using unittest, writing a simple unit test for a module is done by subclassing `TestCase` and writing methods with the test prefix. The previous example, written with it, will look like this:

```
>>> import unittest
>>> class MyTests(unittest.TestCase):
...         def test_average(self):
...                 self.assertEquals(average(1, 2, 3), 2)
...                 self.assertEquals(average(1, -3), -1)
...                 self.assertEquals(average(0, 1), 0.5)
...                 self.assertRaises(TypeError, average)
...
>>> unittest.main()
.
----------------------------------------------------------
Ran 1 test in 0.000s

OK
```

The `main` function scans the context and looks for classes that subclass `TestCase`. It instantiates them, then runs all methods that start with `test`.

If the `average` function is in the `utils.py` module, the `test` class will be called `UtilsTests`, and written in a `test_utils.py` file:

```
import unittest
from utils import average

class UtilsTests(unittest.TestCase):
    def test_average(self):
        self.assertEquals(average(1, 2, 3), 2)
        self.assertEquals(average(1, -3), -1)
        self.assertEquals(average(0, 1), 0.5)
        self.assertRaises(TypeError, average)
if __name__ == '__main__':
    unittest.main()
```

From there, every time the `utils` module evolves, the `test_utils` module gets more tests.

> To work, the `test_utils` module needs to have the `utils` module available in the context. This is either because the two files are in the same folder, or because the test runner puts the `utils` module in the Python path.
>
> The Distutils `develop` command is very helpful here.

Running tests over a whole application presupposes that you have a script that builds a **test campaign** out of all test modules. unittest provides a TestSuite class that can aggregate tests and run them as a test campaign, as long as they are all instances of subclasses of TestCase or TestSuite.

Conventionally, a test module provides a test_suite function that returns a TestSuite instance either used in the __main__ section, when the module is called by the prompt, or used by a test runner:

```
import unittest
from utils import average

class MyTests(unittest.TestCase):
    def test_average(self):
        self.assertEquals(average(1, 2, 3), 2)
        self.assertEquals(average(1, -3), -1)
        self.assertEquals(average(0, 1), 0.5)
        self.assertRaises(TypeError, average)

class MyTests2(unittest.TestCase):
    def test_another_test(self):
        pass

def test_suite():
    """builds the test suite."""
    def _suite(test_class):
        return unittest.makeSuite(test_class)
    suite = unittest.TestSuite()
    suite.addTests((_suite(MyTests), _suite(MyTests2)))
    return suite

if __name__ == '__main__':
    unittest.main(defaultTest='test_suite')
```

Running this module from the shell will print the test campaign output:

```
$ python test_utils.py
..
------------------------------------------------------------
Ran 2 tests in 0.000s

OK
```

Usually, running of all tests is done by a global script that browses the code tree looking for tests and runs them. This is called **test discovery**, and is covered later in this chapter.

doctest

doctest is a module that extracts snippets from docstrings or text files from interactive prompt sessions, and replays them to check that the output written in the example is the same as the real output.

For instance, this text file (test.txt) can be run as a test:

```
Check that the computer CPU is not getting too hot::

    >>> 1 + 1
    2
```

The doctest module provides some functions to extract and run the tests:

```
>>> import doctest
>>> doctest.testfile('test.txt', verbose=True)
Trying:
    1 + 1
Expecting:
    2
ok
1 items passed all tests:
   1 tests in test.txt
1 tests in 1 items.
1 passed and 0 failed.
Test passed.
*** DocTestRunner.merge: 'test.txt' in both testers; summing outcomes.
(0, 1)
```

Using doctest has many advantages:

- Packages can be documented and tested through examples.
- Documentation examples are always up to date.
- Using examples in doctests to write a package helps in having the user's point of view that we have described in the last section.

However, doctests do not make unit tests obsolete; they should be used only to provide human-readable examples in documents. In other words, when the tests are concerning low-level matters or need complex test fixtures that would obfuscate the document, they should not be used.

Some Python frameworks such as Zope are using doctests extensively, and they are at times criticized by people who are new to the code. Some doctests are really hard to read and understand, since the examples break one of the rules of technical writing: They cannot be taken and run in a simple prompt, and they need extensive knowledge. So documents that are supposed to help newcomers are really hard to read because the code examples, which are doctests built through TDD, are based on complex test fixtures or even specific test APIs.

 As explained in the chapter about documentation, when you use doctests that are part of the documentation of your packages, be careful to follow the seven rules of technical writing.

At this stage, you should have a good overview of what TDD brings. If you are still not convinced, you should give it a try over a few modules. Write a package using TDD and measure the time spent in building it, then in debugging it, and refactoring it. You should find out quickly that it is truly superior.

I Do Test

If you are coming from the **I don't do tests** section and are now convinced by TDD, congratulations!

This section describes a few problems developers bump into when they write tests, and some ways to solve them. It also provides a quick review of test runners and tools available in the community.

Unittest Pitfalls

The `unittest` module was introduced in Python 2.1 and has been widely used by developers since then. But some alternative test frameworks were raised in the community made by people who were frustrated by the weaknesses and limitations of `unittest`.

These are the common criticisms that were made:

- The framework is heavy to use because:
    - You have to write all your tests in subclasses of `TestCase`.
    - You have to prefix the method names with `test`.
    - You are invited to use assertion methods provided in `TestCase`.
    - You have to build test suites for the test campaign to be run.

- The framework is hard to extend because it requires massive subclassing of classes or tricks such as decorators.

- Test fixtures are sometimes hard to organize because the `setUp` and `tearDown` facilities are tied to the `TestCase` level, though they run once per test. In other words, if a test fixture concerns many tests modules, it is not simple to organize its creation and cleanup.

- It is not easy to run a test campaign over Python software: Extra scripts have to be written to collect the tests, aggregate them, and then run them.

A lighter approach is needed to write tests without suffering from the rigidity of a framework that looks too much like its big Java brother, JUnit. Since Python does not require working with a 100% class-based environment, it is preferable to provide a more Pythonic test framework that is not based on subclassing.

A common approach would be:

- To provide a simple way to mark any function or any class as a test

- To extend the framework through a plug-in system

- To provide a complete test fixture environment for all test levels: the whole campaign, a group of tests at module level, and at test level

- To provide a test runner based on test discovery, with an extensive set of options

Python core developers are aware of the weaknesses of `unittest`, and some work is being done in Python 3k to enhance it.

 Some people are working on `unittest` replacement for Python 3k.

One project is based on `test_harness` implementation. See `http://oakwinter.com/code/`.

Unittest Alternatives

Some third-party tools try to solve the problems just mentioned by providing extra features in the shape of `unittest` extensions.

The most used ones are:

- `nose`: `http://www.somethingaboutorange.com/mrl/projects/nose`
- `py.test`: `http://codespeak.net/py/dist/test.html`

nose

`nose` is mainly a test runner with powerful discovery features. It has extensive options that allow running all kind of test campaigns in a Python application.

To install it, use `easy_install`:

```
$ easy_install nose
Searching for nose
Reading http://pypi.python.org/simple/nose/
Reading http://somethingaboutorange.com/mrl/projects/nose/
...
Processing dependencies for nose
Finished processing dependencies for nose
```

Test Runner

A new command called `nosetests` is then available at the prompt. Running the tests presented in the first section of the chapter can be done directly with it:

```
$ nosetests -v
test_average (test_utils.MyTests) ... ok
test_another_test (test_utils.MyTests2) ... ok
builds the test suite. ... ok

----------------------------------------------------------

Ran 3 tests in 0.010s

OK
```

`nose` takes care of discovering the tests by recursively browsing the current directory, and building a test suite on its own. This simple feature is already an advantage when compared to the work that has to be done to launch tests in `unittest`. There is no boiler-plate code needed anymore to build and run the test campaign, and the only requirement is writing test classes.

Writing Tests

`nose` goes a step further by running all classes and functions whose name matches the regular expression `((?:^|[b_.-])[Tt]est)` located in modules that matches it too. Roughly, all callables that start with `test` and are located in a module that matches the pattern will also be executed as a test.

For instance, this `test_ok.py` module will be recognized and run by `nose`:

```
$ more test_ok.py
def test_ok():
    print 'my test'
$ nosetests -v
test_ok.test_ok ... ok

----------------------------------------------------------------------
Ran 1 test in 0.071s

OK
```

Regular `TestCase` classes and `doctests` are executed as well.

Last, `nose` provides assertion functions that are similar to `TestCase` methods. But these are provided as functions that use the PEP 8 naming conventions, rather than using the Java convention `unittest` uses (see `http://code.google.com/p/python-nose/wiki/TestingTools`).

Writing Test Fixtures

`nose` supports three levels of fixtures:

- Package level: `setup` and `teardown` functions can be added in the `__init__.py` module of a tests folder containing all tests for the package, for instance.
- Module level: A test module can have its own `setup` and `teardown` functions.
- Test level: The callable can also have fixture functions using the `with_setup` decorator provided.

For instance, to set a test fixture at the module and test level use this code:

```
def setup():
    # setup code, launched for the whole module
    ...

def teardown():
    # tear down code, launched for the whole module
    ...

def set_ok():
    # setup code launched only for test_ok
    ...

@with_setup(set_ok)
def test_ok():
    print 'my test'
```

Integration with setuptools and Plug-in System

Last, `nose` integrates smoothly with `setuptools` and so the `test` command can be used with it (`python setup.py test`). This is done by adding the `test_suite` metadata in `setup.py` like this:

```
setup(
    ...
    test_suite = 'nose.collector'
    ...)
```

`nose` also uses `setuptools` entry point machinery for developers to write `nose` plug-ins, which let them override or modify every aspect of the tool from test discovering to test output.

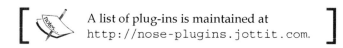 A list of plug-ins is maintained at `http://nose-plugins.jottit.com`.

Wrap-Up

`nose` is a complete testing tool that fixes many of the issues `unittest` has. It is still designed to use implicit prefix names for tests, which remain a constraint for some developers. While this prefix can be customized, it still requires one to follow a convention.

This convention over configuration statement is not bad, and a lot better than the boiler-plate code required in `unittest`. But using explicit decorators, for example, could be a nice way to get rid of the `test` prefix.

Last, the plug-in approach makes it very flexible, and allows a developer to customize to the tool to meet his or her needs.

 You can add a `.noserc` or a `nose.cfg` file in your home directory to specify default options when `nosetests` is launched.
A good practice is to automatically look for `doctests`.
Example of such a file is:

```
[nosetests]
with-doctest=1
doctest-extension=.txt
```

py.test

`py.test` is very similar to `nose`, and this section will just present its particularities. The tool is bundled into a package called `py` that contains other tools.

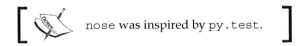

nose was inspired by py.test.

It can be installed with `easy_install` as well:

```
$ easy_install py
Searching for py
Best match: py 0.9.0
Finished processing dependencies for py
```

From there, a new `py.test` command is available at the prompt that can be used exactly like `nosetests`. The tool uses, like `nose`, a pattern-matching algorithm to catch tests to be run. The pattern is stricter than that which `nose` uses and will catch only:

- Classes that starts with `Test`, in a file that starts with `test`
- Functions that start with `test`, in a file that starts with `test`

Be careful to use the right character case: If a function starts with a capital "T", it will be taken as a class, and thus ignored. And if a class starts with a lower case "t", py.test will break because it will try to deal with it as a function.

The test fixture features are similar to `nose`, except that the semantics differ a bit. `py.test` will look for three levels of fixture in each test module from the official documentation:

```
def setup_module(module):
    """ setup up any state specific to the execution
        of the given module.
    """

def teardown_module(module):
    """ teardown any state that was previously setup
        with a setup_module method.
    """

def setup_class(cls):
    """ setup up any state specific to the execution
        of the given class (which usually contains tests).
    """

def teardown_class(cls):
    """ teardown any state that was previously setup
        with a call to setup_class.
    """
```

```
def setup_method(self, method):
    """ setup up any state tied to the execution of the given
        method in a class. setup_method is invoked for every
        test method of a class.
    """

def teardown_method(self, method):
    """ teardown any state that was previously setup
        with a setup_method call.
    """
```

Each function will get the current module, class, or method as an argument. The test fixture will, therefore, be able to work on the context without having to look for it, as with nose. But py.test doesn't provide a way to run a global test fixture such as nose, by allowing addition of setup and a teardown functions at the package level.

The original features of py.test are:

- The ability to disable some test classes
- The ability to distribute tests among several computers
- The fact that tests start immediately, while the tool continues its discovery task

Disabling a Test Class

The tool provides a simple mechanism to disable some tests upon certain conditions. If the disabled attribute is found on the test class, it is checked.

For instance, as its documentation explains, when a test is platform-dependent, the Boolean can be set like this (example from the official documentation):

```
class TestEgSomePosixStuff:
    disabled = sys.platform == 'win32'

    def test_xxx(self):
        ...
```

A callable can be used in order to provide complex conditions:

```
def _disabled():
    # complex work here
    return 0

class Test_2:

    disabled = _disabled()

    def test_one(self):
        pass
```

Unfortunately, this attribute cannot be a method or a property, since `py.test` just calls `getattr(cls, 'disabled', 0)` over the class.

Automated Distributed Tests

An interesting feature of `py.test` is its ability to distribute the tests across several computers. As long as the computers are reachable through SSH, `py.test` will be able to drive each computer by sending to it tests to be performed.

However, this feature relies on the network; if the connection is broken the slave will not be able to continue working since it is fully driven by the master.

A Buildbot approach is preferable when a project has long test campaigns. But the `py.test` distributed model can be used for ad hoc distribution of tests when you are working on an application that consumes a lot of resources to run the tests.

Test Starts Immediately

`py.test` uses an iterator in its discovery process, so the first test it finds can be directly launched. This speeds up the first output, which is nice when the test fixtures are slow. Furthermore, the first failure will occur faster.

Wrap-Up

`py.test` is very similar to `nose` since no boiler-plate code is needed to aggregate the tests in it. Tests fixtures are also enough to layer the setup, but there is no direct way to launch a setup at the package level. Unfortunately, there is no plug-in system here as is in `nose`.

Last, `py.test` focuses on making the tests run fast, and is truly superior compared to other tools in this area.

The tool is part of a bigger framework and could be distributed independently to avoid installing other elements.

Unless you want to use specific features `py.test` has, `nose` should be preferred.

Fakes and Mocks

Writing unit tests presupposes that you isolate the module being tested. Tests feed the function or method with some data and test the output.

This is mainly to make sure the tests:

- Are concerning an atomic part of the application, which can be a function or a class
- Provide deterministic, reproducible results

Sometimes, isolation of a part of the program is not obvious. For instance, if the code sends mails, it will call Python's `smtplib` module, which will work with the SMTP server through a telnet connection. This should not happen when the tests are run. Ideally, unit tests should run on any computer with no external dependencies and side effects.

Thanks to Python's dynamic nature, it is possible to use **monkey patches** to modify the runtime code from the test fixture (see `http://en.wikipedia.org/wiki/Monkey_patch`), to **fake** the behavior of a third-party code or library.

Building a Fake

A fake behavior in the tests can be created by discovering the minimal set of interactions needed for the tested code to work with the external parts. Then the output is manually returned, or uses a real pool of data that has been previously recorded.

This is done by starting an empty class or function and using it as a replacement. The test is then launched, and the fake filled in until it behaves correctly.

Let's take an example with a function called `send` in a module called `mailer` that sends mails:

```
import smtplib
import email.Message
def send(sender, to, subject='None', body='None',
        server='localhost'):
    """sends a message."""
    message = email.Message.Message()
    message['To'] = to
    message['From'] = sender
    message['Subject'] = subject
    message.set_payload(body)
    server = smtplib.SMTP(server)
    try:
        res = server.sendmail(sender, to, message.as_string())
    finally:
        server.quit()

    return res
```

nose will be used to demonstrate Fakes and Mocks in this section.

The corresponding test can be:

```
from mailer import send
from nose.tools import *

def test_send():
    res = send('tarek@ziade.org', 'tarek@ziade.org',
               'topic', 'body')
    assert_equals(res, {})
```

This test will pass and work as long as there is an SMTP server on the local host. If not, it will fail like this:

```
$ nosetests -v

test_mailer.test_send ... ERROR


======================================================================
ERROR: test_mailer.test_send

----------------------------------------------------------------------
Traceback (most recent call last):

...

"...Versions/2.5/lib/python2.5/smtplib.py", line 310, in connect
    raise socket.error, msg
error: (61, 'Connection refused')


----------------------------------------------------------------------

Ran 1 test in 0.169s
```

A patch can be added to fake the SMTP class:

```
from mailer import send
from nose.tools import *
import smtplib

def patch_smtp():
    class FakeSMTP(object):
        pass
    smtplib._SMTP = smtplib.SMTP
    smtplib.SMTP = FakeSMTP
```

```
def unpatch_smtp():
    smtplib.SMTP = smtplib._SMTP
    delattr(smtplib, '_SMTP')

@with_setup(patch_smtp, unpatch_smtp)
def test_send():
    res = send('tarek@ziade.org', 'tarek@ziade.org',
               'topic', 'body')
    assert_equals(res, {})
```

And the test can be run again:

```
$ nosetests -v
test_mailer.test_send ... ERROR

======================================================================
ERROR: test_mailer.test_send
----------------------------------------------------------------------
Traceback (most recent call last):
...
TypeError: default __new__ takes no parameters

----------------------------------------------------------------------
Ran 1 test in 0.066s

FAILED (errors=1)
```

The FakeSMTP class is then completed until the test passes. It will complain about a few methods the class should have:

```
class FakeSMTP(object):
    def __init__(self, *args, **kw):
        # we don't care
        pass

    def quit(self):
        pass

    def sendmail(self, *args, **kw):
        return {}
```

Of course, the fake class can evolve with new tests to provide more complex behaviors. But it should be as short and simple as possible. The same principle can be used with more complex outputs, by recording them to serve them back through the fake API. This is often done with third-party servers such as LDAP or SQL.

Fakes have real limitations. If you decide to fake an external dependency, you may introduce bugs or unwanted behaviors the real server wouldn't or vice-versa.

Using Mocks

Mock objects are generic fake objects (see `http://en.wikipedia.org/wiki/Mock_object`) that can be used to isolate the tested code. They automate the build of input and output. There is a greater use of mock objects in statically typed language, where monkey patching is harder but they are still useful in Python to shorten the code to mimic external APIs.

There are a lot of mock libraries available in Python, and the simplest and easiest one to use is Ian Bicking's `minimock` (see `http://blog.ianbicking.org/minimock.html`).

It is easy installable as usual:

```
$ easy_install minimock
Searching for minimock
Reading http://pypi.python.org/simple/minimock
...
Finished processing dependencies for minimock
```

The library provides three elements:

- `mock`: A function that generates and puts a mock object at the given namespace
- `Mock`: The mock class that can be used to instantiate a mock object manually
- `restore`: A function that removes the patch done by `mock`

In our example, using `minimock` to patch SMTP is way simpler than the manual fake:

```
from mailer import send
from nose.tools import *
import smtplib
from minimock import mock, restore, Mock

def patch_smtp():
    mock('smtplib.SMTP',
```

```
                    returns=Mock('smtp_connection',
                            sendmail=Mock('sendmail',
                                        returns={})
                        )
                )

    def unpatch_smtp():
        restore()

    @with_setup(patch_smtp, unpatch_smtp)
    def test_send():
        res = send('tarek@ziade.org',
                    'tarek@ziade.org', 'topic', 'body')
        assert_equals(res, {})
```

The `returns` attribute allows you to define which element is returned by the call. When the mock object is used, every time an attribute is called by the code, it creates a new mock object for the attribute on the fly. Thus, no exception is raised. This is the case (for instance) for the `quit` method we wrote earlier.

If a method has to return a specific value, a mock object can be manually instantiated for that method with the value to return in its `returns` argument. This special mock object can be passed as a keyword argument. This is done for `sendmail`.

Now let's run the test again:

```
$ nosetests -v -s
test_mailer.test_send ... Called smtplib.SMTP('localhost')
Called sendmail(
    'tarek@ziade.org',
    'tarek@ziade.org',
    'To: tarek@ziade.org\nFrom: tarek@ziade.org\nSubject: topic\n\nbody')
Called smtp_connection.quit()
ok

----------------------------------------------------------

Ran 1 test in 0.122s

OK
```

Notice that the elements called are printed out by `minimock`. This makes it a good candidate for doctests.

Document-Driven Development

doctests are a real advantage in Python compared to other languages. The fact that a text can use code examples that are also runable as tests changes the way TDD can be done. For instance, part of the documentation can be done through doctests during the development cycle. This approach also ensures that the provided examples are up to date and really working.

Building software through doctests rather than regular unit tests is called **Document-Driven Development (DDD)**. Developers explain what the code is doing in plain English, while they are implementing it.

Writing a Story

Writing doctests in DDD is done by building a story about how a piece of code works and should be used. The principles are described in plain English and then a few code usage examples are distributed throughout the text. A good practice is to start to write a text on how the code works, and then add some code examples. This is how the modules in Chapter 6 are written.

Let's look back at the atomisator.parser package doctest. The first version of the text was:

```
==================
atomisator.parser
==================

The parser knows how to return a feed content with
a function available as a top-level function.

This function takes the feed url and returns an iterator
on its content. A second parameter can specify how
many entries have to be returned before the iterator is
exhausted. If not given, it is fixed to 10
```

The example was then completed and the code built with it was:

```
==================
atomisator.parser
==================

The parser knows how to return a feed content, with
the 'parse' function, available as a top-level function::

    >>> from atomisator.parser import parse
```

```
This function takes the feed url and returns an iterator
on its content. A second parameter can specify how
many entries have to be returned before the iterator is
exhausted. If not given, it is fixed to 10::

    >>> res = parse('http://example.com/feed.xml')

    >>> res

    <generator ...>
```

Later, the doctest will probably evolve to take into account new elements or required changes. This doctest is also a good documentation for developers who want to use the package, and should be changed with this usage in mind.

A common pitfall in writing tests in a document is to transform it into an unreadable piece of text. If this happens, it should not be considered as part of the documentation anymore.

That said, some developers that are working exclusively through doctests often group their doctests into two categories: the ones that are readable and usable so that they can be a part of the package documentation, and the ones that are unreadable and are just used to build and test the software.

Many developers think that doctests should be dropped for the latter, in favor of regular unit tests. Others even use dedicated doctests for bug fixes.

So the balance between doctests and regular tests is a matter of taste and is up to the team, as long as the published part of the doctests is readable.

 When DDD is used in a project, focus on the readability and decide which doctests are eligible to be a part of the published documentation.

Summary

This chapter advocated the usage of TDD and provided more information on:

- `unittest` pitfalls
- Third-party tools: `nose` and `py.test`
- How to build fakes and mocks
- Documentation-Driven Development

The next chapter will focus on ways to optimize your programs.

12

Optimization: General Principles and Profiling Techniques

"Premature optimization is the root of all evil in programming."

Donald Knuth

This chapter is about optimization and provides a set of general principles and profiling techniques. It gives the three rules of optimization every developer should be aware of, and provides guidelines on optimization. Last, it focuses on how to find bottlenecks.

The Three Rules of Optimization

Optimization has a price, no matter what the results are. When a piece of code works, it might be better (sometimes) to leave it alone than to try making it faster at all costs. They are a few rules to keep in mind when doing optimization:

- Make it work first.
- Work from the user's point of view.
- Keep the code readable.

Make It Work First

A very common mistake is to try to optimize the code while you are writing it. This is impossible because the real bottlenecks are often located where you would have never thought they would be.

An application is composed of very complex interactions, and it is impossible to get a full picture of what is going on before it is really used.

Of course, this is not a reason to write a function or a method without trying to make it as fast as possible. You should be careful to lower its complexity as much as possible and avoid useless repetition. But the first goal is to make it work. This goal should not be hindered by optimization matters.

For line-level code, the Python philosophy is that there's one and preferably only one way to do it. So as long as you stick with a Pythonic syntax, described in Chapters 2 and 3, your code should be fine. Often, writing less code is better and faster than writing more code.

Don't do any of these things until you have gotten your code working and you are ready to profile:

- Start to write a global dictionary to cache data for a function
- Think about externalizing a part of the code in C or hybrid languages such as Pyrex
- Look for external libraries to do some basic calculation

For very specialized programs, such as scientific calculation programs or games, the usage of specialized libraries and externalization might be unavoidable from the beginning. On the other hand using libraries like Numeric might ease the development of specific features and produce a simpler and faster code at the end. Furthermore, you should not rewrite a function if there is a good library that does it for you.

For instance Soya 3D, which is a game engine on the top of OpenGL (see `http://home.gna.org/oomadness/en/soya3d/index.html`), uses C and Pyrex for fast matrix operations when rendering real-time 3D.

 Optimization is carried out on programs that already work. "Make it work, then make it right, then make it fast"—Kent Beck

Work from the User's Point of View

I have seen teams working on optimizing the startup time of an application server that worked really fine when it was started. Once they finished speeding it, they promoted that work to their customers. They were a bit frustrated to notice that the customers didn't really care about it. This was because the speed-up work was not motivated by the user feedback, but by the developer's point of view. The people who built the system were launching the server everyday. So the startup time mattered to them but not the customer.

While making a program start faster is a good thing from an absolute point of view, teams should be careful to prioritize the optimization work and ask themselves the following questions:

- Have I been asked to make it faster?
- Who finds the program slow?
- Is it really slow, or acceptable?
- How much will it cost to make it go faster? Is it worth it? What parts need to be fast?

Remember that optimization has a cost, and that the developer's point of view is meaningless to customers, unless you are writing a framework or a library and the customer is a developer too.

 Optimization is not a game. It should be done only when necessary.

Keep the Code Readable(and thus maintainable)

Even if Python tries to make the common code patterns the fastest, optimization work might obfuscate your code and make it really hard to read. There's a balance to keep between producing readable, and therefore maintainable code, and defacing it in order to make it faster.

When you have reached 90% of your optimization objectives, and the 10% left to be done makes your code completely unreadable, it might be a good idea to stop the work there or to look for other solutions.

 Optimization should not make your code unreadable. If it happens, you should look for alternative solutions such as externalization or redesign. However, there is always a good compromise between readability and speed.

Optimization Strategy

Let's say your program has a real speed problem you need to resolve. Do not try to guess how to make it faster. Bottlenecks are often hard to find by looking at the code, and a set of tools is needed to find the real problem.

A good optimization strategy can start with three steps:

- Find another culprit: Make sure a third-party server or resource is not faulty.
- Scale the hardware: Make sure the resources are sufficient.
- Write a speed test: Create a scenario with speed objectives.

Find Another Culprit

Often, a performance problem occurs at production level and the customer alerts you that it is not working as it used to when the software was being tested. Performance problems might occur because the application was not planned to work in the real world with a high number of users and an increase of data size.

But if the application interacts with other applications, the first thing to do is to check if the bottlenecks are located on those interactions. For instance, a database server or an LDAP server might be responsible for extra overhead and make everything slower.

The physical links between applications should also be considered: Maybe the network link between your application server and another server in the intranet is getting really slow due to a misconfiguration, or a paranoid anti-virus that scans all TCP packets and slows everything down.

The design documentation should provide a diagram of all interactions and the nature of each link to get an overall picture of the system, and get help when trying to resolve a speed problem.

 If your application uses third-party servers of resources, every interaction should be audited to make sure the bottleneck is not located there.

Scale the Hardware

When there is no more volatile memory available, the system starts to use the hard disk to store data. This is swapping.

This involves a lot of overhead and the performances drop drastically. From a user's point of view, the system is considered dead at this stage. So, it is important to scale the hardware to prevent this.

While having enough memory on a system is important, it is also important to make sure that the applications are not acting crazy and eating too much memory. For instance, if a program works on big video files that can weigh in at several hundreds of megabytes, it should not load them entirely in memory, but rather work on chunks or use disk streams.

Disk usage is also important. A full partition might really slow down your application, if the I/O errors are hidden in the code that tries to write repeatedly on the disk. Furthermore, even if the code only tries the write once, the hardware and OS might try to write multiple times.

Munin is a great system-monitoring tool that you can use to get a snapshot of the system health: `http://munin.projects.linpro.no` Make sure the system is healthy and fits the application need. But make sure the application is not consuming memory and disk space like an ogre.

Write a Speed Test

When starting with optimization work, it is important to work on tests' side rather than running some manual tests continually. A good practice is to dedicate a test module in the application, where the sequence of calls that are to be optimized is written. Having this scenario will help you to track your progress while you are optimizing the application.

You can even write a few assertions where you set some speed objectives. To prevent speed regression, these tests can be left after the code has been optimized:

```
>>> def test_speed():
...     import time
...     start = time.time()
...     the_code()
...     end = time.time() - start
...     assert end < 10, \
...     "sorry this code should not take 10 seconds !"
...
```

Measuring execution speed depends on the power of the CPU used. But we will see in the next section how to write universal duration measures.

Finding Bottlenecks

Finding bottlenecks is done by:

- Profiling CPU usage
- Profiling memory usage
- Profiling network usage

Profiling CPU Usage

The first source of bottlenecks is your code. The standard library provides all the tools needed to perform code profiling. They are based on a deterministic approach.

A **deterministic profiler** measures the time spent in each function by adding a timer at the lowest level. This introduces a bit of overhead, but provides a good idea on where the time is consumed. A **statistical profiler**, on the other hand, samples the instruction pointer usage and does not instrument the code. The latter is less accurate, but allows running the target program at full speed.

There are two ways to profile the code:

- **Macro-profiling**: Profiles the whole program while it is being used, and generates statistics.
- **Micro-profiling**: Measures a precise part of the program by instrumenting it manually.

Macro-Profiling

Macro-profiling is done by running the application in a special mode, where the interpreter is instrumented to collect statistics on the code usage. Python provides several tools for this:

- `profile`: A pure Python implementation
- `cProfile`: A C implementation that provides the same interface as that of the `profile` tool, but has less overhead
- `hotshot`: Another C implementation, which is probably going to be removed from the standard library

Unless your program runs with a Python version below 2.5, the recommended profiler is `cProfile`.

The following is a `myapp.py` module with a main function:

```
import time
def medium():
    time.sleep(0.01)
def light():
    time.sleep(0.001)
def heavy():
    for i in range(100):
        light()
        medium()
        medium()
    time.sleep(2)
def main():
    for i in range(2):
        heavy()
if __name__ == '__main__':
    main()
```

The module can be called directly from the prompt and the results are summarized here:

```
$ python -m cProfile myapp.py
        1212 function calls in 10.120 CPU seconds

    Ordered by: standard name

    ncalls  tottime  cumtime  percall    file
         1    0.000   10.117   10.117 myapp.py:16(main)
       400    0.004    4.077    0.010 myapp.py:3(medium)
       200    0.002    2.035    0.010 myapp.py:6(light)
         2    0.005   10.117    5.058 myapp.py:9(heavy)
         3    0.000    0.000    0.000 {range}
       602   10.106   10.106    0.017 {time.sleep}
```

The statistics provided are a print view of a statistic object filled by the profiler. A manual call of the tool can be:

```
>>> from myapp import main
>>> import cProfile
>>> profiler = cProfile.Profile()
>>> profiler.runcall(main)
>>> profiler.print_stats()
        1209 function calls in 10.140 CPU seconds
    Ordered by: standard name
    ncalls  tottime  cumtime  percall file
         1    0.000   10.140   10.140 myapp.py:16(main)
       400    0.005    4.093    0.010 myapp.py:3(medium)
       200    0.002    2.042    0.010 myapp.py:6(light)
```

```
  2     0.005   10.140    5.070 myapp.py:9(heavy)
  3     0.000    0.000    0.000 {range}
602    10.128   10.128    0.017 {time.sleep}
```

The statistics can also be saved in a file and then read by the `pstats` module. This module provides a class that knows how to handle profile files, and gives a few helpers to play with them like sort methods:

```
>>> cProfile.run('main()', 'myapp.stats')
>>> import pstats
>>> p = pstats.Stats('myapp.stats')
>>> p.total_calls
1210
>>> p.sort_stats('time').print_stats(3)
Thu Jun 19 23:56:08 2008    myapp.stats

        1210 function calls in 10.240 CPU seconds

   Ordered by: internal time
   List reduced from 8 to 3 due to restriction <3>

   ncalls  tottime  cumtime  percall filename:lineno(function)
      602   10.231   10.231    0.017 {time.sleep}
        2    0.004   10.240    5.120 myapp.py:9(heavy)
      400    0.004    4.159    0.010 myapp.py:3(medium)
```

From there, you can browse the code by printing out the callers and callees for each function:

```
>>> p.print_callees('medium')
   Ordered by: internal time
   List reduced from 8 to 1 due to restriction <'medium'>

Function                  called...
                            ncalls  tottime  cumtime
myapp.py:3(lighter)  ->      400    4.155    4.155  {time.sleep}

>>> p.print_callers('light')
   Ordered by: internal time
   List reduced from 8 to 2 due to restriction <'light'>

Function               was called by...
                            ncalls  tottime  cumtime
myapp.py:3(medium)   <-      400    0.004    4.159  myapp.py:9(heavy)
myapp.py:6(light)    <-      200    0.002    2.073  myapp.py:9(heavy)
```

Being able to sort the output allows working on different views to find the bottlenecks. For instance:

- When the number of calls is really high and makes most of the global time, the function or method is probably in a loop and an optimization might be tried to get it out.

- When one function is taking very long, a cache might be a good option if possible.

Another great way to visualize bottlenecks from profiling data is to transform them into diagrams. Gprof2Dot (http://code.google.com/p/jrfonseca/wiki/Gprof2Dot) can be used to turn profiler data into a dot graph. You can download this simple script from http://jrfonseca.googlecode.com/svn/trunk/gprof2dot/gprof2dot.py and use it on the stats as long as Graphviz (see http://www.graphviz.org/) is installed in your box:

```
$ wget http://jrfonseca.googlecode.com/svn/trunk/gprof2dot/
gprof2dot.py
$ python2.5 gprof2dot.py -f pstats myapp.stats | dot -Tpng -o output.png
```

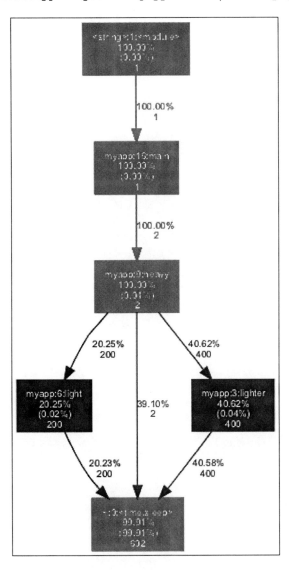

KcacheGrind is also a great vizualization tool to display profile data.
See `http://kcachegrind.sourceforge.net/cgi-bin/show.cgi`.

Macro-profiling is a good way to detect the function that has a problem, or at least its neighborhood. When you have found it, you can jump to micro-profiling.

Micro-Profiling

When the slow function is found, it is sometimes necessary to do more profiling work that tests just a part of the program. This is done by manually instrumenting a part of the code in a speed test.

For instance, the `cProfile` module can be used from a decorator:

```
>>> import tempfile, os, cProfile, pstats
>>> def profile(column='time', list=5):
...     def _profile(function):
...         def __profile(*args, **kw):
...             s = tempfile.mktemp()
...             profiler = cProfile.Profile()
...             profiler.runcall(function, *args, **kw)
...             profiler.dump_stats(s)
...             p = pstats.Stats(s)
...             p.sort_stats(column).print_stats(list)
...         return __profile
...     return _profile
...
>>> from myapp import main
>>> @profile('time', 6)
... def main_profiled():
...     return main()
...
>>> main_profiled()
Fri Jun 20 00:30:36 2008    ...
        1210 function calls in 10.129 CPU seconds
    Ordered by: internal time
    List reduced from 8 to 6 due to restriction <6>
    ncalls  tottime  cumtime  percall filename:lineno(function)
       602   10.118   10.118    0.017 {time.sleep}
         2    0.005   10.129    5.065 myapp.py:9(heavy)
       400    0.004    4.080    0.010 myapp.py:3(lighter)
       200    0.002    2.044    0.010 myapp.py:6(light)
         1    0.000   10.129   10.129 myapp.py:16(main)
         3    0.000    0.000    0.000 {range}
```

```
>>> from myapp import lighter
>>> p = profile() (lighter)
>>> p()
Fri Jun 20 00:32:40 2008    /var/folders/31/
31iTrMYWHny8cxfjH5VuTk+++TI/-Tmp-/tmpQjstAG

        3 function calls in 0.010 CPU seconds

   Ordered by: internal time

   ncalls  tottime  cumtime  percall filename:lineno(function)
        1    0.010    0.010    0.010 {time.sleep}
        1    0.000    0.010    0.010 myapp.py:3(lighter)
```

This approach allows testing parts of the application and sharpens the statistics output.

But at this stage, having a list of callees is probably not interesting, as the function has already been pointed out as the one to optimize. The only interesting information is to know how fast it is, and then enhance it.

timeit fits this need better by providing a simple way to measure the execution time of a small code snippet, with the best underlying timer the host system provides (time.time or time.clock):

```
>>> from myapp import light
>>> import timeit
>>> t = timeit.Timer('main()')
>>> t.timeit(number=5)
10000000 loops, best of 3: 0.0269 usec per loop
10000000 loops, best of 3: 0.0268 usec per loop
10000000 loops, best of 3: 0.0269 usec per loop
10000000 loops, best of 3: 0.0268 usec per loop
10000000 loops, best of 3: 0.0269 usec per loop
5.6196951866149902
```

The module allows to repeat the call, and is oriented to try out isolated code snippets. This is very useful outside the application context, in a prompt for instance, but is not really handy to use within an existing application.

A deterministic profiler will provide results depending on what the computer is doing, and so results may vary each time. Repeating the same test multiple times and making averages provides more accurate results. Furthermore, some computers have special CPU features, such as **SpeedStep**, that might change the results if the computer is idling when the test is launched (see http://en.wikipedia.org/wiki/SpeedStep). So continually repeating the test is a good practice for small code snippets. There are also various caches to keep in mind such as DNS caches or CPU caches.

A decorator similar to the one above is an easier way to time a part of an application. This decorator collects durations, though :

```
>>> import time
>>> import sys
>>> if sys.platform == 'win32':     # same condition in timeit
...     timer = time.clock
... else:
...     timer = time.time
>>> stats = {}
>>> def duration(name='stats', stats=stats):
...     def _duration(function):
...         def __duration(*args, **kw):
...             start_time = timer()
...             try:
...                 return function(*args, **kw)
...             finally:
...                 stats[name] = timer() - start_time
...         return __duration
...     return _duration
...
>>> from myapp import heavy
>>> heavy = duration('this_func_is')(heavy)
>>> heavy()
>>> print stats['this_func_is']
1.50201916695
```

The global `stats` dictionary is filled by the decorator when the code is executed, and can be read after the function has finished its work.

Using such a decorator allows to add inline instrumentation to the application code without disrupting the application itself.

```
>>> stats = {}
>>> from myapp import light
>>> import myapp
>>> myapp.light = duration('myapp.light')(myapp.light)
>>> myapp.main()
>>> stats
{'myapp.light': 0.05014801025390625}
```

This can be done in the context of speed tests.

Measuring Pystones

When measuring execution time, the result depends on the computer hardware. To be able to produce a universal measure, the simplest way is to benchmark the speed of a fixed sequence of code and calculate a ratio out of it. From there, the time taken by a function can be translated to a universal value that can be compared on any computer.

A lot of benchmarking tools are available. For instance, Whetstone was created in 1972 and back then, it provided a computer performance analyzer in Algol 60 (see http://en.wikipedia.org/wiki/ Whetstone_%28benchmark%29). It is used to measure the Millions Of Whetstone Instructions Per Second (MWIPS). A table of results is maintained at http://freespace.virgin.net/roy.longbottom/ whetstone%20results.htm.

Python provides a benchmark utility in its `test` package that measures the duration of a sequence of well-chosen operations. The result is a number of **pystones** per second the computer is able to perform, and the time used to perform the benchmark, which is generally around one second on modern hardware:

```
>>> from test import pystone
>>> pystone.pystones()
(1.0500000000000007, 47619.047619047589)
```

The rate can be used to translate a profile duration into a number of pystones:

```
>>> from test import pystone
>>> benchtime, pystones = pystone.pystones()
>>> def seconds_to_kpystones(seconds):
...     return (pystones*seconds) / 1000
...
...
>>> seconds_to_kpystones(0.03)
1.4563106796116512
>>> seconds_to_kpystones(1)
48.543689320388381
>>> seconds_to_kpystones(2)
97.087378640776762
```

The `seconds_to_kpystones` returns the number of **kilo pystones**. This conversion can be included in the `duration` decorator to yield a value in stones.

```
>>> def duration(name='stats', stats=stats):
...     def _duration(function):
...         def __duration(*args, **kw):
...             start_time = timer()
...             try:
...                 return function(*args, **kw)
...             finally:
...                 total = timer() - start_time
...                 kstones = seconds_to_kpystones(total)
...                 stats[name] = total, kstones
...         return __duration
...     return _duration
>>> @duration()
... def some_code():
...     time.sleep(0.5)
...
>>> some_code()
>>> stats
{'stats': (0.50012803077697754, 24.278059746455238)}
```

Having pystones will allow using this decorator in tests so that you can set assertions on execution times. These tests will be runnable on any computer and will allow developers to prevent speed regressions. When a part of the application has been optimized, they will be able to set its maximum execution time in tests and make sure it won't be breached by further changes.

Profiling Memory Usage

Another problems is memory consumption. If a program that runs starts to eat so much memory that the system swaps, there is probably a place in your application where too many objects are created. This is often easy to detect through classical profiling because consuming enough memory to make a system swap involves a lot of CPU work that can be detected. But sometimes it is not obvious, and the memory usage has to be profiled.

How Python Deals with Memory

Memory usage is probably the hardest thing to profile in Python when you use the CPython implementation. While languages such as C allow you to get the memory size of any element, Python will never let you know how much a given object consumes. This is due to the dynamic nature of the language, and the fact that there is an automatic management of object instantiation: the **garbage collector**. For instance, two variables that point to the same string value might or might not point to the same string-object instance in memory.

The approach of such a memory manager is roughly based on a simple statement: If a given object is not referenced anymore, it is removed. In other words, all local references in a function are removed after the interpreter leaves the function. If there's no more remaining reference to the object, it is removed from the memory as well.

- Makes sure the object is not being used anymore.

 Under normal conditions, the collector will do a nice job. But a del call can be used to help the garbage collector by manually removing the references to an object.

So objects that remain in memory are:

- Global objects
- Objects that are still referenced in some way

Be careful of the **argument inbound outbound** edge-case. If an object is created within the arguments, the argument reference will still be alive if the function returns the object. This can lead to unexpected results if it is used as a default value:

```
>>> def my_function(argument={}):    # bad practice
...     if '1' in argument:
...         argument['1'] = 2
...     argument['3'] = 4
...     return argument
...
>>> my_function()
{'3': 4}
>>> res = my_function()
>>> res['4'] = 'I am still alive!'
>>> print my_function()
{'3': 4, '4': 'I am still alive!'}
```

That is why non-mutable objects should always be used, like this:

```
>>> def my_function(argument=None):    # better practice
...     if argument is None:
...         argument = {}  # a fresh dict is created everytime
...     if '1' in argument:
...         argument['1'] = 2
...     argument['3'] = 4
```

```
...        return argument
...
>>> my_function()
{'3': 4}
>>> res = my_function()
>>> res['4'] = 'I am still alive!'
>>> print my_function()
{'3': 4}
```

Garbage collection is handy and avoids keeping track of objects and therefore we have to manually destroy them. Although this introduces another problem, since developers never clean up instances in memory, it might grow in an uncontrolled way if developers don't pay attention to the way they use data structure.

Usual memory eaters are:

- Caches that grow uncontrolled
- Object factories that register instances globally and do not keep track of their usage, such as a database connector creator, used on the fly every time a query is called
- Threads that are not properly finished
- Objects with a __del__ method and involved in a cycle are also memory eaters. The Python garbage collector will not break the cycle since it cannot be sure which object should be deleted first. Hence, you will leak memory. Using this method is a bad idea in any case.

Profiling Memory

Knowing how many objects are controlled by the garbage collector and their real size is a bit tricky. For instance, knowing how much a given object weighs in bytes would involve crawling down all its attributes, dealing with cross-references, and then summing up everything. It's a pretty difficult problem if you consider the way objects tend to refer to each other. The gc module does not provide high-level functions for this, and would require Python to be compiled in debug mode to have a full set of information.

Often, programmers just ask the system about the memory usage of their application after and before a given operation has been performed. But this measure is approximative and depends a lot on how the memory is managed at system level. Using the top command under Linux or the Task Manager under Windows, for instance, makes it possible to detect memory problems when they are obvious. But it requires painful work on the code side to track down the faulty code block.

Fortunately, there are a few tools available to make memory snapshots, and calculate the number and size of loaded objects. But let's keep in mind that Python does not release memory easily, and prefers to hold on to it in case it is needed again.

A Guppy-PE Primer

Guppy-PE (`http://guppy-pe.sourceforge.net`) is a framework that provides a memory profiler called `Heap`, among other features.

Guppy is `easy_install`-able:

```
$ sudo easy_install guppy
```

From there, an `hpy` function is available under the `guppy` namespace. It returns an object that knows how to display a snapshot of the memory:

```
>>> from guppy import hpy
>>> profiler = hpy()
>>> profiler.heap()
Partition of a set of 22723 objects. Total size = 1660748 bytes.
 Index   Count   %     Size   % Cumulative  % Kind (class / dict of
class)
      0    9948  44   775680  47    775680  47 str
      1    5162  23   214260  13    989940  60 tuple
      2    1404   6    95472   6   1085412  65 types.CodeType
      3      61   0    91484   6   1176896  71 dict of module
      4     152   1    84064   5   1260960  76 dict of type
      5    1333   6    79980   5   1340940  81 function
      6     168   1    72620   4   1413560  85 type
      7     119   1    68884   4   1482444  89 dict of class
      8      76   0    51728   3   1534172  92 dict (no owner)
      9     959   4    38360   2   1572532  95 __builtin__.wrapper_
descriptor
<43 more rows. Type e.g. '_.more' to view.>
```

The output provides memory usage ordered by size, and grouped by the type of objects. The object has many attributes to define how the list is displayed and is used for memory the way `pstats` is used with time.

We can measure how much a specific object weighs using the `iso` method:

```
>>> import random
>>> def eat_memory():
...     memory = []
...     def _get_char():
...         return chr(random.randint(97, 122))
...     for i in range(100):
```

```
...             size = random.randint(20, 150)
...             data = [_get_char() for i in xrange(size)]
...             memory.append(''.join(data))
...         return '\n'.join(memory)
...
>>> profiler.iso(eat_memory())
Partition of a set of 1 object. Total size = 8840 bytes.
 Index   Count   %     Size   % Cumulative  % Kind
     0       1 100     8840 100       8840 100 str
>>> profiler.iso(eat_memory()+eat_memory())
Partition of a set of 1 object. Total size = 17564 bytes.
 Index   Count   %     Size   % Cumulative  % Kind
     0       1 100    17564 100      17564 100 str
```

A `setrelheap` method is also available to reset the profiler, so that it can be used to track down the memory usage of an isolated block of code using `heap`. But this initialization is not perfect because the context will always have a few elements loaded. That is why the size of a freshly-initialized `hpy` instance varies a bit and is not 0:

```
>>> g = hpy()
>>> g.setrelheap()
>>> g.heap().size
1120
>>> g.heap().size
1200
>>> g.heap().size
1144
```

The `heap` method returns a `Usage` object that provides information such as:

- `size`: The total consumed size in bytes
- `get_rp()`: A nice traversal method that will tell where the object code is located in the modules.
- Many ways to sort the results, such as `bytype`

Tracking Memory Usage with Heapy

Heapy is not easy to use and needs a bit of practice. This section will just discuss some simple functions that can be used to provide memory usage information. From there, tracking down the code has to be done by browsing objects through the Heapy API.

The `pkgcore` project's website has a nice example on how Heapy was used to track down memory usage. See `http://www.pkgcore.org/trac/pkgcore/doc/dev-notes/heapy.rst`

It is a good starting point when playing with the tool.

The `duration` decorator (proposed earlier) can be changed to provide the size of the memory used by a function in bytes. This information can be retrieved with the duration and the pystone values, in a dictionary. The full decorator put in a `profiler.py` module looks like this:

```python
import time
import sys
from test import pystone
from guppy import hpy

benchtime, stones = pystone.pystones()

def secs_to_kstones(seconds):
    return (stones*seconds) / 1000

stats = {}
if sys.platform == 'win32':
    timer = time.clock
else:
    timer = time.time

def profile(name='stats', stats=stats):
    """Calculates a duration and a memory size."""
    def _profile(function):
        def __profile(*args, **kw):
            start_time = timer()
            profiler = hpy()
            profiler.setref()

            # 12 corresponds to the initial memory size
            # after a setref call
            start = profiler.heap().size + 12
            try:
                return function(*args, **kw)
            finally:
                total = timer() - start_time
                kstones = secs_to_kstones(total)
                memory = profiler.heap().size - start
                stats[name] = {'time': total,
                               'stones': kstones,
                               'memory': profiler.heap().size}
        return __profile
    return _profile
```

The `start` variable is used to make sure that the calculated memory does not include the memory consumed by Heapy when the `setrelheap` call is made.

Using the decorator with `eat_memory` will provide, besides the duration in seconds and pystones, the memory consumed by the function:

```
>>> import profiler
>>> import random
>>> eat_it = profiler.profile('you bad boy!')(eat_memory)
>>> please = eat_it()
>>> profiler.stats
{'you bad boy!': {'stones': 14.306935999128555, 'memory': 8680,
                                'time': 0.30902981758117676}}
```

Of course, running it several times will lead to different memory sizes when non-mutable objects are involved. But it is still a good indicator.

Another interesting usage of Heapy is to check if a function does not free the used memory, for instance if it produces cached or registered elements. This can be done by repeating function calls and observing whether the memory used grows:

A simple function for this can be:

```
>>> REPETITIONS = 100
>>> def memory_grow(function, *args, **kw):
...       """checks if a function makes the memory grow"""
...       profiler = hpy()
...       profiler.setref()
...       # 12 corresponds to the initial memory size
...       # after a setref call
...       start = profiler.heap().size + 12
...       for i in range(REPEAT):
...           function(*args, **kw)
...       return profiler.heap().size - start
...
>>> def stable():
...       return "some"*10000
...
>>> d = []
>>> def greedy():
...       for i in range(100):
...           d.append('garbage data'*i)
...
```

```
>>> memory_grow(stable)
24
>>> memory_grow(greedy)
5196468
```

C Code Memory Leaks

If the Python code seems perfectly fine and the memory still increases when you loop through the isolated function, the leak might be located on the C side. This happens for instance when a `Py_DECREF` call is missing.

The Python core code is pretty robust and tested for leaks. If you use packages that have C extensions, they might be a good place to look at first.

Profiling Network Usage

As I said earlier, an application that communicates with third-party programs such as a database or an LDAP server can be slowed down when those applications are slow. This can be tracked with a regular code profiling method on the application side. But if the third-party software works fine on its own, the culprit is probably the network.

The problem might be a misconfigured hub, a low-bandwidth network link, or even a high number of traffic collisions that makes computers send the same packets several times.

Here are a few elements to get you in. To find out what is going on, there are three fields to investigate:

- Watch the network traffic using tools such as:
    - ntop: `http://www.ntop.org` (Linux only)
    - wireshark: `www.wireshark.org` (previously name Ethereal)
- Track down unhealthy or misconfigured devices with `net-snmp` (`http://www.net-snmp.org`).
- Estimate the bandwidth between two computers using `Pathrate`, a statistical tool. See `http://www.cc.gatech.edu/fac/Constantinos.Dovrolis/pathrate.html`.

If you want to go further on network performance issues, you might also want to read *Network Performance Open Source Toolkit* by Richard Blum (Wiley). This book exposes strategies to tune the applications that are heavily using the network, and provides a tutorial to scan complex network problems.

High Performance MySQL by Jeremy Zawodny (O'Reilly) is also a good book to read when writing an application that uses MySQL.

Summary

We have seen in this chapter:

- The three rules of optimization:
  - Make it work first.
  - Take the user's point of view.
  - Keep the code readable.
- An optimization strategy based on writing a scenario with speed objectives.
- How to profile code memory, and a few tips for network profiling.

Now that you know how to find problems, the next chapter provides solutions to get rid of them.

13
Optimization: Solutions

Optimizing a program is not a magical process. It is done by following a simple process, synthesized by Stefan Schwarzer at Europython 2006 in an original pseudo-code example:

```
def optimize():
    """Recommended optimization"""
    assert got_architecture_right(), "fix architecture"
    assert made_code_work(bugs=None), "fix bugs"
    while code_is_too_slow():
        wbn = find_worst_bottleneck(just_guess=False,
                                    profile=True)
        is_faster = try_to_optimize(wbn,
                                    run_unit_tests=True,
                                    new_bugs=None)
        if not is_faster:
            undo_last_code_change()
# By Stefan Schwarzer, Europython 2006
```

This chapter presents some solutions to optimize your program through:

- Reducing the complexity
- Multithreading
- Multiprocessing
- Caching

Reducing the Complexity

There are many definitions of what makes a program complex, and many ways to express it. But at the code level, where we want to make an isolated sequence of statements faster, there is a limited number of techniques to quickly detect the lines that are guilty in a bottleneck.

The two main techniques are:

- Measuring the **cyclomatic complexity** of the code
- Measuring the Landau notation also called **Big-O notation**

From there, the optimization process will consist of reducing the complexity so that the code is fast enough. This section provides simple tips for this work by simplifying loops. But first of all, let's learn how to measure complexity.

Measuring Cyclomatic Complexity

Cyclomatic complexity is a metric introduced by McCabe that measures the number of linear paths through the code. All `if`, `for`, and `while` loops are counted to come up with a measure.

The code can then be categorized as follows:

Cyclomatic Complexity	What it means
1 to 10	Not complex
11 to 20	Moderately complex
21 to 50	Really complex
More than 50	Too complex

In Python, this can be done automatically by parsing the **AST (Abstract Syntax Tree)**see `http://en.wikipedia.org/wiki/Abstract_Syntax_Tree`. The `PyMetrics` project from Reg Charney (`http://sourceforge.net/projects/pymetrics`) provides a nice script to calculate the cyclomatic complexity.

Measuring the Big-O Notation

The complexity of a function can be expressed by the Big-O notation (see `http://en.wikipedia.org/wiki/Big_O_notation`). This metric defines how an algorithm is affected by the size of the input data. For instance, does the algorithm scale linearly with the size of the input data or quadratically?

Calculating the Big-O notation manually for an algorithm is the best approach to optimize your code, as it gives you the ability to detect and focus on the parts that will really slow down the code.

To measure the Big-O notation, all constants and low-order terms are removed in order to focus on the portion that really weights when the input data grows. The idea is to try to categorize the algorithm in one of these categories, even if it is approximative :

Notation	Type
O(1)	Constant. Does not depend on the input data.
O(n)	Linear. Will grow as "n" grows.
O(n log n)	Quasi linear
$O(n^2)$	Quadratic complexity
$O(n^3)$	Cubic complexity
...	...
O(n!)	Factorial complexity

For instance, a `dict` look up is O(1) (pronounced "order 1") and is considered constant regardless of how many elements are in the `dict`, whereas looking through a list of items for a particular item is O(n).

Let's take another example:

```
>>> def function(n):
...     for i in range(n):
...         print i
...
```

In that case, the loop speed will depend on "n", and the Big-O notation will be O(n).

If the function has conditions, the notation to keep is the highest one:

```
>>> def function(n):
...     if some_test:
...         print 'something'
...     else:
...         for i in range(n):
...             print i
...
```

In this example, the function can be O(1) or O(n), depending on the test. So the worst case is O(n), which is the notation to keep.

Let's take another example:

```
>>> def function(n):
...     for i in range(n):
...         for j in range(n):
...             print i, j
...
```

A nested loop introduces a quadratic complexity $O(n^2)$, which is very expensive when n is big.

Of course the notation needs to introspect the called functions:

```
>>> def function(n):
...     for i in range(n):
...         print i
...
>>> def other_function(n):
...     if some_test:
...         for i in range(n):
...             function(n)
...     else:
...         function(n)
...
```

The other_function is either calling function, which has O(n) complexity, or else calling it in a loop that has O(n) complexity, so the worst case is O(n*n): $O(n^2)$.

As said earlier, constants and low-order terms should be removed when calculating the notation because they don't really matter when data size is getting big:

```
>>> def function(n):
...     for i in range(n*2):
...         print i
...
```

This function is O(n*2), but since constants are removed we just say O(n).
That said, this simplification should be kept in mind when you are comparing several algorithms.

Be careful, for although we usually assume that an $O(n^2)$ (quadratic) function will be faster than an $O(n^3)$ (cubic) function, this may not always be the case. Sometimes, for smaller values of n, the cubic function is faster, while for larger values of n the quadratic function catches up and is faster. For instance $O(100*n^2)$ that is simplified to $O(n^2)$ is not necessarily faster than $O(5*n^3)$ that corresponds to $O(n^3)$. That is why you should optimize once profiling has shown where to do it.

If you want to practice on Big-O, you can exercise on `http://pages.cs.wisc.edu/`
`~hasti/cs367-common/notes/4.COMPLEXITY.html#bigO`.

> The Big-O notation is a great way to improve your algorithms, but beware that:
>
> • Its calculation implies approximation.
>
> • It's accurate only for pure Python code, which does not depend on external resources.
>
> When you are unable to calculate the complexity of an algorithm, for instance if it has C code that is not easy to dig, switch on tools such as `timeit` or the profile decorator that was presented in the previous chapter, with enough input data to test the algorithm's efficiency.

Simplifying

To reduce the complexity of an algorithm, the way data is stored is fundamental. You should pick your data structure carefully. This section provides a few examples.

Searching in a List

If you need to provide a search algorithm for a list instance, a binary search over a sorted version will reduce the complexity from O(n) to O(log n). The `bisect` module can be used for this since, given a value, it uses a binary search to return the next insertion index for a sorted sequence:

```
>>> def find(seq, el):
...     pos = bisect(seq, el)
...     if pos==0 or (pos==len(seq) and seq[-1]!=el):
...         return -1
...     return pos - 1
...
>>> seq = [2, 3, 7, 8, 9]
>>> find(seq, 9)
4
>>> find(seq, 10)
-1
>>> find(seq, 0)
-1
>>> find(seq, 7)
2
```

Of course, this means that either the list is already sorted or you need to sort it. On the other hand, if you already have a sorted list, you can also insert new items into that list using `bisect` without needing to re-sort the list (i.e. insertion sort; see `http://en.wikipedia.org/wiki/Insertion_sort`).

Using a Set Instead of a List

When you need to build a sequence of distinct values out of a given sequence, the first algorithm that comes in mind is:

```
>>> seq = ['a', 'a', 'b', 'c', 'c', 'd']
>>> res = []
>>> for el in seq:
...       if el not in res:
...            res.append(el)
...
>>> res
['a', 'b', 'c', 'd']
```

The complexity is introduced by the lookup in the `res` list with the `in` operator that costs at the most O(n). It is then called in the global loop, which costs O(n). So the complexity is mostly quadratic.

Using a `set` type for the same work will be faster because the stored values are looked up using hashes such as in the `dict` type. In other words, for each value in `seq`, the time taken to see if it is already in the `set` will be constant:

```
>>> seq = ['a', 'a', 'b', 'c', 'c', 'd']
>>> res = set(seq)
>>> res
set(['a', 'c', 'b', 'd'])
```

This lowers the complexity to *O(n)*.

Of course, this assumes that the rest of the algorithm can use a `set` object, which ignores duplicates.

When you try to reduce the complexity of an algorithm, carefully consider your data structures. There are a range of built-in types, so pick the right one.

It is often better to transform your data before the algorithm is called than to try changing the algorithm to make it faster on the original data.

Cut the External Calls, Reduce the Workload

Part of the complexity is introduced by calls to other functions, methods, classes. In general, get as much of the code out of loops as possible. This is doubly important for nested loops. Don't recalculate those things over and over inside a loop that can be calculated before the loop even begins. Inner loops should be tight.

Using Collections

The collection module provides alternatives to built-in container types. They are available in three types:

- `deque`: A list-like type with extra features
- `defaultdict`: A dict-like type with a built-in default factory feature
- `namedtuple`: A tuple-like type that assigns keys for members (2.6 only)

deque

A `deque` is an alternative implementation for lists. Whereas a list is based on arrays, a `deque` is based on a doubly linked list. Hence, a `deque` is much faster when you need to insert something into its middle or head, but much slower when you need to access an arbitrary index. Of course, modern hardware does memory copies so quickly that the downsides of a list aren't as severe as one might imagine. So be sure to profile your code before switching from a list to a `deque`.

For example, if you want to remove two elements of a sequence located at a given position without creating a second list instance, by using a slice, a `deque` object will be faster:

```
>>> from pbp.scripts.profiler import profile, stats
>>> from collections import deque
>>> my_list = range(100000)
>>> my_deque = deque(range(100000))
>>> @profile('by_list')
... def by_list():
...     my_list[500:502] = []
...
>>> @profile('by_deque')
... def by_deque():
...     my_deque.rotate(500)
...     my_deque.pop()
...     my_deque.pop()
...     my_deque.rotate(-500)
...
```

```
...
>>> by_list();by_deque()
>>> print stats['by_list']
{'stones': 47.836141152815379, 'memory': 396,
 'time': 1.0523951053619385}
>>> print stats['by_deque']
{'stones': 19.198688593777742, 'memory': 552,
 'time': 0.4223711490631035}
```

deque also provides more efficient append and pop methods that work at the same speed from both ends of the sequence. This makes it a perfect type for queues.

For example, a **FIFO (First In First Out)** queue will be much more efficient with a deque:

```
>>> from collections import deque
>>> from pbp.scripts.profiler import profile, stats
>>> import sys
>>> queue = deque()
>>> def d_add_data(data):
...     queue.appendleft(data)
...
>>> def d_process_data():
...     queue.pop()
...
>>> BIG_N = 1000000
>>> @profile('deque')
... def sequence():
...     for i in range(BIG_N):
...         d_add_data(i)
...     for i in range(BIG_N/2):
...         d_process_data()
...     for i in range(BIG_N):
...         d_add_data(i)
...
>>> lqueue = []
>>> def l_add_data(data):
...     lqueue.append(data)
...
>>> def l_process_data():
...     lqueue.pop(-1)
...
>>> @profile('list')
... def lsequence():
...     for i in range(BIG_N):
```

```
...              l_add_data(i)
...          for i in range(BIG_N/2):
...              l_process_data()
...          for i in range(BIG_N):
...              l_add_data(i)
...
>>> sequence(); lsequence()
>>> print stats['deque']
{'stones': 86.521963988031672, 'memory': 17998920, 'time':
1.9380919933319092}
>>> print stats['list']
{'stones': 222.34191851956504, 'memory': 17994312, 'time':
4.9804589748382568}
```

 Python 2.6 provides new useful queue classes such as a LIFO queue (LifoQueue) and a priority queue (PriorityQueue) in the Queue module (which has been renamed to queue in Python 3k).

defaultdict

The defaultdict type is similar to the dict type, but adds a default factory for new keys. This avoids writing an extra test to initialize the mapping entry, and is more efficient than the dict.setdefault method.

The Python documentation provides a usage example for this feature, which runs almost three times faster than dict.setdefault:

```
>>> from collections import defaultdict
>>> from pbp.scripts.profiler import profile, stats
>>> s = [('yellow', 1), ('blue', 2), ('yellow', 3),
...        ('blue', 4), ('red', 1)]
>>> @profile('defaultdict')
... def faster():
...     d = defaultdict(list)
...     for k, v in s:
...         d[k].append(v)
...
...
>>> @profile('dict')
... def slower():
...     d = {}
...     for k, v in s:
...         d.setdefault(k, []).append(v)
...
>>> slower(); faster()
```

```
>>> stats['dict']
{'stones': 16.587882671716077, 'memory': 396,
 'time': 0.35166311264038086}
>>> stats['defaultdict']
{'stones': 6.5733464259021686, 'memory': 552,
 'time': 0.13935494422912598}
```

The defaultdict type takes a factory as a parameter, and can therefore be used with built-in types or classes whose constructor does not take arguments:

```
>>> lg = defaultdict(long)
>>> lg['one']
0L
```

namedtuple

namedtuple is a class factory that takes a type name and a list of attributes, and creates a class out of it. The class can then be used to instantiate a tuple-like object and provide accessors for its elements:

```
>>> from collections import namedtuple
>>> Customer = namedtuple('Customer',
...                       'firstname lastname')
>>> c = Customer(u'Tarek', u'Ziadé')
>>> c.firstname
u'Tarek'
```

It can be used to create records that are easier to write, compared to a custom class that would require some boiler-plate code to initialize values. The generated class can be subclassed to add more operations.

Reducing the complexity is done by storing the data in an efficient data structure that works well with the way the algorithm will use it.

That said, when the solution is not obvious, you should consider dropping and re-writing the incriminated part instead of killing the code readability for the sake of performance.

Often, the Python code can be readable and fast. So try to find a good way to perform the work instead of trying to work around a flawed design.

Multithreading

Threading is often considered to be a complex topic by developers. While this statement is totally true, Python provides high-level classes and functions that ease the usage of threading for the specific use cases this section will present.

To summarize this section, threading should be considered when some tasks can be performed in the background while the main program is doing something else.

What is Multithreading?

A thread is short for a thread of execution. A programmer can split his or her work into threads that run simultaneously and share the same memory context. Unless your code depends on third-party resources, multi-threading will not speed it up on a mono-processor machine, and will even add some overhead for thread management. Multi-threading will benefit from a multiprocessor or multi-core machine and will parallelize each thread execution on each CPU, thus making the program faster.

The fact that the same context is shared among threads means you must protect data from concurrent accesses. If two threads update the same data without any protection, and if the data remains in inconsistent state, a race condition may occur. This is called a **race hazard**, where unexpected results happen because of the code run by each thread making false assumptions about the state of the data.

Lock mechanisms help in protecting data, and thread programming has always been a matter of making sure that the resources are accessed by threads in a safe way. This can be quite hard and thread programming often leads to bugs that are hard to debug, since they are hard to reproduce. The worst problem occurs when, due to a wrong code design, two threads lock a resource and try to get the resource that the other thread has locked. They will wait for each other forever. This is called a **deadlock** and is quite hard to debug. **Reentrant locks** help a bit in this by making sure a thread doen't get locked by attempting to lock a resource twice.

Nevertheless, when threads are used for isolated needs with tools that were built for them, they may increase the speed of programs.

Multithreading is often implemented at the kernel level. When the machine has one single processor with a single core, the system uses a **timeslicing** mechanism. Here, the CPU switches from one thread to another so fast that there is an illusion of parallelization. This is done at the processing level as well. On multiprocessor or multi-core machines, even if timeslicing is used, processes and threads are distributed among CPUs making the program really fast.

How Python Deals with Threads

Unlike some other languages, Python uses multiple kernel-level threads that can each run any of the interpreter-level threads. However, all threads accessing Python objects are serialized by one global lock. This is done because much of the interpreter code as well as third-party C code is not thread-safe and need to be protected.

This mechanism is called the **Global Interpreter Lock (GIL)** and some developers have started to ask for its removal from Python 3k. But, as Guido stated, this would involve too much work and make Python implementation more complex. So the GIL stays.

Stackless Python or **Stackless** is an experimental implementation of the Python programming language, so named because it avoids depending on the C call stack for its stack. The language supports generators, micro-threads, and coroutines, and provides the benefits of thread-based programming without the performance and complexity problems associated with conventional threads.

See: http://www.stackless.com.

Although some developers are frustrated by this limitation, many developers understand the fundamental difficulty of doing multithreaded programming correctly. Hence, many Python programmers will often opt to use multiple processes instead of multiple threads. Because processes have separate memory contexts, they aren't quite as susceptible to data corruption as threads are.

So what is the point of multithreading in Python?

When threads contain only pure Python code, there is no point in using threads to speed up the program since the GIL will serialize it. However, multiple threads can do IO operations or execute C code in certain third-party extensions parallelly.

For non-pure code blocks where external resources are used or C code involved, multithreading is useful to wait for a third-party resource to return results. This is because a sleeping thread that has explicitly unlocked the GIL can stand by and wake up when results are back. Last, whenever a program needs to provide a responsive interface, multithreading is the answer even if it uses timeslicing. The program can interact with the user while doing some heavy computing in the so-called background.

See Shannon Behrens article on Dr Dobb's on concurrency for more details: http://ddj.com/linux-open-source/206103078.

The next section tries to cover common use cases.

When Should Threading Be Used?

Despite the GIL limitation, threads can be really useful in some cases. They can help in:

- Building responsive interfaces
- Delegating work
- Building multi-user applications

Building Responsive Interfaces

Let's say you ask your system to copy files from a folder to another through a graphical user interface. The task will possibly be pushed into the background and the windows will be constantly refreshed by the main thread, so you get live feedback on the operation. You will also be able to cancel the operation. This is less irritating than a raw `cp` or `copy` command that does not provide any feedback until the whole work is finished, and that has to be stopped through a *Ctrl+C*.

A responsive interface also allows a user to work on several tasks. For instance, Gimp will let you play around with a picture while another one is being filtered, since the two tasks are independent.

 When you are building a user interface, try to push long running tasks into the background, or at least try to provide constant feedback to the user.

Delegating Work

If your process depends on third-party resources, threads might really speed up everything.

Let's take the case of a function that indexes files in a folder and pushes the built indexes into a database. Depending on the type of file, the function calls a different external program. One is specialized in PDF and another one in OpenOffice files, for example.

Instead of treating each file in a sequence, by calling the right program and then storing the result into the database, your function can set up a thread for each converter and push jobs to be done to each one of them through a queue. The overall time taken by the function will be closer to the slowest converter than to the sum of all the work.

This consumers-producer pattern is often used to provide a shared space for threads, and will be presented in this chapter.

Converter threads can be initialized from the start and the code in charge of pushing the result into the database can also be a thread that consumes available results in the queue.

Multi-User Applications

Threading is also used as a design pattern for multi-user applications. For instance, a web server will push a user request into a new thread and then will idle, waiting for new requests. Having a thread dedicated to each request simplifies a lot of work, but requires the developer to take care of locking the resources. But this is not a problem when all shared data is pushed into a relational database that takes care of the concurrency matters. So threads in a multi-user application act almost like a process and are under the same process only to ease their management at the application level.

For instance, a web server will be able to put all requests in a queue and wait for a thread to be available to send the work to it. Furthermore, it allows memory sharing that can boost up some work and reduce the memory load.

Using processes costs more resources since it loads a new interpreter for each one. Sharing data between processes also requires more work.

Consider using threads for any multi-user application.

The **Twisted** framework, which comes with a callback-based programming philosophy, has ready-to-use patterns for server programming.

Last, **eventlet** (see http://wiki.secondlife.com/wiki/Eventlet) is another interesting approach, probably simpler than Twisted.

Simple Example

Let's take a small example of an application that recursively scans a directory to process text files. Each text file is opened and processed by an external converter. Using threads will possibly make it faster because the indexation work can be done simultaneously on several files.

The external converter is a small Python program that does some complex work:

```
#!/usr/bin/python
for i in range(100000):
    i = str(i) + "y"*10000
```

This script saved into `converter.py` takes around 25 kpystones, which is around half a second on a MacBook Intel Core Duo 2.

In a multi-threaded solution, the main program deals with a pool of threads. Each thread takes its work from a queue. In this use case, threads are called **workers**. The queue is the shared resource where the main program adds files it has found walking in the directory. The workers take the files out of the queue and process them.

The `Queue` module (which will be renamed `queue` in Python 3k) from the standard library is the perfect class for our program. It provides a multi-consumer, multi-producer FIFO queue that internally uses a `deque` instance and is thread-safe.

So if we want to process files that are in that queue, we just use the `get` method together with `task_done`, which lets the `Queue` instance know that the task has to be finished for `join` to work:

```
>>> from Queue import Queue
>>> import logging
>>> import time
>>> import subprocess
>>> q = Queue()
>>> def index_file(filename):
...     logging.info('indexing %s' % filename)
...     f = open(filename)
...     try:
...         content = f.read()
...         # the content is not used in our example
...         # external process is here
...         subprocess.call(['converter.py'])
...         time.sleep(0.5)
...     finally:
...         f.close()
...
>>> def worker():
...     while True:
...         index_file(q.get())
...         q.task_done()
...
```

The `worker` function, which will be called through a thread, takes file names from the queue and processes them by calling the `index_file` function. The `sleep` call simulates the process done by an external program, and makes the thread wait for the results, and therefore unlock the GIL.

The main program can then launch workers, scan for files to be processed, and feed the queue with them.

This is done by creating `Thread` instances with the `worker` method. The `setDaemon` is necessary so that the threads automatically get shut down when the program exits. Otherwise, the program would hang forever waiting for them to exit. This can be manually managed but it is not useful here.

At the end of the `index_files` function, the `join` method will wait for the queue to be fully processed.

Let's create a full script called `indexer.py` that runs a multithreaded version, and a single thread to index a directory structure containing text files:

```
from threading import Thread
import os
import subprocess
from Queue import Queue
import logging
import time
import sys
from pbp.scripts.profiler import profile, print_stats
dirname = os.path.realpath(os.path.dirname(__file__))
CONVERTER = os.path.join(dirname, 'converter.py')

q = Queue()

def index_file(filename):
    f = open(filename)
    try:
        content = f.read()
        # process is here
        subprocess.call([CONVERTER])
    finally:
        f.close()

def worker():
    while True:
        index_file(q.get())
        q.task_done()

def index_files(files, num_workers):
    for i in range(num_workers):
        t = Thread(target=worker)
        t.setDaemon(True)
        t.start()
    for file in files:
        q.put(file)
    q.join()

def get_text_files(dirname):
    for root, dirs, files in os.walk(dirname):
        for file in files:
            if os.path.splitext(file)[-1] != '.txt':
```

```
                continue
            yield os.path.join(root, file)
@profile('process')
def process(dirname, numthreads):
    dirname = os.path.realpath(dirname)
    if numthreads > 1:
        index_files(get_text_files(dirname), numthreads)
    else:
        for f in get_text_files(dirname):
            index_file(f)
if __name__ == '__main__':
    process(sys.argv[1], int(sys.argv[2]))
    print_stats()
```

This script can be used with any directory as long as it contains text files. It takes two parameters:

1. The name of the directory
2. The number of threads

When name of the directory is used alone, no threads are launched and the directory is processed in the main thread.

Let's run it on the same MacBook, on a directory containing 36 files with 19 text files. The directory is composed of a structure of 6 directories:

```
$ python indexer.py zc.buildout-1.0.6-py2.5.egg 1
process : 301.83 kstones, 6.821 secondes, 396 bytes

$ python indexer.py zc.buildout-1.0.6-py2.5.egg 2
process : 155.28 kstones, 3.509 secondes, 2496 bytes

$python indexer.py zc.buildout-1.0.6-py2.5.egg 4
process : 150.42 kstones, 3.369 secondes, 4584 bytes

$python indexer.py zc.buildout-1.0.6-py2.5.egg 8
process : 153.96 kstones, 3.418 secondes, 8760 bytes

$python indexer.py zc.buildout-1.0.6-py2.5.egg 12
process : 154.18 kstones, 3.454 secondes, 12948 bytes

$python indexer.py zc.buildout-1.0.6-py2.5.egg 24
process : 161.84 kstones, 3.593 secondes, 25524 bytes
```

It appears that two threads are twice as fast as one thread and that adding more threads is not changing anything. Twenty-four threads are even a bit slower than 12 threads, due to the overhead.

These results may vary depending on the number of files since the disk access is also adding some overhead. But we can safely say that multithreading made the code two times faster, when used on a dual-core.

Multithreading should be used to build responsive interfaces and to delegate some work to third-party applications.

Since memory is shared, the danger of data corruption and race conditions is always present. This danger is greatly mitigated if you use the queue module as the only way for the threads to communicate and pass data to one another.

It's a reasonable policy to never let two threads touch the same mutable data.

Multiprocessing

The GIL limitation makes it impossible to speed up programs that make heavy use of pure Python that is CPU bound. The only way to achieve it is to use separate processes. This is usually done by **forking** the program at some point. A fork is a system call available through os.fork, which will create a new child process. The two processes then continue the program in their own right after the forking:

```
>>> import os
>>> a = []
>>> def some_work():
...     a.append(2)
...     child_pid = os.fork()
...     if child_pid == 0:
...         a.append(3)
...         print "hey, I am the child process"
...         print "my pid is %d" % os.getpid()
...         print str(a)
...     else:
...         a.append(4)
...         print "hey, I am the parent"
...         print "the child is pid %d" % child_pid
...         print "I am the pid %d " % os.getpid()
...         print str(a)
...
>>> some_work()
```

```
hey, I am the parent
the child is pid 25513
I am the pid 25411
[2, 4]
hey, I am the child process
my pid is 25513
[2, 3]
```

 Be careful: Running this example at the prompt will lead to a messed-up session.

The memory context is also copied at the fork and then each process deals with its own address space. To communicate, processes need to work with system-wide resources or use low-level tools like **signals**.

Unfortunately, os.fork is not available under Windows, where a new interpreter needs to be spawned in order to mimic the fork feature. So the code may vary depending on the platform.

When the processes are created, they might need to communicate. If the processes are used to do some isolated job using a relational database (for instance), a shared space is usually the best pick.

Working with signals is painful. Shared memory, pipes, or sockets are simpler to work with. This is usually the case when processes are not one-shot workers, but rather interactive.

There is one library that makes processing really easy to deal with: pyprocessing.

Pyprocessing

pyprocessing provides a portable way to work with processes as if they were threads.

To install it, look for processing with easy_install:

$ easy_install processing

The tool provides a Process class that is very similar to the Thread class, and can be used on any platform:

```
>>> from processing import Process
>>> import os
>>> def work():
...     print 'hey i am a process, id: %d' % os.getpid()
...
```

```
>>> ps = []
>>> for i in range(4):
...     p = Process(target=work)
...     ps.append(p)
...     p.start()
...
hey i am a process, id: 27457
hey i am a process, id: 27458
hey i am a process, id: 27460
hey i am a process, id: 27459
>>> ps
[<Process(Process-1, stopped)>, <Process(Process-2, stopped)>,
<Process(Process-3, stopped)>, <Process(Process-4, stopped)>]
>>> for p in ps:
...     p.join()
...
```

When the processes are created, the memory is forked. The most efficient usage of processes is to let them work on their own after they have been created to avoid overhead, and check on their states from the main thread. Besides the memory state that is copied, the Process class also provides an extra `args` argument in its constructor so that data can be passed along.

`pyprocessing` also provides a queue-like class that can be used to share data among processes in a shared memory space fully managed by the package.

> `processing.sharedctypes` also provides functions to share objects from `ctypes` amongst processes.
>
> See `http://pyprocessing.berlios.de/doc/sharedctypes.html`.

The previous worker example can, therefore, use processes instead of threads as long as the `Queue` instance is replaced by a `processing.Queue` one.

Another nice feature of `pyprocessing` is the `Pool` class that automatically generates and manages a collection of workers. If not provided, the number of workers will be the same as that of the number of CPUs available on the computer, given by the `cpuCount` API:

```
>>> import processing
>>> import Queue
>>> print 'this machine has %d CPUs' \
...        % processing.cpuCount()
this machine has 2 CPUs
```

```
>>> def worker():
...     file = q.get_nowait()
...     return 'worked on ' + file
...
>>> q = processing.Queue()
>>> pool = processing.Pool()
>>> for i in ('f1', 'f2', 'f3', 'f4', 'f5'):
...     q.put(i)
...
>>> while True:
...     try:
...         result = pool.apply_async(worker)
...         print result.get(timeout=1)
...     except Queue.Empty:
...         break
...
worked on f1
worked on f2
worked on f3
worked on f4
worked on f5
```

The `apply_async` method will call the `worker` function through the pool, and immediately return a result object that can be used by the main process to get back the result. The `get` method can be used to wait for a result with a timeout.

Last, an `Array` and a `Value` class provide shared memory spaces. However, their usage should be avoided by design since they introduce bottlenecks in the parallelization, and increase code complexity.

> The `pyprocessing` website has a lot of code examples that are worth a read to reuse this package in your programs. By the time this book was written, this package was claimed on python-dev to become part of the standard library, and this should be effective in the 2.7 series. So `pyprocessing` is definitely the recommended multiprocessing tool.

Caching

The result of a function or a method that is expensive to run can be cached as long as:

- The function is deterministic and results have the same value every time, given the same input.

- The return value of the function continues to be useful and valid for some period of time (non-deterministic).

A deterministic function always returns the same result for the same set of arguments, whereas a non-deterministic one returns results that may vary.

Good candidates for caching are usually:

- Results from callables that query databases
- Results from callables that render static values, like file content, web requests, or PDF rendering
- Results from deterministic callables that perform complex calculations
- Global mappings that keep track of values with expiration times, like web session objects
- Some data that needs to be accessed often and quickly

Deterministic Caching

A simple example of deterministic caching is a function that calculates a square. Keeping track of the results allows you to speed it up:

```
>>> import random, timeit
>>> from pbp.scripts.profiler import profile, print_stats
>>> cache = {}
>>> def square(n):
...     return n * n
...
>>> @profile('not cached')
... def factory_calls():
...     for i in xrange(100):
...         square(random.randint(1, 10))
...
>>> def cached_factory(n):
...     if n not in cache:
...         cache[n] = square(n)
...     return cache[n]
...
>>> @profile('cached')
... def cached_factory_calls():
...     n = [random.randint(1, 10) for i in range(100)]
...     ns = [cached_factory(i) for i in n]
...
>>> factory_calls(); cached_factory_calls();
>>> print_stats()
not cached : 20.51 kstones, 0.340 secondes, 396 bytes
cached : 6.07 kstones, 0.142 secondes, 480 bytes
```

Of course, such a caching is efficient as long as the time taken to interact with the cache is less than the time taken by the function. If it's faster to simply re-calculate the value, by all means do so! Also caches can be dangerous if used incorrectly. For instance, you might end up using stale data, or you might end up gobbling memory with an ever larger cache.

That's why setting up a cache has to be done only if it's worth it; setting it up properly has a cost.

In the preceding example, we used an argument to the function as key for the cache. This only works if the arguments are hashable. For instance, this works with `int` and `str`, but not with `dict`. When arguments are getting complex and are not necessarily hashable, they have to be manually processed and translated into a unique key used for the cache:

```
>>> def cache_me(a, b, c, d):
...     # we don't care about d for the key
...     key = 'cache_me:::%s:::%s:::%s' % (a, b, c)
...     if key not in cache:
...         print 'caching'
...         cache[key] = complex_calculation(a, b, c, d)
...     print d    # d is just use for display
...     return cache[key]
...
```

It is possible, of course, to automatically create the key by looping over each argument. But there are many special cases where we will need to calculate the key manually, as in the example above.

This behavior is called **memoizing** and can be turned into a simple decorator:

```
>>> cache = {}
>>> def get_key(function, *args, **kw):
...     key = '%s.%s:' % (function.__module__,
...                       function.__name__)
...     hash_args = [str(arg) for arg in args]
...     # of course, will work only if v is hashable
...     hash_kw = ['%s:%s' % (k, hash(v))
...                for k, v in kw.items()]
...     return '%s::%s::%s' % (key, hash_args, hash_kw)
...
>>> def memoize(get_key=get_key, cache=cache):
...     def _memoize(function):
...         def __memoize(*args, **kw):
...             key = get_key(function, *args, **kw)
```

```
...                 try:
...                     return cache[key]
...                 except KeyError:
...                     cache[key] = function(*args, **kw)
...                     return value
...             return __memoize
...         return _memoize
...
...
>>> @memoize()
... def factory(n):
...     return n * n
...
>>> factory(4)
16
>>> factory(4)
16
>>> factory(3)
9
>>> cache
{"__main__.factory:::['3']::[]": 9,
 "__main__.factory:::['4']::[]": 16}
```

The decorator uses a callable to calculate a key, and a default `get_key` does argument introspection. It will raise an exception if the keyword argument is not hashable. Nevertheless, this function can be adapted to special cases. The mapping that stores values is also made configurable.

A common practice is to calculate the **MD5** hash (or **SHA**) of arguments. But beware that such a hash has a real cost, and the function itself needs to be slower than the key calculation for the cache to be useful. For our `factory` function, it is barely the case:

```
>>> import md5
>>> def get_key(function_called, n):
...     return md5.md5(str(n)).hexdigest()
...
>>> @memoize(get_key)
... def cached_factory(n):
...     return n * n
...
>>> factory_calls(); cached_factory_calls();
>>> print_stats()
cached : 6.96 kstones, 0.143 secondes, 1068 bytes
not cached : 7.61 kstones, 0.157 secondes, 552 bytes
```

Non-Deterministic Caching

Non-deterministic functions are functions that may produce a different output even when given the same input. For example, database queries are sometimes cached for a given amount of time. For instance, if an SQL table holds information on users, caching queries for all functions that display user data is a good practice, as long as this table is not updated often. Another example is a server configuration file that does not change after the server has started. Putting those values in a cache is a good practice. Many servers can be sent a signal as a sign that they should clear their cache and re-read their configuration files. Last, a web server will probably cache complete pages and the logo used on all page headers for at least a few hours, using a cache server such as SQUID. In the logo case, the client-side browser also maintains a local cache as well but deals with SQUID to know if the logo has been modified.

 The cache duration is set according to the average update time of the data.

The `memoize` cache can have an extra `age` argument in order to invalidate cached values that are too old:

```
def memoize(get_key=get_key, storage=cache, age=0):
    def _memoize(function):
        def __memoize(*args, **kw):
            key = get_key(function, *args, **kw)
            try:
                value_age, value = storage[key]
                expired = (age != 0 and
                              (value_age+age) < time.time())
            except KeyError:
                expired = True

            if not expired:
                return value
            storage[key] = time.time(), function(*args, **kw)
            return storage[key][1]
        return __memoize
    return _memoize
```

Let's say we have a function that displays the current time. Dropping the seconds, we can cache it with a 30 seconds age to get a reasonably accurate cache:

```
>>> from datetime import datetime
>>> @memoize(age=30)
... def what_time():
...     return datetime.now().strftime('%H:%M')
```

```
...
>>> what_time()
'19:36'
>>> cache
{'__main__.what_time:::[]::[]': (1212168961.613435, '19:36')}
```

Of course, the cache invalidation could be done asynchronously by another function that removes expired keys to speed up the memoize function. This is common for web applications that need to occasionally expire old sessions.

Pro-Active Caching

There are a lot of caching strategies to speed up an application. For instance, if an intranet gets a high load every morning from its users who read the news posted the previous afternoon, it makes sense to cache the results of rendering the articles so that they don't have to be rendered for every new web request. A good caching strategy would be to mimic these users once at night time through a cron job, to fill the cache with data with a maximum age of 12 hours.

Memcached

If you want to be serious about caching, Memcached (see http://www.danga.com/memcached) is the tool you would want to use. This cache server is used by big applications such as Facebook or Wikipedia to scale their websites. Among simple caching features, it has clustering capabilities that makes it possible to set up a very efficiently distributed cache system in no time.

The tool is Unix-based, but can be driven from any platform and from many languages. The Python client is really simple and our memoize function can be adapted to work with it very easily.

Beaker is a WSGI implementation of a caching middleware using Memcached. See http://pypi.python.org/pypi/Beaker.

Caching can save your day, but it should not be used to hide the slowness of a badly designed or poorly implemented function.

It is often safer to simply improve the code so that you don't have to worry about stale caches, infinite memory growth, or a bad design. It has to be used only on code that cannot be optimized anymore.

Cache size should always be controlled by a maximum age and/or by a maximum size.

Also Memcached should be used for efficient caching.

Summary

In this chapter we have learned:

- How to measure the complexity of the code, and some approaches to reduce it
- How threads work in Python and what they are good for
- A simple way to use processes
- A bit of caching theory and how to use it

The next chapter is dedicated to design patterns.

14
Useful Design Patterns

A design pattern is a reusable, somewhat language-specific solution to a common problem in software design. The most popular book on this topic is *Design Patterns: Elements of Reusable Object-Oriented Software*, written by Gamma, Helm, Johnson, and Vlissides a.k.a. the *Gang of Four* or *GoF*. It is considered as a major writing in this area, and provides a catalogue of 23 design patterns with examples in SmallTalk and C++.

While designing a code application, these patterns are good and known references. They ring a bell to all developers since they describe proven development paradigms. But they should be studied with the used language in mind, since some of them do not make sense in some languages or are already built-in.

This chapter describes the most useful patterns in Python or that are interesting to discuss, with toy implementation examples. The following are the three sections that correspond to design pattern categories defined by the GoF:

- **Creational patterns**: Patterns that are used to generate objects with specific behaviors
- **Structural patterns**: Patterns that help in structuring the code for specific use cases
- **Behavioral patterns**: Patterns that help in structuring processes

Creational Patterns

A creational pattern provides a particular instantiation mechanism. It can be a particular object factory or even a class factory.

This is an important pattern in compiled languages such as C, since it is harder to generate types on-demand at run time.

But this feature is built-in in Python, for instance the `type` built-in, which lets you define a new type by code:

```
>>> MyType = type('MyType', (object,), {'a': 1})
>>> ob = MyType()
>>> type(ob)
<class '__main__.MyType'>
>>> ob.a
1
>>> isinstance(ob, object)
True
```

Classes and types are built-in factories and you can interact with class and object generation using meta-classes, for instance (see Chapter 3). These features are the basics to implement the **Factory** design pattern and we won't further describe it in this section.

Besides Factory, the only other creational design pattern from the GoF that is interesting to describe in Python is **Singleton**.

Singleton

 Singleton restricts instantiation of a class to one object.

The Singleton pattern makes sure that a given class has always only one living instance in the application. This can be used, for example, when you want to restrict a resource access to one and only one memory context in the process. For instance, a database connector class can be a Singleton that deals with synchronization and manages its data in memory. It makes the assumption that no other instance is interacting with the database in the meantime.

This pattern can simplify a lot the way concurrency is handled in an application. Utilities that provide application-wide functions are often declared as Singletons. For instance, in web applications, a class that is in charge of reserving a unique document ID would benefit from the Singleton pattern. There should be one and only one utility doing this job.

Implementing the Singleton pattern is straightforward with the __new__ method:

```
>>> class Singleton(object):
...     def __new__(cls, *args, **kw):
...         if not hasattr(cls, '_instance'):
...             orig = super(Singleton, cls)
```

```
...            cls._instance = orig.__new__(cls, *args, **kw)
...            return cls._instance
...
>>> class MyClass(Singleton):
...      a = 1
...
>>> one = MyClass()
>>> two = MyClass()
>>> two.a = 3
>>> one.a
3
```

Although the problem with this pattern is subclassing; all instances will be instances of MyClass no matter what the method resolution order (__mro__) says:

```
>>> class MyOtherClass(MyClass):
...      b = 2
...
>>> three = MyOtherClass()
>>> three.b
Traceback (most recent call last):
  File "<stdin>", line 1, in ?
AttributeError: 'MyClass' object has no attribute 'b'
```

To avoid this limitation, Alex Martelli proposed an alternative implementation based on shared state called **Borg**.

The idea is quite simple. What really matters in the Singleton pattern is not the number of living instances a class has, but rather the fact that they all share the same state at all times. So Alex Martelli came up with a class that makes all instances of the class share the same __dict__:

```
>>> class Borg(object):
...      _state = {}
...      def __new__(cls, *args, **kw):
...          ob = super(Borg, cls).__new__(cls, *args, **kw)
...          ob.__dict__ = cls._state
...          return ob
...
>>> class MyClass(Borg):
...      a = 1
...
>>> one = MyClass()
>>> two = MyClass()
>>> two.a = 3
>>> one.a
```

```
3
>>> class MyOtherClass(MyClass):
...        b = 2
...
>>> three = MyOtherClass()
>>> three.b
2
>>> three.a
3
>>> three.a = 2
>>> one.a
2
```

This fixes the subclassing issue, but is still dependent on how the subclass code works. For instance, if __getattr__ is overridden, the pattern can be broken.

Nevertheless, Singletons should not have several levels of inheritance. A class that is marked as a Singleton is already specific.

That said, this pattern is considered by many developers as a heavy way to deal with uniqueness in an application. If a Singleton is needed, why not use a module with functions instead, since a Python module is a Singleton?

The Singleton factory is an implicit way of dealing with the uniqueness in your application. You can live without it. Unless you are working in a framework à la Java that requires such a pattern, use a module instead of a class.

Structural Patterns

Structural patterns are really important in big applications. They decide how the code is organized and give developers recipes on how to interact with each part of the application.

The most well-known implementation of structural patterns in the Python world is the **Zope Component Architecture** (**ZCA**, see http://wiki.zope.org/zope3/ComponentArchitectureOverview). It implements most of the patterns described in this section and provides a rich set of tools to work with them. The ZCA is intended to run not only in the Zope framework, but also in other frameworks such as Twisted. It provides an implementation of interfaces and adapters among other things.

So it should be considered instead of re-writing such patterns from scratch, even if it is not a big work.

There are a lot of structural patterns derived from the GoF 11 originals.

Python provides a Decorator-like pattern, for instance, that allows decorating a function using the @decorator syntax, but not at run time. This will be extended to classes in the future version of the language (see http://www.python.org/dev/peps/pep-3129).

Other popular patterns are:

- Adapter
- Proxy
- Facade

Adapter

 Adapter wraps a class or an object A so that it works in a context intended for a class or an object B.

When some code is intended to work with a given class, it is fine to feed it with objects from another class as long as they provide the methods and attributes used by the code. This forms the basics of the duck-typing philosophy in Python.

 If it walks like a duck and talks like a duck, then it's a duck!

Of course, this assumes that the code isn't calling instanceof to verify that the instance is of a specific class.

 I said that it was a duck; there's no need to check its DNA!

The Adapter pattern is based on this philosophy and defines a wrapping mechanism, where a class or an object is wrapped in order to make it work in a context that was not primarily intended for it. StringIO is a typical example, as it adapts the str type so it can be used as a file type:

```
>>> from StringIO import StringIO
>>> my_file = StringIO(u'some content')
>>> my_file.read()
u'some content'
>>> my_file.seek(0)
>>> my_file.read(1)
u's'
```

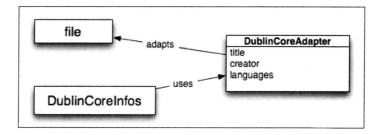

Let's take another example. A `DublinCoreInfos` class knows how to display Dublin Core information (see `http://dublincore.org/`) for a given document. It reads a few fields such as the author's name or the title, and prints them. To be able to display Dublin Core for a file, it has to be adapted the same way `StringIO` does. The figure gives an UML-like diagram of the pattern.

`DublinCoreAdapter` wraps a file instance and provides metadata access over it:

```
>>> from os.path import split, splitext
>>> class DublinCoreAdapter(object):
...     def __init__(self, filename):
...         self._filename = filename
...     def title(self):
...         return splitext(split(self._filename)[-1])[0]
...     def creator(self):
...         return 'Unknown'    # we could get it for real
...     def languages(self):
...         return ('en',)
...
>>> class DublinCoreInfo(object):
...     def summary(self, dc_ob):
...         print 'Title: %s' % dc_ob.title()
...         print 'Creator: %s' % dc_ob.creator()
...         print 'Languages: %s' % \
...                 ', '.join(dc_ob.languages())
...
>>> adapted = DublinCoreAdapter('example.txt')
>>> infos = DublinCoreInfo()
>>> infos.summary(adapted)
Title: example
Creator: Unknown
Languages: en
```

Besides the fact that it allows substitution, the Adapter pattern can also change the way developers work. Adapting an object to work in a specific context makes the assumption that the class of the object does not matter at all. What matters is that this class implements what `DublinCoreInfo` is waiting for. And this behavior is fixed or completed by an adapter. So the code can simply tell somehow whether it is compatible with objects that are implementing a specific behavior. This can be expressed by **interfaces**.

Interfaces

An interface is a definition of an API. It describes a list of methods and attributes a class should have to implement with the desired behavior. This description does not implement any code, but just defines an explicit contract for any class that wishes to implement the interface. Any class can then implement one or several interfaces in whichever way it wants.

While Python prefers duck typing over explicit interface definitions, it may be better to use them sometimes. For instance, explicit interface definition makes it easier for a framework to define functionalities over interfaces.

The benefit is that classes are loosely coupled, which is considered as a good practice. For example, to perform a given process, a class A does not depend on a class B, but rather on an interface I. Class B implements I, but it could be any other class.

This technique is built-in in Java, for instance, where the code can deal with objects that implement a given interface, no matter what kind of class it comes from. It is an explicit duck-typing behavior: Java uses interfaces to verify a type safety at compile time rather than using duck typing to tie things together at run time.

Many developers request that interfaces be added to Python as a core language feature. Currently, those who wish to make use of explicit interfaces are forced to use Zope Interfaces (see `http://pypi.python.org/pypi/zope.interface`) or PyProtocols (see `http://peak.telecommunity.com/PyProtocols.html`).

Previously, Guido rejected the request to add interfaces to the language since they don't fit in Python's dynamic, duck-typing nature. However, interface systems have proven their worth in certain situations, so Python 3000 will come with a feature called **optional type annotations**. This feature can be used as syntax for third-party interface libraries.

Abstract Base Classes (ABC) support was added lately in Python 3000 (see http://www.python.org/dev/peps/pep-3119). extract from the PEP:

"ABCs are simply Python classes that are added into an object's inheritance tree to signal certain features of that object to an external inspector"

 Adapter is perfect to loosely couple a class and an execution context.

But if you use Adapter like a programming philosophy rather than a quick fix to force an object in a specific process, you should also consider using interfaces.

Proxy

 Proxy provides indirect access to an expensive or a distant resource.

A **Proxy** is between a **Client** and a **Subject**, as shown in the figure. It is intended to optimize Subject accesses if they are expensive. For instance, the `memoize` decorator described in the previous chapter can be considered as a Proxy.

A Proxy can also be used to provide smart access to a subject. For instance, big video files can be wrapped into proxies to avoid loading them into memory when the user just asks for their titles.

An example is given by the `urllib2` module. `urlopen` is a proxy for the content located at a remote URL. When it is created, headers can be retrieved independently from the content itself:

```
>>> class Url(object):
...     def __init__(self, location):
...         self._url = urlopen(location)
...     def headers(self):
...         return dict(self._url.headers.items())
...     def get(self):
...         return self._url.read()
...
>>> python_org = Url('http://python.org')
```

```
>>> python_org.headers()
{'content-length': '16399', 'accept-ranges': 'bytes', 'server':
'Apache/2.2.3 (Debian) DAV/2 SVN/1.4.2 mod_ssl/2.2.3 OpenSSL/0.9.8c',
'last-modified': 'Mon, 09 Jun 2008 15:36:07 GMT', 'connection':
'close', 'etag': '"6008a-400f-91f207c0"', 'date': 'Tue, 10 Jun 2008
22:17:19 GMT', 'content-type': 'text/html'}
```

This can be used to decide whether the page has been changed before getting its body to update a local copy, by looking at the last-modified header. Let's take an example with a big file:

```
>>> ubuntu_iso = Url('http://ubuntu.mirrors.proxad.net/hardy/ubuntu-
8.04-desktop-i386.iso')
>>> ubuntu_iso.headers['last-modified']
'Wed, 23 Apr 2008 01:03:34 GMT'
```

Another use case of proxies is **data uniqueness**.

For example, let's consider a website that presents the same document in several locations. Extra fields specific to each location are appended to the document, such as a hit counter and a few permission settings. A proxy can be used in that case to deal with location-specific matters, and also to point to the original document instead of copying it. So a given document can have many proxies and if its content changes, all locations will benefit from it without having to deal with version synchronization.

Use Proxy as a local handle of something that may live somewhere else to:
- Make the process faster.
- Avoid external resource access.
- Reduce memory load.
- Ensure data uniqueness.

Facade

Facade provides a high-level, simpler access to a subsystem.

A Facade is nothing but a shortcut to use a functionality of the application, without having to deal with the underlying complexity of a subsystem. This can be done, for instance, by providing high-level functions at the package level.

See *Tracking Verbosity* in Chapter 4 for examples.

Facade is usually done on existing systems, where a package's frequent usage is synthesized in high-level functions. Usually, no classes are needed to provide such a pattern and simple functions in the __init__.py module are sufficient.

 Facade simplifies the usage of your packages. Facades are usually added after a few iterations with usage feedback.

Behavioral Patterns

Behavioral patterns are intended to simplify the interactions between classes by structuring the processes with which they interact.

This section provides three examples:

- Observer
- Visitor
- Template

Observer

 This is used to notify a list of objects with a state change.

Observer allows adding features in an application in a pluggable way by de-coupling the new functionality from the existing code base. An event framework is a typical implementation of the Observer pattern and is described in the figure that follows. Every time an event occurs, all observers for this event are notified with the subject that has triggered this event.

An event is when something happens. In graphical user interface applications, event-driven programming (see http://en.wikipedia.org/wiki/Event-driven_programming) is often used to link the code to user actions. For instance, a function can be linked to the MouseMove event and so it is called every time the mouse moves over the window. In that case, de-coupling the code from the window management matters simplifies the work a lot: Functions are written separately and then registered as event observers. This approach exists from the earliest versions of Microsoft's MFC framework (see http://en.wikipedia.org/wiki/Microsoft_Foundation_Class_Library), and in all GUI development tools such as Delphi:

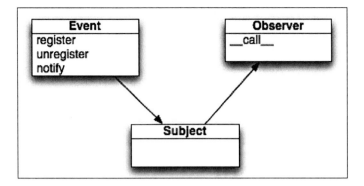

But the code can also generate events. For instance, in an application that stores documents in a database, DocumentCreated, DocumentModified, and DocumentDeleted can be three events provided by the code.

A new feature that works on documents can register itself as an observer to get notified every time a document is created, modified, or deleted, and do the appropriate work. A document indexer could be added that way in an application. Of course, this requires that all the code in charge of creating, modifying, or deleting documents is triggering events. But this is rather easier than adding indexing hooks all over the application code base!

An Event class can be implemented for registration of observers in Python by working at the class level:

```
>>> class Event(object):
...     _observers = []
...     def __init__(self, subject):
...         self.subject = subject
...
...     @classmethod
...     def register(cls, observer):
...         if observer not in cls._observers:
...             cls._observers.append(observer)
...
...     @classmethod
...     def unregister(cls, observer):
...         if observer in cls._observers:
...             self._observers.remove(observer)
...
...     @classmethod
...     def notify(cls, subject):
...         event = cls(subject)
...         for observer in cls._observers:
...             observer(event)
...
```

The idea is that observers register themselves using the `Event` class method and get notified with `Event` instances that carry the subject that triggered them:

```
>>> class WriteEvent(Event):
...     def __repr__(self):
...         return 'WriteEvent'
...
>>> def log(event):
...     print '%s was written' % event.subject
...
>>> WriteEvent.register(log)
>>> class AnotherObserver(object):
...     def __call__(self, event):
...         print 'Yeah %s told me !' % event
...
>>> WriteEvent.register(AnotherObserver())
>>> WriteEvent.notify('a given file')
a given file was written
Yeah WriteEvent told me !
```

This implementation could be enhanced by:

- Allowing the developer to change the order
- Making the event object hold more information than just the subject

De-coupling your code is fun and Observer is the right pattern to do it. It componentizes your application and makes it extensible.

If you want to use an existing tool, try **Pydispatch**. It provides a nice multi-consumer and multi-producer dispatch mechanism. See http://www.sqlobject.org/module-sqlobject.include.pydispatch.html.

Visitor

Visitor helps in separating algorithms from data structures.

Visitor has a similar goal to that of the Observer. It allows extending the functionalities of a given class without changing its code. But Visitor goes a bit further by defining a class that is responsible for holding data, and pushes the algorithms into other classes called `Visitors`. Each visitor is specialized in one algorithm and can apply it on the data. This behavior is quite similar to the MVC paradigm (see `http://en.wikipedia.org/wiki/Model-view-controller`) where documents are passive containers pushed to views through controllers, or where models contain data that is altered by a controller.

Visitor is done by providing an entry point in the data class that can be visited by all kinds of visitors. A generic description is a `Visitable` class that accepts `Visitor` instances and calls them, as shown in the figure below:

The `Visitable` class decides how it calls the `Visitor` class, for instance, by deciding which method is called. For instance, a visitor in charge of printing built-in type content can implement `visit_TYPENAME` methods, and each of these types can call the given method in its `accept` method:

```
>>> class vlist(list):
...     def accept(self, visitor):
...         visitor.visit_list(self)
...
...
>>> class vdict(dict):
...     def accept(self, visitor):
...         visitor.visit_dict(self)
...
>>> class Printer(object):
...     def visit_list(self, ob):
...         print 'list content :'
...         print str(ob)
...     def visit_dict(self, ob):
...         print 'dict keys: %s' % ','.join(ob.keys())
...
>>> a_list = vlist([1, 2, 5])
>>> a_list.accept(Printer())
list content :
[1, 2, 5]
>>> a_dict = vdict({'one': 1, 'two': 2, 'three': 3})
>>> a_dict.accept(Printer())
dict keys: one,three,two
```

But this pattern means that each visited class needs to have an `accept` method to be visited, which is quite painful.

Since Python allows code introspection, a better idea is to automatically link visitors and visited class:

```
>>> def visit(visited, visitor):
...     cls = visited.__class__.__name__
...     meth = 'visit_%s' % cls
...     method = getattr(visitor, meth, None)
...     if method is not None:
...         method(visited)
...
>>> visit([1, 2, 5], Printer())
list content :
[1, 2, 5]
>>> visit({'one': 1, 'two': 2, 'three': 3}, Printer())
dict keys: three,two,one
```

This pattern is used in this way in the `compiler.visitor` module, for instance, by the `ASTVisitor` class that calls the visitor with each node of the compiled code tree. This is because Python doesn't have a match operator like Haskell.

Another example is a directory walker that calls Visitor methods depending on the file extension:

```
>>> def visit(directory, visitor):
...     for root, dirs, files in os.walk(directory):
...         for file in files:
...             # foo.txt → txt
...             ext = os.path.splitext(file)[-1][1:]
...             if hasattr(visitor, ext):
...                 getattr(visitor, ext)(file)
...
>>> class FileReader(object):
...     def pdf(self, file):
...         print 'processing %s' % file
...
>>> visit('/Users/tarek/Desktop', FileReader())
processing slides.pdf
processing shol123.pdf
```

If your application has data structures that are visited by more than one algorithm, the Visitor pattern will help in separating concerns: It is better for a data container to focus only on providing access to data and holding them, and nothing else.

A good practice is to create data structures that do not have any method, like a `struct` in C would be.

Template

 Template helps in designing a generic algorithm by defining abstract steps, which are implemented in subclasses.

Template uses the **Liskov substitution principle**, which says:

"If S is a subtype of T, then objects of type T in a program may be replaced with objects of type S without altering any of the desirable properties of that program." (Wikipedia)

In other words, an abstract class can define how an algorithm works through steps that are implemented in concrete classes. The abstract class can also give a basic or partial implementation of the algorithm, and let developers override its parts. For instance, some methods of the Queue class in the Queue module can be overridden to make its behavior vary.

Let's implement an example shown in the figure that follows. Indexer is an indexer class that processes a text in five steps, which are common steps no matter what indexing technique is used:

- Text normalization
- Text split
- Stop words removal
- Stem words
- Frequency

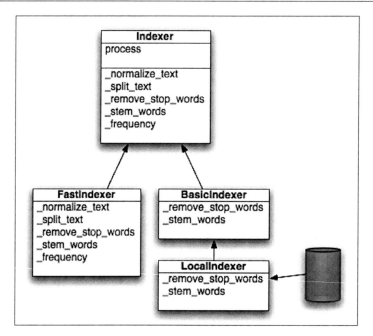

An `Indexer` provides a partial implementation for the process algorithm, but requires `_remove_stop_words` and `_stem_words` to be implemented in a subclass. `BasicIndexer` implements the strict minimum, while `LocalIndex` uses a stop word file and a stem words database. `FastIndexer` implements all steps and could be based on a fast indexer such as **Xapian** or **Lucene**.

A toy implementation can be:

```
>>> class Indexer(object):
...     def process(self, text):
...         text = self._normalize_text(text)
...         words = self._split_text(text)
...         words = self._remove_stop_words(words)
...         stemmed_words = self._stem_words(words)
...         return self._frequency(stemmed_words)
...     def _normalize_text(self, text):
...         return text.lower().strip()
...     def _split_text(self, text):
...         return text.split()
...     def _remove_stop_words(self, words):
...         raise NotImplementedError
...     def _stem_words(self, words):
...         raise NotImplementedError
```

```
...      def _frequency(self, words):
...          counts = {}
...          for word in words:
...              counts[word] = counts.get(word, 0) + 1
```

From there, a `BasicIndexer` implementation can be:

```
>>> from itertools import groupby
>>> class BasicIndexer(Indexer):
...      _stop_words = ('he', 'she', 'is', 'and', 'or') ...
...      def_remove_stop_words(self, words):
...          return (word for word in words
...                  if word not in self._stop_words)
...      def _stem_words(self, words):
...          return ((len(word) > 2 and word.rstrip('aeiouy')
...                  or word)
...                  for word in words)
...
>>> indexer = BasicIndexer()
>>> indexer.process(('My Tailor is rich and he is also '
...                  'my friend'))
{'tailor': 1, 'rich': 1, 'my': 2, 'als': 1, 'friend': 1}
```

Template should be considered for an algorithm that may vary and can be expressed into isolated sub-steps.

This is probably the most used pattern in Python.

Summary

Design patterns are reusable, somewhat language-specific solutions to common problems in software design. They are a part of the culture of all developers, no matter what language they use.

So having implementation examples for the most used patterns for a given language is a great way to document it. There are implementations in Python of each of the GoF design patterns on various websites when it makes sense. The Python Cookbook at http://aspn.activestate.com/ASPN/Python/Cookbook/ in particular is a good place to look.

Python provides some built-in features to use some pattern, and this chapter shows how to implement a few other design patterns:

- Singleton
- Adapter
- Proxy
- Facade
- Observer
- Visitor
- Template

For more information on Design Patterns:

Watch Alex Martelli's talk: `http://www.youtube.com/watch?v=0vJJ1VBVTFg`.

A nice pattern by Shannon Behrens is at: `http://www.linuxjournal.com/article/8747V`

Index

macro-profiling 280-284
micro-profiling 284-286
bottlenecks, finding
CPU usage, profiling 280
memory usage, profiling 288
network usage, profiling 295
Buildbot, continuous integration
about 202
installing 202-204
setting up, Apache used 205
setting up, Mercurial used 204
buildout
building 180
distributing 178
packages, releasing 178
release configuration file, adding 179, 180
release configuration file, creating 179
releasing 178, 180
built-in type
subclassing 63-65
superclass 65
built-in type, subclassing
collection module types 64, 65
distinctdict class code, showing 64, 65
list type 64, 65

C

caching
callables qualities 318
deterministic caching 318-320
Memcached 322
memoizing behaviour 319
non-deterministic caching 321
non-deterministic caching, example 321
pro-active caching 322
caching decorator
duration parameter 53
example 53
Memcached feature 54
memoizing behavior 52
centralized system, VCS
about 184-186
concurrent version system 186
conflict resolution mechanism 184, 185
class names 106

class names, examples
prefix, using 106
suffix, using 106
CloneDigger tool
installing 115
using 115
code editor, working environment
Emacs 25
vim 25, 26
code quality, TDD
improving, tips 254
collection module, using
defaultdict type 305
deque type 303, 304
namedtuple type 306
types 303
continous integration
about 200
Buildbot 201, 202
Mercurial, using 202
zc.buildbot, using 202
complexity, reducing
Big-O notation, categorizing 298
Big-O notation, defining 298
Big-O notation, measuring 299, 300
collection module, using 303
Cyclomatic Complexity, categorizing 298
Cyclomatic Complexity, measuring 298
data, sorting 301
external calls, reducing 303
list, sorting 301
set type, using 302
techniques 298
configuration file, zc.buildout
develop option 169
find-links option 169, 170
minimum configuration file 169
uses 169
constants, variables
naming 93, 94
using 93, 94
consumer's layout, document landscape
Sphinx 245
context decorator
about 55
lock coding 56

arguments 98
controversial rule 97
normal method 98
special methods 98
Zope developer 96

G

generator expression
  uses 43
generators
  about 37
  close method 40
  features 38, 39
  send method 39
  template 40
  throw method 40
  tokenize module 38
genexp
  uses 43
GIL 308
Global Interpreter Lock. *See* **GIL**
groupby function
  example 45
  uses 46

H

helpers, contextlib module
  closing function 59
  nested function 59

I

IDE 25
IDE, working environment
  Eclipse, enriching features 29
  Eclipse, installing 31
inline markup, reST elements
  text, styling 232
installing
  CloneDigger tool 115
  pylint tool 113
  Python 10, 14, 15
  setuptool 13
introspection descriptor
  about 77
  Epydoc 77

non-data descriptor, example 78
iPython
  about 20
  features 20
  installing 20
IronPython 11
iterator
  about 36, 37
  creating 36
  custom iterator, creating 36
  fibonacci series, writing 37
  iter method 36
  itertools module 44
  methods 36
  next method 36
itertools module
  count function 46
  cycle function 46
  dropwhile function 46
  groupby function 45
  ifilterfalse function 47
  ifilter function 46
  imap function 47
  islice 44
  islice function 44
  islice function, using 45
  izip function 47
  repeat function 47
  starmap function 47
  takewhile function 47
  tee function 45
itertools module. functions
  chain function 46
iteration, life cycle
  about 210
  development phase, tasks 212
  duration 212
  global debug 212
  phases 211
  planning phase 212
  release phase 213
iterative development approach 208
iterative development model
  about 210
  disadvantages 211

J

Java Runtime Environment. *See* JRE
JRE 29
Jython 10

L

life cycle
  defining 210, 211
  global planning 211
  iteration 210
  train approach 210
lifecycle, projecting with trac
  cleaning phase 221
  development phase 221
  release phase 221
  release phase, components 221
links, reST elements
  internal link, using 233, 234
Linux, Python
  commands, running 12
  gcc, installing 13
  installing 12
  package, installing 12, 13
  package-management tools, installing 13
  python-dev, installing 13
  python-profier, installing 13
list comprehensions 34, 35
lists, reST elements 232
literal block, reST elements
  using 232, 233

M

Mac OS X, Windows installation
  installing 17
  installing, ways 17
  package, installing 18
macro-profiling
  about 284-286
  uses 284
memory usage, bottlenecks
  C Code memory 295
  dealing with 288, 289
  Guppy-PE Primer 291
  heap method 292

Heapy, using 294
memory eaters 290
 profiling 288, 290
tracking, with Heapy 292, 294
variable, measuring 291
Mercurial
  about 180, 190
  Apache, configuring 195-198
  authorization, setting up 198, 199
  client side, setting up 199
  hgwebdir, configuring 194, 195
  installing 192
  repositories, managing 193
  repositories, setting up 193, 194
  server, installing 193
meta-programming
  about 84
  definition 81
meta-programming, methods
  _metaclass_method 86, 87
  _new_method 84
meta descriptor
  about 79
  implementations 79, 80
MinGW, Windows installation
  hooking, into distutils 23
  installing 15, 16
Minimal System *See* MSYS
Method Resolution Order *See* MRO
mocks
  about 267
  library elements 271
  test, running 272
  using 271, 272
MSYS
  about 16
  installing 16
module
  names 107
MRO
  about 66
  Base Base class 66
  computing 66
  reference document location 66
  understanding 66
module helper, usage documentation
  about 241

installing 25
vimrc file 27

W

Windows installation, Python
  installing 14, 15
  installing, steps 15
  Mac OS X, installing 17
  MinGW, installing 15, 16
  MSYS, installing 16
with statement
  code, logging 59
  compatible items 57
  context example 59
  contextlib module 58
  enter method 57, 58
  exit method 57, 58
  file, working with 56
  using 56
working environment
  another editor, using 27
  binaries, installing 28

creating 148
IDE, using 28
packages structure, adding 148
setting 146, 147
test runner, adding 148

X

XML-Remote Procedure Call. *See*
    XML-RPC;
XML-RPC 50

Z

zc.buildout
  buildout command 170, 171
  configuration file structure 168
  elements 168
  features 168
  overview 167
  recipes 172, 173

Thank you for buying
Expert Python Programming

Packt Open Source Project Royalties

When we sell a book written on an Open Source project, we pay a royalty directly to that project. Therefore by purchasing Expert Python Programming, Packt will have given some of the money received to the Python Software Foundation.

In the long term, we see ourselves and you—customers and readers of our books—as part of the Open Source ecosystem, providing sustainable revenue for the projects we publish on. Our aim at Packt is to establish publishing royalties as an essential part of the service and support a business model that sustains Open Source.

If you're working with an Open Source project that you would like us to publish on, and subsequently pay royalties to, please get in touch with us.

Writing for Packt

We welcome all inquiries from people who are interested in authoring. Book proposals should be sent to authors@packtpub.com. If your book idea is still at an early stage and you would like to discuss it first before writing a formal book proposal, contact us; one of our commissioning editors will get in touch with you.

We're not just looking for published authors; if you have strong technical skills but no writing experience, our experienced editors can help you develop a writing career, or simply get some additional reward for your expertise.

About Packt Publishing

Packt, pronounced 'packed', published its first book "Mastering phpMyAdmin for Effective MySQL Management" in April 2004 and subsequently continued to specialize in publishing highly focused books on specific technologies and solutions.

Our books and publications share the experiences of your fellow IT professionals in adapting and customizing today's systems, applications, and frameworks. Our solution-based books give you the knowledge and power to customize the software and technologies you're using to get the job done. Packt books are more specific and less general than the IT books you have seen in the past. Our unique business model allows us to bring you more focused information, giving you more of what you need to know, and less of what you don't.

Packt is a modern, yet unique publishing company, which focuses on producing quality, cutting-edge books for communities of developers, administrators, and newbies alike. For more information, please visit our website: www.PacktPub.com.

PUBLISHING

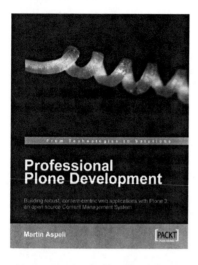

Professional Plone Development

ISBN: 978-1-847191-98-4   Paperback: 398 pages

Building robust, content-centric web applications
with Plone 3, an open source Content Management
System

1. Plone development fundamentals

2. Customizing Plone

3. Developing new functionality

4. Real-world deployments

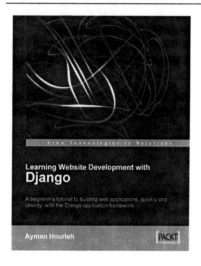

Learning Website Development
with Django

ISBN: 978-1-847193-35-3   Paperback: 264 pages

A beginner's tutorial to building web applications,
quickly and cleanly, with the Django application
framework

1. Create a complete Web 2.0-style web
   application with Django

2. Learn rapid development and clean, pragmatic
   design

3. Build a social bookmarking application

4. No knowledge of Django required

Please check **www.PacktPub.com** for information on our titles

CherryPy Essentials

ISBN: 978-1-904811-84-8   Paperback: 272 pages

Design, develop, test, and deploy your Python web applications easily

1. Walks through building a complete Python web application using CherryPy 3

2. The CherryPy HTTP:Python interface

3. Use CherryPy with other Python libraries

4. Design, security, testing, and deployment

Mastering OpenLDAP

ISBN: 978-1-847191-02-1   Paperback: 400 pages

Install, Configure, Build, and Integrate Secure Directory Services with OpenLDAP server in a networked environment

1. Up-to-date with the latest OpenLDAP release

2. Installing and configuring the OpenLDAP server

3. Synchronizing multiple OpenLDAP servers over the network

4. Creating custom LDAP schemas to model your own information

5. Integrating OpenLDAP with web applications

Please check **www.PacktPub.com** for information on our titles

Printed in the United Kingdom by
Lightning Source UK Ltd., Milton Keynes
139803UK00001B/129/P